M000201779

Too Weak to Govern

Too Weak to Govern investigates the power of the majority party in the U.S. Senate through a study of the appropriations process over a period of nearly four decades. It uses quantitative analysis, case studies, and interviews with policy makers to show that the majority party is more likely to abandon routine procedures for passing spending bills in favor of creating massive "omnibus" spending bills when it is small, divided, and ideologically distant from the minority. This book demonstrates that the majority party's ability to influence legislative outcomes is greater than previously understood but that it operates under important constraints. The majority party's actions protect the party's reputation by helping it pass a budget and by protecting it from politically damaging votes on amendments. However, the majority generally cannot use its power to push its preferred policies through to approval. Overall, the weakness of the Senate majority party is a major reason for the breakdown of the congressional appropriations process over the past forty years.

Peter Hanson is an assistant professor of political science at the University of Denver and a former staff member in the office of Senator Tom Daschle (D-SD). He has been interviewed by national and international media organizations, including the BBC, Agence France-Presse, the *New York Times' FiveThirtyEight* blog, *USA Today*, Minnesota Public Radio, Colorado Public Radio, Rocky Mountain PBS, and the *Denver Post*. He co-led the University of Denver's "Colorado Voter Poll" in 2012.

Too Weak to Govern

Majority Party Power and Appropriations in the U.S. Senate

PETER HANSON
University of Denver

CAMBRIDGE
UNIVERSITY PRESS

CAMBRIDGE
UNIVERSITY PRESS

32 Avenue of the Americas, New York, NY 10013-2473, USA

Cambridge University Press is part of the University of Cambridge.

It furthers the University's mission by disseminating knowledge in the pursuit of education, learning, and research at the highest international levels of excellence.

www.cambridge.org
Information on this title: www.cambridge.org/9781107635876

© Peter Hanson 2014

First published 2014

Printed in the United States of America

A catalog record for this publication is available from the British Library.

Library of Congress Cataloging in Publication data
Hanson, Peter, 1973– author.
Too weak to govern : majority party power and appropriations in the U.S. Senate /
Peter Hanson, University of Denver.
    pages   cm
Includes bibliographical references and index.
ISBN 978-1-107-06315-0 (hardback) – ISBN 978-1-107-63587-6 (paperback)
1. United States. Congress. Senate. Committee on Appropriations.   2. United States –
Appropriations and expenditures.   3. United States – Politics and government –
1945–1989.   4. United States – Politics and government – 1989–   I. Title.
KF4987.A67H36   2014
328.73'07658–dc23   2014020952

ISBN 978-1-107-06315-0 Hardback
ISBN 978-1-107-63587-6 Paperback

For Rebecca

Contents

Figures

Tables

Preface

This is a book about party power in the Senate. How much power does the majority party in the Senate have to shape legislative outcomes to its liking? What are the sources of its power, and when is the majority likely to use it? How effectively can the majority party manage a chamber that is notoriously individualistic and so subject to delays and filibusters that the actual passage of legislation appears at times to be miraculous?

These are important questions. At stake is not just whether the Senate majority party can push its own legislative program to passage but whether it can pass any legislative program at all in today's highly polarized environment. Dismal evaluations of the Senate abound. "Sit and watch us for seven days – just watch the floor," Senator Michael Bennet (D-CO) lamented. "You know what you'll see happening? Nothing."[1] The power granted by Senate rules to individual senators appears to have paralyzed the chamber rather than allow for the serious debate intended by the framers of the Constitution.

Former leaders of the chamber agree that there are few tools available to force action in the chamber. "When I was whip back in 2007 and McConnell was leader, we were trying to move the ethics in lobbying reform bill to conference," former Senate majority leader Trent Lott recalled. "Jim DeMint objected and Senator McConnell said, 'Hey, whip, go over there and see if you can get him to relent.' I tried. I tried. I got my chief deputy whip to go talk to him. I got his buddies to talk to him.

---

[1] Packer, George, "The Empty Chamber: Just How Broken Is the Senate?" *New Yorker*, August 9, 2010.

He wouldn't relent. The result was, we didn't get to go to conference" (interview with author, March 7, 2012).

Lott's tale of obstruction and gridlock is a common one. It is also alarming given the variety of serious policy challenges facing the United States. If the deck is stacked against the ability of senators to make hard choices, then there is little hope that they can put the nation's fiscal house in order or address threats such as global warming. Concerns like these have sparked an important debate within the Senate about modifying the filibuster. The Senate took a first step toward reform when Democrats abolished the ability of senators to filibuster presidential nominations in November 2013, but senators can still demand a supermajority vote before legislation can be adopted. Absent further change to the Senate's rules, what can reasonably be expected of the Senate majority party?

In this book, I explore the nature of party power in the Senate by investigating how the majority party manages the annual passage of the appropriations bills that fund the government. One of the most important changes in the appropriations process since the 1960s is the crumbling of the "regular order" – a time-tested system of passing a dozen or so appropriations bills covering separate jurisdictions by bringing each bill to the floor for individual debate, amendment, and a vote. The regular order has been replaced by an ad hoc practice of packaging appropriations bills together into massive omnibus spending bills worth hundreds of billions of dollars. Omnibus packages may allocate up to one-third of the federal budget in a single bill and establish policies that affect millions of Americans.

The magnitude of this change is substantial and sometimes unappreciated. While omnibus spending bills are widely disparaged, there is little recognition among scholars that they have displaced something valuable in the regular order. In a *Washington Post* editorial, political scientist Jonathan Bernstein (writing about a process related to appropriations – passing a budget resolution) observed, "There's nothing sacred about the 'regular order' – the real question is whether [members of Congress are] getting their important business done, not what procedures they follow."[2] I think this view is mistaken. Rules and procedures are ways of allocating power and making decisions about policy in every legislative body. The "regular order" in appropriations is a permissive set of procedures that allows any member of the majority or minority to participate

---

[2] Bernstein, Jonathan, "Useful Reminder: They Don't Believe What They're Saying," *Washington Post*, July 1, 2013.

in lawmaking by offering amendments or making motions. Congress abandons this open environment and centralizes power in the hands of a few key players when it creates omnibus spending bills. As Senator Susan Collins (R-ME) explains,

> [The regular order] means we would bring up each of the individual bills, they would be open to full and fair debate, they would be amended, they would be voted on, and we would avoid having some colossal bill at the end of the year that combines all the appropriations bills. Those bills are often thousands of pages in length. A lot of times some of the provisions have not had the opportunity to be thoroughly vetted. They really are not very transparent. They contribute to the public's concern about the way we do business here in Washington.... The best way for us to achieve these goals is for each and every one of the appropriations bills to come before the full Senate and for us to work our will on those bills. That is the way the Senate should operate. It is the way we must operate in order to restore the faith of the American people in this institution.[3]

The most potent criticism of omnibus bills captured by Senator Collins is that they are undemocratic because their creation and passage are marked by a lack of broad participation, transparency, and accountability. The packages are often written behind closed doors by a few key members of Congress. Rank-and-file members of Congress may have little opportunity to read, debate, or amend omnibus bills before voting on them. "No member knew, or could have known, all that was in those huge stacks of paper before voting on them," the *New York Times* fumed after Congress approved a 2,000-page, $600 billion omnibus in 1987.[4] Omnibus packages may also contain spending or policies buried in their pages that would not pass on their own. An eleven-bill package in 2003 eased logging restrictions on Alaska national forests at the behest of Appropriations Chairman Ted Stevens (R-AK). Adding the forestry provision and other riders to the package was "irresponsible and anti-democratic" the *Washington Post* charged. "What is 'omnibus appropriations legislation,' after all, except a bundle of 11 complex bills, debated and discussed in a few days and finalized in secret?"[5]

Criticism of omnibus bills comes from presidents and members of Congress, Democrats and Republicans, and the minority and majority alike. President Reagan called for an end to omnibus bills from his lectern in his 1988 State of the Union address. Former Senate majority leader

---

[3] *Congressional Record*, February 27, 2012, S1041.
[4] "New Session, Old Odor," *New York Times*, January 26, 1988.
[5] Applebaum, Anne, "No Bottom to This Barrel," *Washington Post*, February 12, 2003.

Tom Daschle called the practice "a symptom of the dysfunctionality of Congress these days" (interview with author, February 15, 2012). In 2009, members of the Republican minority in the Senate signed a letter to Majority Leader Harry Reid (D-NV) observing that "omnibus bills have not allowed for adequate public review [of appropriations bills] and have clouded what should otherwise be a transparent process."[6] Two years later, their call to return to the regular order was echoed by Senate Appropriations Committee chair Daniel Inouye (D-HI) as he expressed his own frustration about omnibus packages.[7]

These criticisms point to the fact that the majority's decision to create an omnibus bill is not one of legislative style over substance. It is a decision to replace one system of passing legislation with another. More fundamentally, it is an exercise of power. Running twelve bills through the regular order or packaging them together into an omnibus bill is a choice between an open and permissive system for considering legislation versus one that is centralized and restrictive. Rank-and-file members recognize that creating an omnibus means fewer opportunities for them to participate in lawmaking, claim credit for accomplishments, and take positions important to their constituents than they would likely receive in the regular order.

Given the homage so many members pay to the regular order, what accounts for the frequency with which it is abandoned? Congress has created omnibus bills in twenty-four of the last thirty-eight years. As of this writing, it has packaged every appropriations bill into an omnibus package since 2010. In some recent years, the powerful subcommittees of the Appropriations Committee in the House and Senate have not even approved the individual spending bills assigned to them – a fact that would have astounded observers just ten years ago. Congress now lurches from budget crisis to budget crisis, and its orderly system for adopting appropriations bills is broken.

I show that Senate majority parties that have a narrow margin of control, are ideologically divided, or are especially ideologically distant from the minority are likely to conclude that the regular order is harming the party and to abandon it in favor of creating an omnibus package. Abandoning the regular order limits amending in the Senate and helps ensure the passage of the budget, protecting the reputation of the

---

[6] Letter to Senate Majority Leader Harry Reid, March 24, 2009. http://www.src.senate .gov/files/03-24-09_Letter_to_Reid.pdf. Accessed July 2, 2013.
[7] *Congressional Record*, March 10, 2011, S1541.

majority party. Interestingly, the Senate abandons the regular order more frequently than the House does and at times forces the creation of omnibus bills through its failure to deal with bills individually. The greater likelihood that the Senate majority party will abandon the regular order is a reflection of the Senate's individualistic rules and the difficulty of managing the Senate floor. It is likely that we would see fewer and smaller omnibus bills if the United States had two legislative branches like the House of Representatives.

These findings offer important lessons for two ongoing debates about party power in Congress. One debate is over the extent of the Senate majority party's ability to influence legislative outcomes in its favor. For example, can the majority party win a vote by pressuring a wavering senator to support the party or block the minority from offering a policy that might win majority support? Traditionalists such as Barbara Sinclair and Steven Smith maintain that the Senate's rules prevent the majority party from exercising substantial influence in this fashion. Recent studies by political scientists such as Chris Den Hartog and Nate Monroe challenge this view with findings that the Senate majority party can often meet its policy goals in the chamber. I chart a middle course between these two positions. I show that the majority party's influence is generally insufficient to meet policy goals but that its manipulation of the appropriations process helps it to meet electoral goals by protecting its party reputation. The Senate majority party has a limited, but important, ability to influence legislative outcomes.

The second debate is about the conditions under which majority party influence is likely to be used. My findings challenge well-known partisan theories of Congress such as Conditional Party Government (CPG). CPG was developed by John Aldrich and David Rohde to describe the House of Representatives, but it is sometimes assumed to describe the far different dynamics of the Senate as well. Aldrich and Rohde maintain that the majority party's ability and incentive to influence legislative outcomes are conditioned on the unity of its members and their overall ideological distance from the minority. When these conditions are met, members of the majority have a strong sense of common purpose. They delegate power to their leaders to influence the legislative process and enact their preferred policies. An observation of the majority party influencing the legislative process is a sign of a strong, unified party exercising powers that have been delegated to it by its members.

These expectations do not match the reality of the Senate. The majority party in the Senate is more likely to abandon the regular order and create omnibus bills when it has characteristics that make its job managing the floor more difficult – in short, when it is weak. Omnibus bills are more likely when the majority is small and divided because that is when it has trouble summoning the votes it needs to overcome opposition, deal with troublesome amendments, and pass individual spending bills. The packages are also more likely when large ideological gulfs between the parties generate more intense minority opposition and raise the risk of gridlock, making the passage of spending bills in the regular order more difficult. Omnibus bills help the majority overcome gridlock and pass a budget. Their creation is the sign of a weak Senate majority party struggling to avoid harm rather than a vigorous majority dominating the floor. As the title of this book suggests, they emerge when the majority party is too weak to govern using its traditional procedures.

One objective of this book is to provide clarity about what it means for a majority party to be "strong" or "weak" in the Senate. Political scientists commonly use the term "strong" to identify parties with the ability to influence legislative outcomes and "weak" to identify those that cannot. This shorthand unhelpfully muddles the debate over the kinds of party characteristics and circumstances that are associated with majority party influence. Properly speaking, a strong majority party is one that can meet its legislative goals regardless of whether it has to manipulate the legislative process to do so. The strongest Senate majority party is one that can win votes outright because it has a large margin of control and is ideologically unified. Weak majority parties are those with small margins of control or ideological divisions or that are facing vigorous minority delaying tactics. Parties in these situations can influence legislative outcomes to meet a limited set of goals, but they achieve less overall than what they could gain with more (or more unified) members. True majority party strength in the Senate is found in numbers and ideological unity, not the limited means by which parties can manipulate legislative outcomes.

This book utilizes a mixed methodological approach to make its case, including interviews with policy makers, quantitative analysis, and case studies. I take this approach because it is the best way to support an argument that depends on understanding the flow of business on the Senate floor. I take some pride in the fact that it demonstrates the value of books and qualitative analysis in a field that is increasingly dominated by short articles presenting quantitative findings. I am a proponent of the research method known as the "soak and poke" – hanging around Congress to see matters and develop questions firsthand. I had an unparalleled opportunity to observe the daily chess match for control over the Senate floor in my twenties as a legislative assistant to Senate Democratic Leader Tom Daschle. Complaints about the efforts of the Republican majority to stifle debate and block amendments were commonplace at weekly Democratic strategy sessions held in the Lyndon Baines Johnson Room. Leadership aides would urge staff members representing each senator to uphold filibusters designed to prevent the majority from cutting off debate and, with it, the right to amend a bill. "They're trying to turn this place into the House of Representatives!" was the rallying cry. The notion of being under the majority's thumb like members of the House was alarming to those accustomed to the Senate's individualistic traditions. In the colorful words of one Senate staff member, the majoritarian House was no better than the "Gulag" – the old Stalinist system of prison camps in the Soviet Union. The fierce procedural battles I observed left me deeply curious about the nature of majority party power in the Senate and the ways in which it could be exercised.

Later, in graduate school at Berkeley, I came to admire books by scholars such as Richard Fenno, Nelson Polsby, and Richard Hall, whose "hanging around" in Congress led to remarkable works of scholarship. This book follows their lead by incorporating interviews with former Senate majority leaders Tom Daschle and Trent Lott, as well as senior staff members, with decades of experience working with appropriations. The insights of policy makers offer critical guidance in the interpretation of data and help connect the dots in the sprawling annual debates over spending bills. It is my hope that more researchers will utilize interviews as part of their research to add depth to their work. Staff members who have served for years on Capitol Hill understand legislative procedures, care deeply about Congress as an institution, and are eager to talk about their observations. I am grateful to all of the individuals who spoke with me as part of this project.

The quantitative evidence presented in the book comes from an analysis of a unique data set of the legislative history of the appropriations process. Most studies of the Congress rely on the record of roll call votes to analyze decisions made on the floor. By definition, such studies cannot measure with any certainty why some bills receive a vote and others do not. My approach builds on the routine nature of the appropriations process and the norm of following the regular order. It is widely understood that Congress writes twelve (formerly thirteen) appropriations bills each year and generally seeks to pass them on an individual basis. I mark a failure to vote on one of these bills as a moment in which Congress departs from the regular order in favor of an alternate path. I analyze the majority's decision not to call a vote to understand how, when, and why the majority party controls the legislative agenda and what it accomplishes by doing so. I build on these statistical findings with detailed case studies to demonstrate how the patterns visible in the quantitative data manifest on the floor of the Senate. Where possible, I draw directly from debates in the *Congressional Record* and transcripts of press conferences with Senate leaders to make my points using the words of members themselves.

The lessons about the strength of the Senate majority party offered in this book give reason for both skepticism and hope about the ability òf senators to navigate the rules of the institution to make tough decisions about policy. The good news is that the majority party largely has been able to fulfill its basic duty of funding the government even in the most challenging circumstances. The bad news is that it has done so with legislative tactics that have sacrificed transparency, accountability, and participation in the legislative process by most members. The appropriations process is now badly broken, and there appears to be little immediate hope that it will return to health. Absent further changes to the Senate's rules, the Senate majority party will continue to muddle its way through and meet its basic responsibilities. The question is whether the world's greatest deliberative body can do better than muddle along. Senators must find a way to govern again by providing opportunities for members to perform basic legislative functions such as evaluating legislation, weighing alternatives and making improvements to bills without the process breaking down. Senate leaders must create an enduring new balance between protecting the Senate's tradition of individualism and ensuring that important decisions can be made in a timely manner.

Chapter 1 outlines the ongoing debate over the extent of majority power in the Senate and presents a theoretical framework for the majority's management of the appropriations process, drawing from interviews with senior policy makers and past scholarship. Omnibus packages have become an increasingly common way of passing appropriations bills in the last thirty-eight years, but there is little research into the reason for this change. Interviews with top policy makers, such as former Senate majority leaders Tom Daschle and Trent Lott, suggest that the bills arise when a weak majority party loses control of the Senate floor. Members weigh the opportunity to participate in lawmaking in the regular order against the risks of troublesome amendments or that they may fail to pass a budget. Members of the majority party abandon the regular order and create an omnibus bill when they judge that the risk to their party reputation outweighs the benefits they receive from participating in the legislative process.

Chapter 2 presents quantitative data and analysis to test three major expectations of the theory. The results show that the Senate majority party is more likely to abandon the regular order and create an omnibus package when it is small, divided, and distant from the minority. Not calling a vote on individual spending bills and passing an omnibus bill instead also tends to reduce the opportunity of members to offer amendments. Finally, omnibus bills generally receive bipartisan support. Together, these findings show that creating omnibus bills is a strategy used by weak parties to pass the budget and protect their reputations.

Chapter 3 provides an account of key debates on appropriations bills in the 1980s to illustrate how and why Congress transitioned from passing spending bills individually to packaging them together as omnibus bills. In 1981, the Republican majority that assumed control of the Senate was hampered by a small margin of control and severe ideological divisions in its membership. Liberals such as Senator Lowell Weicker (R-CT) and conservatives such as Senator Jesse Helms (R-NC) faced off over abortion, school prayer, and desegregation on appropriations bills. These floor debates occurred in the context of difficult budget fights sparked by President Ronald Reagan's efforts to reduce federal spending. Internal Republican disputes prevented Majority Leader Howard Baker (R-TN) from passing individual spending bills at times and led him to add them to omnibus packages instead.

Chapter 4 investigates a crucial seven-year period from 1988 to 1994 in which Congress stopped creating omnibus bills and returned to passing appropriations bill in the regular order. This case study shows that the transition was sustained by the ability of a unified and powerful Democratic majority to resolve frequent disputes over social policy on spending bills without resorting to packaging the bills together. This period came to a sharp end in 1995 when Republicans resumed control of Congress. Congress resumed passing omnibus bills as appropriations bills became the focal point of budget disputes with the president and because the narrow Republican majority left the party vulnerable to Democratic obstructive tactics. This chapter also investigates the role of presidents in the creation of omnibus bills. Presidents can make the creation of omnibus bills more or less likely, but they have different judgments about the strategic value of bargaining with Congress over a single omnibus bill versus a dozen individual spending bills.

Chapter 5 analyzes the majority's management of the appropriations process in the early 2000s during the presidency of George W. Bush. During this era, a unified Republican majority was vulnerable to obstruction and being rolled by the minority on votes because of its narrow margin of control. It responded by creating omnibus spending bills that allowed it to avoid difficult votes and ensure passage of the budget. Influence from President Bush tilted the bills in a more conservative direction by overturning some of the policy decisions made on the Senate floor, but voting patterns show that the bills still received substantial bipartisan support.

Chapter 6 concludes by outlining the challenge facing congressional leaders today. The unorthodox strategy of creating omnibus bills is increasingly accepted as a standard way of doing business. Intense minority opposition has made it difficult for any majority to pass spending bills, and the budget process established in 1974 appears to be on the verge of collapse. As we enter into the fourth decade of the modern budget process, the future is deeply uncertain.

Acknowledgments

This book has its roots in my experiences working in the U.S. Senate for Tom Daschle (D-SD) from 1996 to 2002. I was fortunate to work for a dedicated public servant and with an immensely talented group of fellow staff members. I am deeply grateful to Pete Rouse, Laura Petrou, Ann Mills, Eric Washburn, Kelly Fado, Tim Mitrovitch, Nancy Erickson, and many others who had faith in me and gave me responsibility beyond my years. It was through my work in the Daschle office that I gained my first exposure to the annual appropriations process. I learned how the schedule of Congress revolved around the need to pass a budget and got to know many of the hardworking staff members who served the Appropriations Committee. My years in the Senate left me with a lasting respect for the men and women who work there and with an abiding interest in the institution.

The first draft of this book was written as my dissertation in the political science program at the University of California, Berkeley. I am grateful to all the faculty, students, and staff at Berkeley I met during my time there. They were a constant source of friendly and good-humored guidance and, at least once a week, cookies. Eric Schickler and Rob Van Houweling introduced me to academic research on Congress and helped me to draw larger lessons from my practical experience in politics. Their criticism and advice helped me to form my ideas, and I could not have written this book without them. Gordon Silverstein was a friend, mentor, and one of the best teachers I have seen. Jack Citrin supervised my first major research project and gave me advice and support at crucial points during my graduate program. Bruce Cain had faith in my potential and helped to secure my admission to the program at Berkeley. And Nelson

Polsby helped to keep me on the academic path with a firm "Tell them no!" when my old colleagues in Washington tried to lure me back with a job.

I am also grateful for the support of the talented group of graduate students I met at Berkeley who are now teaching students of their own across the country. Devin Caughey read many drafts of my work, usually with little to no advance warning, and never failed to give thoughtful advice. Thank you as well to Bruce Huber, Alex Theodoridis, Lee Drutman, Michael Salamone, Josh Green, Pat Egan, Megan Mullin, Angelo Gonzalez, Alison Gash, Jill Greenlee, Manoj Mate, Matthew Wright, Sarah Reckhow, Matt Grossman, David Hopkins, John Hanley, Rebecca Hamlin, Amanda Hollis-Brutsky, Adrienne Hosek, Chloe Thurston, Erin Hartman, Rachel VanSickle-Ward, and many others who helped me to learn and grow during those years.

It is a victory to complete graduate school both happy and well fed, and I am very grateful to my friends in Berkeley who helped me to do that. Nat Lewis, Nydia MacGregor, Madison and Georgia, and the Thursday Night Dinner crew provided dinner, whiskey, and music (not always in that order). Brent Blackaby and Larry Huynh were constant companions and great friends.

This book was completed at the University of Denver, where I have benefited from the support of an outstanding group of colleagues: Lisa Conant, Nancy Wadsworth, Jing Sun, David Ciepley, Spencer Wellhofer, Susan Sterett, Joshua Wilson, Jonathan Sciarcon, and Andrea Stanton. I am particularly appreciative of Seth Masket, who read drafts of my work and always gave feedback that improved the project. My undergraduate research assistant, Ben Horblit, provided invaluable help. His computer wizardry is entirely responsible for the automated method used to count amendments in the appropriations process in this book. University of Denver senior Alex Johnson copyedited the final text. I am also grateful to Miranda Yaver, Anthony Madonna, Ken Shotts, Frances Lee, Gregory Koger, and Sarah Binder, who read earlier drafts of my work and gave useful feedback. Whatever flaws this book may have, they are fewer in number thanks to the many people who helped me to avoid pitfalls and express my ideas more clearly.

Finally, I would like to thank my family. Unqualified love and support can take you far in life, and that is what they have always given me. My parents, Gary and Julie, my sister, Siri, and my brother, Jon, are all the true authors of this book because it would not be possible without them.

Jon, a fellow political scientist, encouraged me, helped me solve knotty statistical problems, and always had a thoughtful word of advice. He's a pretty fantastic big brother. And, of course, I thank my wife, Rebecca. There is not a day that goes by that I do not think how lucky I am to have found her.

I

The Limited Influence Theory of the Senate

The short walk under the Capitol dome from the House to the Senate connects two sharply different institutions. The framers of the Constitution aimed to give the House of Representatives and the Senate distinctive roles and personalities in the American political system. The House was meant to have an "immediate dependence on, and an intimate sympathy" with the people, while the Senate was meant to be insulated from popular passions and a "defence to the people against their own temporary errors and delusions."[1] The designs of the two chambers reflect these divergent goals. House members are elected for two years, senators for six. House members represent small, often homogenous districts, while senators represent much more diverse state populations. Today, the framers' enduring stamp on the two chambers is evident in the fiery, tempestuous character of the House and the staid, tradition-bound Senate.

Other crucial distinctions between the House and Senate do not stem from the Constitution but from the rules that have been adopted by each chamber. The rules of the Senate protect the right of individual senators to participate in the legislative process but place a low priority on the efficient passage of legislation, while the rules of the House restrict a member's opportunity to participate in order to expedite the passage of bills. These rules, in combination with the constitutional design of the two chambers, give each a unique and equally important impact on the production of legislation. Despite this fact, the Senate is more poorly understood than the House is. Scholars of Congress have filled the pages of academic journals and books with studies of the House because its large membership and

---

[1] Federalist 52 and 63.

firm rules of majority party control have made it amenable to quantitative analysis. The Senate has been comparatively neglected.

There has been a welcome change in that trend in recent years. Rising polarization in Congress has led to renewed interest in the role that political parties play in the Senate, and there is an emerging debate over the extent of the power they wield. Scholars have generally concluded that powerful majority parties are more likely to be found in the House than in the Senate because the rules of the House more easily lend themselves to majority party control (Aldrich and Rohde 2001; Cox and McCubbins 2005). The Senate has been viewed as an idiosyncratic institution in which power rests with individual senators and political parties are on the sidelines (Fenno 1989; Sinclair 1986; Smith 2005). The Senate's rules empower members with the right to unlimited debate and to offer amendments on any subject. So armed, individual senators can tie the chamber in knots with delaying tactics or force a vote on a policy of their choosing. The breadth of this power has led the majority party to coordinate closely with the minority and to accommodate the needs of individual members in order to move legislation toward passage.

The traditional view of the Senate is being challenged by new evidence. Recent studies describe a variety of ways in which political parties shape legislative outcomes in the Senate. By one account, the two parties exacerbate gridlock and make it harder for the nation to address critical problems (Sinclair 2002). As reaching an accommodation has grown more difficult, Democrats and Republicans have taken advantage of Senate rules to block action by the other side, and the two parties coexist in a frustrating legislative stalemate. Another contingent of scholars maintains that the Senate bears important similarities to the House of Representatives (Den Hartog and Monroe 2011; Gailmard and Jenkins 2007; Monroe and Roberts 2008). Party leaders have adopted new legislative strategies to help them pass legislation tilted toward the views of the majority. The Senate majority can take on the minority in fierce legislative battle and often win the day rather than accept compromise.

This book offers a new perspective on the role of the Senate majority party that I call the theory of limited influence (Hanson 2014). I study the majority party's management of the annual appropriations process to show that it has an important but constrained ability to influence legislative outcomes on the Senate floor. The appropriations process is well suited to the study of majority party power because it occurs annually, and variation in the majority's method of passing spending bills can be observed over time. Congress traditionally follows a routine set of practices known as the "regular order" to pass spending legislation. In the regular order, a dozen bills to fund the government are written in committee in the House and Senate and brought to the floor of each chamber for debate, amendment, and final passage. I show how the Senate majority party manipulates the appropriations process by abandoning the regular order and instead packaging bills together into massive "omnibus" bills. The one-two punch of skipping individual debate on a bill and then creating a package helps the majority party limit troublesome amendments and pass the budget at the cost of reducing the opportunity for all members to participate in lawmaking. The majority party protects its reputation and strengthens the reelection prospects of its members with this strategy, but it cannot systematically secure its policy goals.

In the last three decades, the most dominant parties in the Senate have been likely to follow the regular order. Majority parties that are small, divided, and ideologically distant from the minority have been likely to depart from this tradition. They have shut down debate and created omnibus packages that reduce the transparency of the legislative process and centralize decision-making authority in a few key players. This finding appears counterintuitive from the standpoint of some partisan theories of Congress, but it is consistent with a broader understanding of party power. Majority parties in a dominant position in the Senate can meet their goals without taking unusual steps to influence the legislative process. Those in a weaker position use their influence to manage a floor that is slipping out of their control.

In the remainder of this chapter, I lay the groundwork for these arguments. The chapter begins with a general review of party power in Congress and turns to focus on the debate over the role of parties in the Senate, weaving in the words of former Senate majority leaders Tom Daschle and Trent Lott and other policy makers to give additional insight into academic debates. I explain the annual budget and appropriations process and why scholars have used it as a window into Congress to view larger trends. I integrate theories of parties and omnibus formation in a way that takes full account of the Senate's distinctive role in the constitutional system. Finally, I draw a set of expectations from this new theory to test in chapters to come.

PARTY POWER IN CONGRESS

What does it mean to say that a political party in Congress is powerful? The answer to this question begins with the individual members who make up parties. It has been common since the publication of David Mayhew's *Congress: The Electoral Connection* (1974) and Richard Fenno's *Congressmen in Committees* (1973) to characterize individual members of the House and Senate as strategic actors who systematically pursue a set of goals. The first goal is the desire to win reelection. Individual senators can only stay in office with the periodic approval of the voters of their states in elections. To meet this goal, they cast votes aimed at winning the support of voters and avoid issues that will cause them trouble. They send out press releases and give interviews to the media to generate name recognition and claim credit for their accomplishments. They hire staff devoted to solving the problems of their constituents (Fiorina 1989). They secure funds to support projects such as constructing a bridge or purchasing equipment for law enforcement (Evans 2004). They raise money to build campaign war chests. The list goes on. Members have other goals in addition to winning election, such as the adoption of particular policies or gaining influence in the chamber, but reelection is generally regarded as the first and most important goal since it is the prerequisite to accomplishing anything else.

Political parties are valuable because they help members meet their goals. A member's party identification acts as a "brand name" that conveys key information about the member's views to the electorate and helps voters identify like-minded candidates on Election Day (Aldrich 2011). Members also benefit at the ballot box by associating with a party that has a positive reputation for legislative accomplishment (Cox and McCubbins 2005; Lee 2009). Parties provide members with resources such as money, staff, and advice to run political campaigns (Jacobson 2009). Finally, they offer an organizational structure that allows members to coordinate to meet common legislative goals (Aldrich 2011). They can exercise negative agenda control to keep troublesome issues off the floor, or positive agenda control to help push desired legislation to final passage.

The strength of a political party in Congress is typically defined in terms of its ability to influence the legislative process so that the results will meet the goals of its members (Aldrich 2011; Aldrich and Rohde 2001; Cox and McCubbins 2005; Kiewiet and McCubbins 1991; Krehbiel 1998; Smith 2007). As John Aldrich explains, "[A] party will be 'strong' when it helps its members win what they collectively desire as partisans rather than winning what might be achievable from a majority formed on some other basis" (2011, 220). The 100 members of the Senate could theoretically form a variety of different winning coalitions to pass legislation. Many of these coalitions could "roll" the majority party by passing legislation that most of its members oppose. For example, forty-nine members of the minority party could join together with two members of the majority party to form a winning coalition for a bill that is opposed by the remaining members of the majority party. A "strong" party is one that can influence the legislative process to narrow the list of potential outcomes to those that meet the goals of the members of the majority party.

Not all scholars have accepted that parties have a meaningful ability to influence legislative outcomes. Keith Krehbiel (1992, 1998) maintains that most legislative outcomes can be explained as the result of the preferences of members and that the two parties at best offset each other in their efforts to influence the legislative process. In Krehbiel's view, the passage of a bill on which sixty members of the majority party in the Senate agree simply reflects the shared preferences of members. The existence of the party did not contribute in a meaningful way to the outcome of the vote. One result of his challenge was to lead scholars to a more careful identification of ways in which parties add value to members' efforts above and beyond what they can achieve on their own. A substantial body of research on party influence in the House of Representatives has since satisfied most scholars that parties do influence legislative outcomes, at least in the House (Aldrich 2011; Binder 1997; Cox and McCubbins 2005; Smith 2007). As I discuss later in this chapter, there is far more contention about the existence of party influence in the Senate.

A brief survey of partisan theories of Congress reveals a wide-ranging debate about the conditions under which the majority party is able and likely to influence outcomes and whether it meets policy or electoral goals through its efforts. One well-known framework is the theory of Conditional Party Government (CPG) in which members who are unified and have preferences distinct from the minority delegate authority to their leaders to influence outcomes in order to pursue shared policy goals (Aldrich and Rohde 2001). Smith offers an alternative framework in which party influence is exercised to pursue electoral and policy goals "when the party's small size or lack of cohesiveness puts floor victories at risk. Weakness in the majority party generates the need for influence" (2007, 78). A third alternative is the "cartel" theory in which party members have a continuous ability and incentive to influence legislative outcomes in order to enhance their party reputation in the pursuit of reelection goals (Cox and McCubbins 2005). These three frameworks are quite different in spirit. In the first, a dominant majority party uses its influence to extend its control over the floor. In the second, a struggling majority party uses its influence to stave off defeat. In the third, the majority party influences outcomes without regard to the strength or weakness of its position.

The diversity of these approaches reveals a problem in the common shorthand used by political scientists to describe a party that can influence outcomes as "strong" and one that cannot as "weak." This language unhelpfully conflates a party's descriptive characteristics with its ability and inclination to influence outcomes. The implication is that parties observed wielding influence are also strong in other ways, such as being large and unified. This conclusion tacitly endorses the argument that influence arises out of majority party dominance and masks the important debate about the conditions under which a party is able and likely to influence legislative outcomes. As Smith notes, a large and unified party might not be observed influencing outcomes because it has no need to do it. "A large majority party can win votes without the support of some of its members. A very cohesive majority party can win votes without having to ask its members to vote differently than they would otherwise. A large and cohesive party makes life particularly easy for the majority party leadership" (Smith 2007, 78).

The most serious problem with the standard jargon is that it may obscure the real situation on the floor. A small and divided majority party that finds itself in deep trouble on the floor and influences the legislative process to escape is considered "strong" by the standard definition. A party that is so large and unified that it gets its way without influencing the legislative process appears "weak" because it has taken no observable action to shape the outcome. Black is white. Up is down. Shorthand jargon that was intended to simplify matters has now confused them. A more useful approach, and the one I take in this book, is to use the terms "strong" and "weak" as summary descriptions of the majority party's ability to meet its legislative goals based on its overall strategic position in the chamber. Large and unified parties are strong. Small and divided parties are weak. In the Senate, a large ideological gulf between the two parties weakens the majority by intensifying minority opposition and raising the risk of gridlock.

I use the term "influence" to refer to the majority party taking action that shifts legislative outcomes away from what would occur without the party's efforts. Influence may be directly observable, such as when the House adopts a closed rule, or indirectly observable through measures such as majority party roll rates. The task of legislative scholars is to identify different forms of influence, the conditions under which the majority party is able and likely to use them, and the goals it can achieve by doing so. As I show in this book, abandoning the regular order and forming an omnibus bill are directly observable forms of influence that the Senate majority party is most likely to use when it encounters serious trouble on the floor because it is weak. The majority party's influence over the legislative process helps it meet electoral goals and protect its party reputation by limiting amendments and passing a budget.

This conception of party power fits poorly with CPG and the cartel theory, but these theories were written to describe the House of Representatives rather than the Senate. An obvious point of disagreement is that Aldrich and Rohde (2000; 2001) predict majority party homogeneity both creates the ability to influence the legislative process and increases the likelihood that influence will be observed. I show that members are able and more likely to package bills together when they are divided. One of the broad objectives of this book is to demonstrate that common conceptions of party power such as CPG do not fit well in the Senate because they were not designed with its distinctive rules in mind. This is less an indictment of CPG, which by many accounts fits well in the House of Representatives, than it is a statement about the need for a partisan theory of the Senate. This book takes an important step toward creating such a theory by demonstrating the important but limited nature of majority party influence in the Senate and the conditions under which it is likely to be used.

MAJORITY PARTY INFLUENCE IN THE SENATE

The traditional understanding of the Senate places its emphasis on the majority party's inability to influence legislative outcomes. This understanding originated in the 1980s as researchers took note of a rising degree of activism among individual senators. Once, members respectfully deferred to those with seniority and labored patiently in committee for years to develop policy expertise. The new Senate was more independent and entrepreneurial. Senators were active in dozens of policy areas, offering amendments and speaking their minds in a way that would have violated deeply held norms in the decades before. In this freewheeling arena, power rested with individual senators, and the majority party was seen as having little ability to change legislative outcomes beyond what could be achieved on the floor (Fenno 1989; Sinclair 1986; Smith 1989).

The individualistic Senate rests on a foundation created by two crucial rules that make it difficult for the majority to control the agenda. First, debate in the Senate is famously unlimited, and most parliamentary motions are debatable. Members can speak for as long as they wish unless sixty votes are secured for cloture (Koger 2010). Second, senators are generally free to offer amendments regardless of their germaneness to the topic at hand (Smith 2005).[2] The combination of these two rules is potent. Together, they are said to make it virtually impossible for the majority to conduct the routine business of the chamber without the cooperation of the minority or to exercise firm control over the legislative agenda. Instead, the majority governs the Senate through "unanimous consent" agreements negotiated with the minority that set the terms of debate for legislation. In the words of Senate scholar Barbara Sinclair: "Keeping the Senate functioning as a legislature requires broad accommodation; it dictates satisfying every senator to some extent. A reasonably cohesive majority party can run the House without consulting the minority. The Senate only runs smoothly when the majority leader and the minority leader cooperate and not always then" (Sinclair 2005, 13).

An important consequence of the Senate's rules in the traditional understanding is that the policies that emerge from the chamber are likely to be the product of decisions on the floor rather than the majority's preferred policy (Smith 2005). Senators are free to amend any legislation put forward by the majority and can delay matters indefinitely to enforce that right if necessary. In the absence of effective tools to control the agenda, the policies favored by the typical member of the majority party are likely to be moderated as they are amended to the satisfaction of the senators whose support is needed to win passage on the floor. It is also difficult for the majority to avoid voting on issues it would prefer to leave off the agenda. Democrats demonstrated this principle in 1996 when they offered a non-germane amendment raising the minimum wage to every bill that came to the floor and brought the Senate to a standstill until the Republican majority agreed to allow a vote on it (Sinclair 2012). The amendment passed.

As parties in Congress have grown more ideologically unified and distinct from each other, scholars have turned their attention toward

---

[2] There is an exception to the rule that amendments do not have to be germane. Amendments to appropriations bills must be germane according to Rule 16 of the Standing Rules of the Senate and may be challenged on those grounds if a senator raises a point of order during debate.

identifying whether the role of parties has changed. A common finding of this work is that unified parties that are ideologically distant from each other contribute to gridlock (Brady and Volden 2006; Rae and Campbell 2001). Sinclair explains that the compromises needed to run the Senate have grown more elusive as the parties have grown farther apart. Actual or threatened filibusters stemming from the predilection of individual members or minority strategy now routinely delay the passage of legislation in the Senate and force the majority to seek sixty votes for bills to clear the floor (Sinclair 2002). Lacking strong tools to control the floor, the majority is often powerless to push legislation through to passage. Sinclair describes the Senate as the "choke point" in the American legislative process and reports that "the Senate floor proved to be the single greatest obstacle and the place that the greatest attrition occurred" once bills clear committee (Sinclair 2002, 258–259). In a similar vein, Steve Smith reviewed a variety of procedural changes thought to enhance the power of the majority in the Senate in recent decades and concluded that they were part of a "parliamentary arms race" in which "the minority is quick to obstruct and the majority is quick to restrict" (Smith 2010, 1–2). In a polarized Senate, gridlock is a more likely outcome than a strong majority party grip on the floor.

Accounts such as these remain rooted in the traditional understanding of the Senate. They identify important party effects, but they do not maintain that the Senate majority party has strong tools of agenda control or can shift policy outcomes toward the party's preferred position. Gridlock is a typical outcome precisely because the majority party lacks real power to control the agenda. This traditional understanding has come under challenge by a new group of scholars who argue that the Senate majority party has a greater ability to control outcomes than previously understood. The opening salvo in the revisionist account of the Senate came in a volume of collected essays entitled *Why Not Parties?* (Monroe and Roberts 2008). Nathan Monroe, Jason Roberts, and David Rohde argue in the introductory chapter of the book that party effects should be visible in the Senate even if they are not as pronounced as those in the House of Representatives. The book's essays provide evidence for a variety of party effects, ranging from a majority party advantage in the distribution of pork barrel spending to evidence of negative and positive agenda control in the chamber. Subsequent work has developed this line of reasoning and identified disagreements over whether parties meet electoral or policy goals by influencing the legislative process.

Frances Lee identifies a role for parties structuring conflict and meeting electoral goals in her book *Beyond Ideology* (2009). She finds that the efforts of parties to enhance their own party reputation and damage their opponent's are a major source of conflict on the Senate floor. Majority party members routinely support their leadership on procedural votes aimed at securing control over the agenda, while minority members seek to embarrass and disrupt the majority by forcing it to vote on politically damaging issues. These efforts do not lead to systematic policy "wins" for each side. Indeed, in Lee's account, much of this conflict lacks a clear ideological basis.

Other scholars find that the Senate majority party can exercise a substantial degree of agenda control. Sean Gailmard and Jeffrey Jenkins (2007, 698) describe a "coalescing theoretical agreement" in favor of negative agenda control in the Senate and present indirect evidence of it by demonstrating that the Senate majority party is rolled by the minority no more often than the House majority party. Chris Den Hartog and Nathan Monroe analyze the consideration of amendments and legislation that pass the Senate and conclude that successful legislation typically moves policy in the ideological direction of the majority party. "When it comes to pushing its proposals through various stages of the legislative process, the majority is never worse off than its opponents, and is often better off" (Den Hartog and Monroe 2011, 185). Together, these arguments challenge the heart of the traditional account of the Senate. A Senate majority party that can keep unwanted items off the agenda and push its own proposals through to passage can wield a substantial degree of influence and is more similar to the House majority party than has been commonly understood.

I evaluate both the traditional and revisionist assessments of the majority party in the Senate and conclude that neither accurately characterizes its influence. The evidence from the appropriations process shows that the majority party has more of an ability to influence legislative outcomes than traditionalists have found. The party can package bills together in a way that makes passage of the budget more likely and reduces the opportunity to offer amendments – clearly important forms of positive and negative agenda control. But the benefits it receives from its influence are constrained. There is little evidence that the majority party can systematically win the adoption of its preferred policies in the manner suggested by Den Hartog and Monroe. Over the last thirty-eight years, omnibus bills have been much more likely to win bipartisan support than to provoke partisan divisions. The majority party's ability to keep items off the agenda by suppressing amendments is also limited. Debate on amendments is reduced but not eliminated by the omnibus process. Finally, the majority party is most likely to create an omnibus package when it is small, divided, and threatened by gridlock. The simplest interpretation of this evidence is that the majority party has a limited ability to control the agenda that it uses to stave off defeat and avoid political harm when it is threatened rather than to dominate the floor as the majority party can in the House. It meets electoral goals with its efforts to protect the party's reputation, but it cannot systematically advance a partisan policy agenda.

MAJORITY PARTY POWER FROM THE LEADER'S PERSPECTIVE

One way to gauge alternative views of majority party power in the Senate is by talking to those elected to manage the chamber: Senate majority leaders. Interviews are a particularly valuable form of data because elected officials are in a direct position to observe matters of interest and importance to researchers. Outstanding works of scholarship such as Richard Fenno's *The Power of the Purse*, Nelson Polsby's *How Congress Evolves*, and Richard Hall's *Participation in Congress* adeptly demonstrate that interviews in conjunction with other forms of data gathering can generate insights that other methods alone cannot. They support "generalization about expectations, perceptions and attitudes, norms, roles and role behavior, plus the mechanisms operating to maintain harmony among these elements of a political system" (Fenno 1966, xxviii).[3] For this book, I interviewed former Senate majority leaders Tom Daschle and Trent Lott and seven current and former senior staff members in both chambers and of both parties with substantial experience in the appropriations process and decades of service in Congress.[4] Their accounts provide valuable context and interpretative guidance for the findings of this book.

[3] Richard Fenno notes in the introduction to *The Power of the Purse*: "An effort has been made to follow David Truman's wise advice to the student of political institutions to 'perform his task in quantitative terms if he can and in qualitative terms if he must.' In describing the appropriations process in Congress, one 'can' and one 'must.'" His observation remains valid today.

[4] All quotes are verbatim quotations transcribed in notes taken during the interview or from recordings of the interview (leaders only). Staff members currently working in Congress are understandably reluctant to be identified by name or indirectly through the details of their job descriptions. For that reason, I give only general descriptions of the positions held by staff members and identify them with the letters A–G. All interviews were conducted in the winter of 2012.

Senators Lott and Daschle both gave accounts that are more consistent with the traditional view of majority party influence than with revisionist accounts when asked about their experience leading the Senate. In Senator Lott's view, the tools at the disposal of the majority leader to control the floor are painfully inadequate. The majority party cannot control the Senate on its own and must seek cooperation from the minority in order to conduct business:

> [Leading the Senate] is on the back of the majority leader with the acquiescence of the minority leader. For the most part, the only real power he has is the respect for the position and the power of his personal persuasion. He's not like the Speaker who has a Rules Committee he can call over and say, "Bring this bill up now and I don't want any amendments." [In the House,] you go to the floor. Your party votes with you. You decide what the bill's going to be, how long it's going to be debated, and if it's going to be amended, by what. There's not something comparable to that in the Senate. Now, I used to be accused by [Senator Robert] Byrd of trying to change that, to try to make the Senate a mini-House. I didn't want that. I didn't like the messiness of the Senate, but the fact of the matter is, that is the Senate. I've never been in any other body that was more dependent upon the strength and ability of the leaders of the two parties. (Interview with author, March 7, 2012)

Similarly, Senator Daschle emphasized the traditional story of leading the Senate through painstaking work to build coalitions in the chamber. In his telling, the successful passage of legislation in the chamber is a consequence of having shared purpose among members, providing enough time for proposals to ripen for consideration, and making members feel invested in the process by including them in it (interview with author, February 15, 2012). This is a challenging task. Senators are independent and trying to lead them is like "loading frogs into a wheelbarrow."

In Daschle's view, a leader has three major tools to lead the chamber. The most important is the right of first recognition that grants the leader the right to be heard before other members on the Senate floor. "It's a powerful tool to get what you want," Daschle observed. The value of this tool is that it gives the majority the ability to call up a bill and make the first procedural moves on it to gain an advantage in setting the agenda. For example, the majority party can temporarily block the ability of the minority to offer amendments by calling up a bill and immediately offering a series of amendments that fill the limited number of slots available at that moment under parliamentary rules – a tactic known as "filling the amendment tree" (Davidson, Oleszek, and Lee 2012, 243). Second,

Daschle noted that a leader has the "capacity to do favors for senators, whether it's committee assignments, fundraising in their state or at an event ... speaking to their constituents, meeting with people" (interview with author, February 15, 2012). Third, a leader has his or her persuasive ability.

One striking fact that emerges from the leaders' accounts is the difficulty of passing legislation on the Senate floor even when that legislation is widely supported. Former Senator majority leader Trent Lott recounted this story:

> I remember one time Ted Kennedy objected to a bill. This was not long after I'd been elected leader, 1996. And he objected to going to conference. I called the senior staff person in, a lady, and I said, "I want to get this done." "Well, you can't." I said, "What do you mean, 'You can't'?" She said, "Oh, there are multiple hurdles. He could demand the bill be read. We'd have to have six or seven votes to break the filibuster." I said, "Look me in the eyes. I don't care if it takes the rest of the year. This bill is going to conference so go out there and tell 'em to start reading it." That was like seven o'clock. I went down to the dining room and started having supper. About 9:20, she showed up and said, "Senator Kennedy has decided maybe we don't need to read that bill." Sure enough, it took me until the following Thursday. It kept the Senate in an extra week to force action on this bill. I got it done. The final vote was like 98–2. But the Senate had to go through a whole week, and jump through all these hoops and over all these hurdles to get the result that passed overwhelmingly. So, it's tough in the Senate to force things to a result. That's why it is critical that the majority leader have some modicum of cooperation from the minority leader. (Interview with author, March 7, 2012)

Stories like this underscore how members can use the procedural tools available to them to slow the passage of legislation through the Senate even when most members support it. Much as Sinclair describes in her account of the Senate, the possibility of gridlock is a continual threat, and leaders run the chamber as best they can through persuasion and by seeking to reach accommodations with the minority and individual members. While the majority party may have some tools at its disposal to influence the Senate's agenda, they are not enough to shift the balance of power decisively in its direction.

The views of the leaders offer a helpful perspective on academic debates about the role of parties in the Senate. Their emphasis on the need for persuasion and the paucity of tools available to the majority leader reinforces the need to rely on the traditional understanding of the Senate as a starting point for analysis. The Senate's rules place firm limits on the majority party, and gridlock is a common result. Senator Lott's lament about the concerted effort it took to pass a bill that ultimately received the support of ninety-eight senators is particularly instructive. His tale suggests that the Senate's rules make it difficult to pass even broadly supported legislation, but that majority party influence can help to overcome these difficulties. A useful lesson from his example is that analyzing legislation that neither party has an interest in blocking may offer a clear view of majority party influence in the Senate.

Appropriations bills are an example of such legislation. With rare exception, both parties agree that the bills should be passed and the government funded even if they disagree over the details. Gridlock is an unacceptable outcome to both sides since it may result in a damaging government shutdown. Passing spending legislation also takes considerable effort by the majority party since it traditionally requires the party to debate and pass a dozen complicated bills. Senator Ted Stevens (R-AK), the former chair of the Senate Appropriations Committee, would don a tie with a picture of the Incredible Hulk when he managed spending bills on the floor to symbolize the Herculean effort he was undertaking. My approach in this book is to analyze how party characteristics affect the majority party's ability to manage the floor and its choice of strategy when it seeks to pass spending bills. Focusing only on appropriations bills no doubt limits my ability to make broad claims about the role of parties in the Senate, but, as Lee (2009) demonstrated in her analysis of "good government" legislation in *Beyond Ideology*, analyzing subsets of legislation based on selected characteristics (in her case, nonideological bills) can shed light on poorly understood aspects of party power. Appropriations bills offer the opportunity to show how parties influence the legislative process when gridlock is not a desired outcome.

Next, I review the appropriations process and how omnibus spending bills have become an important feature of it. I explain theories about how omnibus appropriations bills form and report why policy makers believe that the practice of packaging bills together has become common. Finally, I integrate these ideas into a new theory of majority party influence over the appropriations process. I show that the Senate majority party uses the limited influence at its disposal to avoid harm when it is small, divided, or distant from the minority by abandoning the regular order and creating omnibus spending bills to ease the passage of the budget and limit amending. Its efforts help it protect its party reputation but fall short of meeting partisan policy goals.

THE BUDGET AND APPROPRIATIONS PROCESS

Scholars have long recognized the advantages to studying the appropriations process to understand a wide range of topics in Congress, including the role of parties, distributive politics, the filibuster, and other matters (Aldrich and Rohde 2000; Evans 2004; Fenno 1966; Kiewiet and McCubbins 1991; Schickler and Sides 2000; Shepsle and Weingast 1981; Shepsle et al. 2009; Smith 2010; Stein and Bickers 1994a, 1994b; Stewart 1989; Wawro and Schickler 2006). These advantages stem from the fact that appropriations bills are considered every year, and so variation in this annual process can be used to identify trends in Congress and observe how they unfold over time.

The Appropriations Committee is widely regarded as one of the most powerful committees in Congress. James Madison argued in Federalist 58 that the "power over the purse may, in fact, be regarded as the most complete and effectual weapon with which any constitution can arm the immediate representatives of the people, for obtaining a redress of every grievance, and for carrying into effect every just and salutary measure." Few today would disagree with Madison's assessment. Tax dollars fuel the operations of government. They pay for programs, fund worker salaries, purchase equipment, and keep the lights on in government offices. New programs cannot take effect until Congress appropriates funds to carry them out, and cutting off funds is the most potent check Congress can place on federal action. As constitutional scholar Gordon Silverstein (2009) often notes, the Vietnam War did not end when Congress revoked the Gulf of Tonkin resolution but when it finally cut off appropriations for the war.

Today the committee is responsible for allocating around a third of the federal budget, or $1.1 trillion dollars in fiscal year 2013, according to the Congressional Budget Office.[5] This includes all "discretionary" spending on matters such as defense, education, scientific research, or housing. The remainder of the budget consists of spending on entitlement programs such as Social Security, Medicare, and Medicaid or interest payments on the federal debt. Spending on entitlement programs is commonly referred to as "mandatory" spending. Permanent law authorizes the Treasury to spend these funds automatically without the need for annual action by Congress.

---

[5] Elmendorf, Doug, "Changes in Discretionary Funding during the Past Few Years," March 26, 2013. Congressional Budget Office. http://www.cbo.gov/publication/44020. Accessed July 24, 2013.

The Appropriations Committees of the House and Senate were created in 1865 and 1867, respectively. Early histories of the committee focus on the House of Representatives and trace efforts to centralize and decentralize of power over spending in the committee between 1865 and 1921 (Stewart 1989). Richard Fenno's *The Power of the Purse* (1966) is the classic study of the appropriations process in both chambers. Fenno studied the committee's activities between 1947 and 1962, drawing from extensive case studies and interviews of committee members. The process he described was orderly and bipartisan. Power over spending was distributed among the subcommittees of the House and Senate Appropriations Committees, which ranged in number from nine to fifteen during Fenno's period of study. There was no formal structure in Congress to set an overall budget, but committee norms emphasized frugality and effectively constrained federal spending. The Appropriations Committee is still regarded as bipartisan today, although not as much as in the past (Aldrich and Rohde 2000). It is often noted for following the practice of "universalism" in which benefits are granted to all members regardless of party as a way to build a large coalition of support for the passage of its bills (Evans 2004; Madonna 2011; Weingast 1979).[6]

The modern budget process was created in the 1970s. Aaron Wildavsky and Naomi Caiden (2004) explain that the orderly process described by Fenno began to collapse shortly after the publication of *The Power of the Purse* in 1966. Slow economic growth and rising government spending led to deficits and intense new conflicts over the budget between the Democratic Congress and Republican President Richard M. Nixon. Congress was poorly positioned to challenge the president in this debate. The Budget and Accounting Act of 1921 had centralized budgetary expertise in the Executive Branch and placed the power to propose a budget in

---

[6] Several of my interview subjects repeated the same phrase to describe the perceived lack of partisanship among appropriators: "There are Republicans, there are Democrats and there are appropriators." I saw the committee's bipartisanship firsthand during the summer of 2004 while working for the most junior member of the House minority, Democratic Representative Stephanie Herseth Sandlin (SD-AL). Committee staff informed our office that the Republican leadership had directed that no earmarks be provided to the new representative in order to prevent her from claiming credit for them at election time. The Republican appropriations staff responded to this directive by cooperating with Democrats to recommend funding in a way that would not be directly traceable to Herseth Sandlin's at-large district in the state of South Dakota. The report accompanying the fiscal year 2005 Commerce, Justice, and State bill directed the Department of Justice to consider providing a grant to the "County of Minnehaha" without identifying it as being located in South Dakota. It was the only county on an extensive list that was not also identified by state. See House Report 108-576, page 47.

the hands of the president. Congress lacked its own budget experts and the decentralized appropriations process made it difficult for members to understand trade-offs or to set and enforce spending targets. Its response was to pass the Congressional Budget and Impoundment Control Act of 1974. The new law expanded the capacity of Congress to make budgetary decisions by creating the Congressional Budget Office and new Budget Committees in the House and Senate. It also established a set of procedures and timetables to create an annual budget and to incorporate the writing and passage of appropriations bills into a central budgetary framework (LeLoup 2005; Schick 2007).

The Congressional Budget and Impoundment Control Act requires the federal budget to be developed and passed in Congress between January and the beginning of a new fiscal year on October 1. The process begins with the submission of the president's budget to Congress at the beginning of each year. The House and Senate review the president's request and are required to pass a budget resolution setting out recommended funding levels by April 15. The budget resolution does not have force of law but it is the basis for a 302(a) allocation to the House and Senate Appropriations Committees that sets out the total amount of money the committee may spend that year. The committee divides these funds among its subcommittees (currently numbered at twelve) in a second distribution referred to as a 302(b) allocation. Each subcommittee is responsible for writing an appropriations bill to provide funding for federal agencies and programs under broad jurisdictional categories, such as agriculture or defense. The subcommittees are not automatically required to follow spending recommendations contained in the budget resolution, but appropriations bills may be subject to a point of order on the floor if they exceed a subcommittee's 302(b) allocation (Keith and Schick 2003).

The writing and adoption of appropriations bills in the House and Senate are structured by a powerful set of norms and traditions known as the "regular order" (Oleszek 2007; Schick 2007). Under the regular order, the House of Representatives acts first on appropriations bills. Its subcommittees write and approve the initial draft of each spending bill. The bills are approved by the full House Committee on Appropriations and brought to the floor of the House for debate, amendment, and final passage by early summer. The Senate acts second. In earlier years, Senate subcommittees did their work by modifying the House versions of the bills. Today, Senate subcommittees write their own appropriations bills. They are then approved in full committee and brought to the floor for debate, amendment, and final passage. The process concludes when the two chambers meet in conference to resolve their differences and send the bills back to each chamber for a final vote.

The budget process established by the Congressional Budget and Impoundment Control Act of 1974 is now in shambles. Both the House and Senate routinely miss the April 15 deadline for passing a budget resolution. It is also common for one or both chambers to fail to pass a budget resolution or for the two chambers to fail to agree on a final version of the resolution. When this occurs, the Appropriations Committees in the two chambers are left without clear guidance about their budget allocation and the writing and passage of appropriations bills is made more difficult. The adoption of spending bills through the regular order has also grown increasingly rare. One staff member recalled: "The appropriations process used to be the most reliable thing in town....We pretty much always got it done. We pretty much always took the individual bills to the floor" (Staff Interview E 2012). Today, Congress routinely fails to bring individual spending bills to the floor for debate.

The abandonment of the regular order is an important change in the way members of Congress conduct their business. Rules, procedures, and budgetary structures are ways of allocating power in Congress and shape the way in which policies are formed (Binder 1997; Stewart 1989). The regular order is characterized by the fact that it is an open and permissive system that gives rank-and-file members of both parties an ability to participate in lawmaking (Schick 2007; Green and Burns 2010). Appropriations bills are brought to the floor individually, and members have an opportunity to make speeches, offer amendments, and cast votes to gain a variety of opportunities for position taking and credit claiming.[7] When the regular order is abandoned, some of the appropriations bills may never be brought to the floor for debate on an individual basis at all. Members lose opportunities to offer amendments and claim credit for their accomplishments. Instead, they must look for alternative ways to pass the budget that offer considerably fewer opportunities to participate in lawmaking. The most common alternative is bring a group of appropriations bills to the floor as a single package rather than individually.

There are two types of packages that may take the place of regular appropriations bills once the regular order is abandoned: traditional

---

[7] In my own experience working in the Senate, the consideration of the annual spending bills offered a bonanza of press opportunities to claim credit for spending on favored programs and projects. A press release announcing funding levels would accompany every stage in the appropriations process from subcommittee approval of a bill to its final passage.

omnibus bills and full-year continuing resolutions. Traditional omnibus bills combine two or more regular appropriations bills along with unrelated legislation into a single legislative package. The most favorable circumstances for lawmaking on an omnibus package occur when party leaders package a group of bills together and then bring the package to the floor for an open debate. Members can offer amendments as usual, although many complain that omnibus bills are called up against tight budgetary deadlines that have the practical effect of shortening debate. A second method of creating an omnibus bill occurs during conference negotiations – the last stage of the legislative process in which House and Senate negotiators create an identical version of a bill for final approval by both chambers. Party leaders create the package by finding a bill that is already is conference and adding other bills to the end of it. This method of creating an omnibus package sharply curtails the opportunity for amendment because conference reports are not amendable when they are returned to the floor of the House and Senate for a final vote.[8] The effect is compounded for any bill that is added to the package without first being debated on the floor in the regular order. These bills are effectively passed under the equivalent of a closed rule without any opportunity for members to amend them at all.[9] In theory, senators could exercise their right to unlimited debate and filibuster an omnibus conference report in order to protect their right to amend, but such a strategy is perceived as costly because members who filibuster a bill could be blamed for a government shutdown. As Chapter 5 explains, Senate Majority Leader Tom Daschle's effort to filibuster a conference report ended when eleven Democrats joined with Republicans to vote for cloture. Between 1975 and 2012, eight omnibus packages were brought to the floor as conference reports.

Full-year continuing resolutions are related to traditional omnibus bills but have a different origin. The term "continuing resolution" (or a CR in Capitol Hill jargon) refers to legislation that provides funding

---

[8] House and Senate negotiators may be unable to resolve a dispute and report an item as being "in disagreement" among the conferees. When this occurs, members of the House and Senate vote separately on items in disagreement until they reach a compromise.

[9] One longtime staff member recalled being "horrified" when he first saw a bill that had not been considered on the Senate floor added to an omnibus package in conference. The staff member explained: "[Because of obstruction], the only policy people in either body get to do is appropriations. If you take away the ability to set policy in appropriations bills, you have eliminated people as participating in overseeing the government" (Staff Interview C 2012).

by extending the previous year's appropriations bills. CRs are normally temporary measures that provide an additional few weeks or months of funding for the government if Congress fails to pass the regular appropriations bills by the beginning of the new fiscal year on October 1. A full-year CR extends the previous year's appropriations bills for the remainder of the fiscal year. In theory, this means that Congress has abandoned its effort to pass a new set of regular appropriations bills. In practice, full-year CRs often contain new legislation or the full text of regular appropriations bills and may be indistinguishable in a practical sense from traditional omnibus bills.[10] Some care needs to be taken when describing CRs for that reason. My approach is to use the terms adopted by policy makers to describe different varieties of CRs. A "temporary" CR is a simple extension of the previous year's bills that lasts a few weeks or months. A "clean" CR (either temporary or full year) is one that contains only an extension of the previous year's bills as opposed to new legislation. A "legislative" CR (my own term) is one that includes new legislation.

In the interviews and case studies presented in this book, policy makers often describe a CR as an undesirable alternative to the passage of an omnibus bill. The concern being expressed by policy makers is that Congress will adopt a clean CR that keeps the government running but prevents members from writing new legislative language that will allow them to claim credit for funding new projects, tinker with ongoing programs, or issue guidance to federal agencies. Clean CRs are so unpopular that it is rare to find a full-year CR that qualifies as "clean" in practice. For example, H.J. Res. 395, a CR for fiscal year 1988, consisted entirely of the full texts of regular appropriations bills rather than extensions of old bills.[11] H.R. 933, the "Consolidated and Further Continuing Appropriations Act" for fiscal year 2013, provided funding in place of all twelve regular appropriations bills.[12] The CR included full

---

[10] Regular appropriations bills may also be incorporated into continuing resolutions by reference rather than by including the full text of the bill. In this case, the language of the continuing resolution states that a specific bill referred to by its bill number is deemed passed. For example, H.J. Res. 465, the continuing appropriations act for fiscal year 1986, incorporates H.R. 3037, the agriculture appropriations bill that had been finalized in conference, "as if such Act had been enacted into law."

[11] "$603.9 Billion Omnibus Funding Bill Clears," in *CQ Almanac 1987*, 43rd ed., 480–488 (Washington, DC: Congressional Quarterly, 1988). http://library.cqpress.com/cqalmanac/cqal87-1145568.

[12] See Chacko, Sarah, and Emily Holden, "With Little Ado, CR Sent to Obama's Desk," *CQ Weekly*, March 25, 2013, 580–581. http://library.cqpress.com/cqweekly/weeklyreport113-000004245454.

legislative language for five of the bills and funded the remaining seven (with several pages of exceptions) under the terms and conditions of the fiscal year 2012 versions of the bills. The "cleanest" CR in recent years was H.J. Res 20, which provided funding for fiscal year 2007. It provided funding in place of nine regular appropriations "under the authority and conditions" of their fiscal year 2006 counterparts but added more than fifty pages of new legislative language spelling out exceptions, establishing new funding levels, and specifying the terms under which spending could take place. Most full-year CRs in the last four decades have provided funding through some mix of new legislation and extensions of old bills.

Like omnibus bills, CRs are normally open to amendment in the Senate unless they come to the floor as conference reports or a unanimous consent agreement is in place. For example, H.R. 933 (described earlier) was amended on the Senate floor with a provision that restricted National Science Foundation research funds for political science to projects that advance economic or national security goals, much to the chagrin of political scientists. Also as with omnibus bills, members often complain that they have fewer opportunities to debate and amend a CR compared with the opportunities they would have considering each bill individually in the regular order.

Full-year CRs are close enough cousins to traditional omnibus bills to treat both as part of a family of packages that I give the generic label "omnibus." They share three key similarities. First, policy makers say in interviews that members generally prefer the regular order to either a traditional omnibus bill or a full-year CR. Second, both types of packages are multidimensional. They provide funding for different categories of the budget either through new legislation or by extending old legislation. Third, both types of packages limit the ability of members to participate in the legislative process. I offer further support for all of these points in the remainder of this chapter.

Table 1.1 illustrates the abandonment of the regular order and the creation of an omnibus package using the thirteen spending bills debated in 1996 as an example. In this case, the House of Representatives started out following the regular order. It passed each of the thirteen spending bills individually and sent them to the Senate. There, the regular order broke down. The Senate passed nine bills individually but did not adopt four: Commerce, Justice, and State; Interior; Labor–Health and Human Services; and Treasury-Postal. As Chapter 4 discusses in detail, the Republican majority faced a wave of Democratic amendments to those bills that forced Republicans to vote on issues they feared would damage

TABLE 1.1. *Legislative History of Fiscal Year 1997 Appropriations Bills*

Bill	House Vote	Senate Vote	Method of Adoption
Agriculture	Yes	Yes	Regular Order
Commerce, Justice, and State	Yes	No	Omnibus
District of Columbia	Yes	Yes	Regular Order
Defense	Yes	Yes	Omnibus
Energy and Water Development	Yes	Yes	Regular Order
Foreign Operations	Yes	Yes	Omnibus
Interior	Yes	No	Omnibus
Labor–Health and Human Services	Yes	No	Omnibus
Legislative Branch	Yes	Yes	Regular Order
Military Construction	Yes	Yes	Regular Order
Treasury-Postal	Yes	No	Omnibus
Transportation	Yes	Yes	Regular Order
Veterans Administration–Housing and Urban Development	Yes	Yes	Regular Order

them in an upcoming election. In response, the Republican leadership pulled two bills from the floor before a final vote and never brought the other two bills to the floor on an individual basis at all.

Funding for the government must be appropriated each year, and so the failure of the Senate to vote on the four bills meant that leaders had to find an alternative way of passing a budget. In this case, Republican leaders opted to create an omnibus package using the Defense bill as the foundation for the package. The Defense bill had been passed by both chambers already and was in conference negotiations. Republicans created a six-bill omnibus by adding the four unpassed bills and the Foreign Operations bill to the conference report for the Defense bill. The strategy meant the Senate would never have a chance to give individual consideration to the two bills that had not been brought to the floor.[13] Both chambers passed the omnibus with minimal debate and bipartisan support. The remaining seven spending bills were all passed in regular order.

This example is instructive for several reasons. First, the House succeeded in passing bills in the regular order, but the Senate did not. In this

[13] Normally, this strategy also would prevent amendments from being offered to the omnibus because it would be brought to the floor as a conference report. For reasons explained in Chapter 4, the final omnibus could have been amended, but both parties agreed not to do so.

case, the Senate majority party could not bring the bills to closure and faced potential political damage because of the Senate's open process for offering amendments. Second, the result of the majority party's action was the successful passage of a budget that drew bipartisan support. There is no evidence from voting patterns the majority won substantial policy victories with its strategy. Quite the opposite. As Chapter 4 explains, the bill was viewed by many as a victory for Democratic President Bill Clinton. Third, the Senate majority party's actions curtailed opportunities for members to offer amendments. The net effect of abandoning the regular order and creating an omnibus was to give the majority party an important, but limited, degree of control over the legislative process. It passed a budget, avoided some tough votes, and lived to fight another day. Patterns like this are consistent in years when an omnibus bill is created. The Senate majority party abandons the regular order when it faces a breakdown of its control over the floor and creates an omnibus bill in order to extricate itself from the difficulties it is facing.

Table 1.2 illustrates patterns in the appropriations process from 1975 to 2012. Congress abandoned the regular order partially or completely in twenty-four of the thirty-eight years under study, with the Senate taking the lead in not calling floor votes on individual spending bills. The Senate did not vote on 127 (26 percent) of the 485 bills written during those years as compared with 60 (12 percent) that were not voted on by the House. A total of 190 bills (39 percent) were adopted as part of package.[14] A total of 295 (61 percent) were passed in the regular order. There are two waves of omnibus bill creation. The first extends from 1979 to 1987 and the second from 1995 through today. In the first wave, Congress adapted the routine practice of passing temporary CRs into a mechanism to provide full-year funding for government agencies and to enact bills that had not passed in regular order. From 1979 to 1981, CRs were "clean" – only a few pages long and limited to formulaic extensions of the previous year's bills. The resolutions expanded in page length starting in 1982 and began to incorporate significant, new legislative provisions or the entire text of appropriations bills.[15] These legislative CRs were brought to the floor of each chamber and debated under normal rules. By the end of the

---

[14] For the purpose of this statistic, I count the total number of bills covered by a package either with a funding extension or with new legislative language. For example, H.R. 933 (discussed earlier) contained legislative language for five bills and funding extensions for seven. I treat it as a twelve-bill package.

[15] See Tellestrup, Jessica, "Continuing Resolutions: Overview of Components and Recent Practices," *Congressional Research Service*, August 6, 2012, 17.

TABLE 1.2. *The Fate of the Annual Appropriations Bills, 1975–2012*

Year	Omnibus Bill Number	No Floor Vote (House)	No Floor Vote (Senate)	Bills in Omnibus
1975	Regular Order	0	0	0
1976	Regular Order	0	0	0
1977	Regular Order	0	0	0
1978	Regular Order	0	0	0
1979	H.J. Res. 440	1	1	2
1980	H.J. Res. 644	1	4	5
1981	H.J. Res. 370[a]	1	4	3
	H.J. Res. 409			
1982	H.J. Res. 631	3	7	6
1983	H.J. Res. 413	1	2	3
1984	H.J. Res. 648	3	5	8
1985	H.J. Res. 465	1	3	7
1986	H.J. Res. 738	2	6	13
1987	H.J. Res. 395	3	3	13
1988	Regular Order	0	0	0
1989	Regular Order	0	0	0
1990	Regular Order	0	0	0
1991	Regular Order	0	1	0
1992	Regular Order	0	0	0
1993	Regular Order	0	0	0
1994	Regular Order	0	0	0
1995	H.R. 3019, S. 1594	0	1	5
1996	H.R. 3610, Defense[b]	0	4	6
1997	Regular Order	0	0	0
1998	H.R. 4328, Transportation[c]	1	3	8
1999	H.R. 3194, District of Columbia[c]	1	0	5
2000	H.R. 4577, Labor[c,d]	0	2	3
	H.R. 4635, VA-HUD			2
2001	Regular Order	0	0	0
2002	H.J. Res 2[e]	8	10	11
2003	H.R. 2673, Agriculture[c]	0	1	7
2004	H.R. 4818, Foreign Operations[c]	1	7	9
2005	Regular Order	0	0	0
2006	H.J. Res. 20[e]	1	8	9
2007	H.R. 2764, State-Foreign Operations	0	5	11
2008	H.R. 1105[e]	11	12	9
	H.R. 2638, Homeland Security[d]			3

Year	Omnibus Bill Number	No Floor Vote (House)	No Floor Vote (Senate)	Bills in Omnibus
2009	H.R. 3288, Transportation-HUD[c]	0	3	6
2010	H.R. 1473	10	12	12
2011	H.R. 2112, Agriculture	6	11	3
	H.R. 2055, Mil-Vets[c]			9
2012	H.R. 933	5	12	12
	Total	60	127	190

[a] H.J. Res. 370 provided funding through March 31, 1982. H.J. Res. 409 provided funding for the remainder of the fiscal year.

[b] Prior to the passage of H.R. 3610, the Senate adopted an identical bill (H.R. 4278). H.R. 4278 was amendable and brought to the floor prior to H.R. 3610, a nonamendable conference report carrying the omnibus package, under a bipartisan agreement intended to avoid setting a precedent in which the Senate considered an omnibus package without an opportunity to offer amendments. In later years, the Senate dispensed with this formality and brought omnibus conference reports to the floor without the opportunity to offer amendments.

[c] Omnibus package created in conference.

[d] Congress passed two separate packages in 2000, 2008 and 2011.

[e] Omnibus passed by the next Congress.

Bill names (Defense, Labor, etc.) indicate that a regular appropriations bill carried the omnibus package.

first wave, the packages had transformed completely from their humble origins and consisted entirely of new legislation rather than extensions of the previous year's bills.[16] In the second wave, packages were sometimes brought to the floor as original legislation or as CRs and debated under the usual rules in each chamber. At other times, omnibus packages were created in conference and brought to the floor as nonamendable conference reports.

CAUSES OF OMNIBUS LEGISLATION

The shift from passing bills in the regular order to creating omnibus packages is a modern phenomenon and the most important change to take place in the appropriations process since the passage of the Congressional Budget and Impoundment Control Act of 1974. An omnibus bill had been passed only once in 1950 prior to the period under study and the

[16] Congress continued to label the packages as "continuing resolutions" despite the fact that they were no longer simple extensions of the previous year's funding.

practice was abandoned under intense criticism from members (Nelson 1953). The reasons for rise of omnibus legislating in the last four decades have gone largely unexplored (but see Hanson 2014 and Smith 2014). Several good studies by Glen Krutz (2000, 2001a, 2001b) investigate the broad practice of packaging bills together, but they do not focus on omnibus appropriations bills in particular and are now more than a decade old. Barbara Sinclair (2012) takes note of omnibus spending bills in her book *Unorthodox Lawmaking* but does not give a comprehensive analysis of the reasons for their creation. It is surprising that such a common, controversial, and consequential practice has been overlooked in research on Congress. This section presents the findings of existing scholarship on legislative packages to review what is known about their causes and consequences. I supplement these findings by reporting the results of interviews with policy makers to shed additional light on the specific dynamics of omnibus appropriations bills.

Theoretical investigations of the ways in which members of Congress make decisions offer some useful insight into the advantages of packaging bills together. It is common to model decision making in Congress by assuming that members can be arrayed on a line from left to right according to their preferences. The likelihood that the chamber will adopt a policy depends on the relative closeness of the policy and its alternative (such as the status quo) on the line to the "pivotal" voter whose support is needed to win final passage (Krehbiel 1998). The model is complicated by the presence of veto points on the line (such as the sixtieth vote needed to break a filibuster or the sixty-seventh vote needed to overcome a presidential veto) that create a large gridlock zone in which no legislation can be passed (Brady and Volden 2006).

This approach models dynamics among members as they consider a single policy dimension, such as defense spending. The dynamics of decision making change substantially when Congress considers two or more policy dimensions simultaneously, as it does when omnibus bills are created. It has been long understood that considering several policy dimensions simultaneously disrupts the voting coalitions that would form for the same policies if considered one at a time. Different policy domains can be combined together in a variety of ways that will attract majority support even if a particular component of the package might fail when considered on its own (Black 1958; Riker 1982; Shepsle and Bonchek 1997). Some members of Congress may oppose social welfare programs and support defense spending, while others support welfare and want to cut defense. Voted on separately, bills providing funding for each category of program might face gridlock on the floor. A package combining both policies can break gridlock by giving both camps something to support. This is exactly the advantage modern observers attribute to omnibus bills. "Joining several bills in a single package can help leaders garner support. In such megabills, sweeteners can be added to woo supporters, and provisions that could not win majority support in stand-alone bills can be tucked out of sight" (Davidson, Oleszek, and Lee 2012, 172).

Glen Krutz's study of omnibus legislating is the most comprehensive assessment of the causes and effects of packaging bills together in Congress. He finds that omnibus bills are created to overcome difficulties on the floor (Krutz 2001b). Contextual factors such as large budget deficits, divided government, divided control of Congress, and minority obstruction create challenging legislative environments that make it more difficult to pass legislation. Leaders package bills together to overcome these difficulties and are particularly likely to package bills facing opposition (Krutz 2001b). "An agenda-control and coalition-building tool, the omnibus bill is typically assembled in order to get something passed that otherwise faces uncertainty" (Krutz 2000, 533). Sinclair reviews omnibus appropriations bills in *Unorthodox Lawmaking* and similarly concludes that divided government, partisan polarization, deficit politics, and "severe policy and political problems" in the consideration of individual spending bills give rise to omnibus spending bills (2012, 116). Together, these arguments suggest that omnibus bills are more likely when broad contextual factors in the political environment make the passage of legislation difficult. Omnibus bills are a strategy turned to when times are hard.

The utility of packaging bills together raises an important question: why not do it all the time? One reason is that omnibus bills are controversial among members (Davidson, Oleszek, and Lee 2012). Krutz theorizes that rank-and-file members calculate the costs and benefits of forming omnibus packages when making a decision about whether to support them. The packages benefit members by giving them distributive benefits that improve their chance of reelection and by giving members of the majority a chance to pursue policy goals. On the other hand, "members lose opportunities for participation and influence" (Krutz 2001b, 212). Sinclair similarly finds that omnibus bills, even if technically open to amendment, "reduce the opportunities for careful scrutiny of the legislation's provisions and for broad participation by rank-and-file members" (2012, 111).

These studies suggest that omnibus bills are used more often during hard legislative times because that is when members are willing to swallow their objections and accept a reduced policy-making role in order to meet other goals. A corollary to this reasoning is that member calculations about how best to pursue their interests constrain the ability of party leaders to package bills. Omnibus bills are convenient problem-solving tools for leaders, but members of the majority party are not always willing to accept the opportunity cost the bills impose on their ability to participate in the legislative process.

These assumptions offer a helpful framework for analyzing the creation of omnibus appropriations bills. First, any assessment of a specific role for the Senate in the creation of omnibus bills needs to take into account the influence of contextual factors such as divided control of Congress and the roles of the House of Representatives and the president. Second, creating an omnibus bill is not a preferred strategy for rank-and-file members. Members recognize that omnibus bills reduce their opportunities to engage in credit claiming and position taking, and their preferences constrain the ability of a leader to create omnibus packages. Third, omnibus bills arise out of hard legislative times. Members turn to omnibus bills when their ability to meet their legislative goals is threatened.

THE VIEW FROM THE HILL

This framework is a useful point of departure, but it needs to be adapted to the specific circumstances of the appropriations process. I do so in the last two sections of this chapter. This section reports the findings of interviews with policy makers on the causes and consequences of omnibus spending bills. The final section integrates their views with previous research into a broader theory of how members of the Senate majority party manage the appropriations process to help them meet their legislative goals.

Policy makers explain that the majority party sets out to pass spending bills in regular order each year but abandons this strategy and creates an omnibus package when it encounters difficulties. "I don't ever remember starting a year where it was the majority's goal to have an omnibus bill" one longtime staff member reported (Staff Interview D 2012). In Senator Daschle's view, members prefer to pass bills in the regular order but turn to omnibus bills as a response to challenges on the floor:

> I don't think [creating an omnibus bill is] really even a decision. It's an
> evolving set of circumstances that bring you to the conclusion that you

don't have any choice. Actually, the choice is either a CR or an omnibus, and CRs are never very popular because it's generally an extension of current law and there are things you want to change.... So, I think it's a set of circumstances where, by default, members come to the realization that if we're going to get something passed short of a CR it has to be an omnibus. But, I think it's a clear result of the failure to pass the individual bills, which for the most part, is still everyone's preference. (Interview with author, February 15, 2012)

According to Senator Lott, the Senate typically completes action on bills with bipartisan support, but "the ones that ... are gonna be a huge fight they just shove off to the end. They wrap 'em up in a package and send 'em over in a block" (interview with author, March 7, 2012).

Policy makers note that problems passing bills in the regular order are particularly acute in the Senate. One staff member observed: "To avoid an omnibus, you need to do twelve bills. Right now, the Senate ... cannot functionally do twelve bills on the Senate floor" (Staff Interview F 2012). The first problem is the need to overcome threatened filibusters and holds. One staff member recalled an Energy and Water appropriations bill in 2010 that cleared the House without controversy but hit a roadblock in the Senate when two senators placed a hold on it for unrelated reasons. Majority Leader Harry Reid "worked his ass off" for a month to secure cloture and pass the bill. Giving all bills the same amount of time was not realistic in the compressed Senate calendar and would elbow other matters off the agenda (Staff Interview C 2012).

A second problem is that members and their staffs bring large numbers of amendments to the floor regardless of their chances of being passed or germaneness to the topic at hand, sparking negotiations, long quorum calls, and votes (Staff Interview B 2012). The noncontroversial Military Construction appropriations bill used to take thirty minutes, one staff member recalled. Today the Senate is doing well if it clears the bill in a week (Staff Interview A 2012). Large numbers of amendments raise an additional concern for the majority: the risk of taking tough votes. Senator Lott explained:

As the years went by, the appropriations bills – since we didn't do as many authorizations, there were not as many opportunities to vent the senators' frustrations and be able to offer amendments – then the appropriations bills became the magnets for amendments, legitimate and otherwise. And as the years went by, they also became the magnet or the opportunity for each side of the aisle to make political statements by forcing votes on controversial issues that were unrelated perhaps to the appropriations bill that was pending, discouraging the leaders on either side from wanting to bring appropriations bills up, because your members then had to cast tough [votes on] unnecessary, political, and irrelevant amendments quite often. (Interview with author, March 7, 2012)

One staff member with experience in the Democratically controlled Senate in 2012 explained that the Interior bill would force Democrats to vote on global warming while the Homeland Security bill would force them vote on immigration, and so many members of the majority preferred to keep the bills off the floor. Following the regular order can be "hard on the party in power" (Staff Interview A 2012). In the words of one staff member, Senate leaders conclude, "There's a much easier way to do this – we just won't take things to the Senate floor" (Staff Interview C 2012).

Similarly, a staff member with decades of experience working in Senate appropriations recalled sitting in an appropriations strategy session with Senate Majority Leader Bill Frist, chairman of the Senate Appropriations Committee Thad Cochran, and Senator Mitch McConnell. Chairman Cochran proposed debating all twelve spending bills in regular order on the Senate floor. Senator McConnell opposed this idea, worrying that "the Democrats will offer amendments that senators with challenging races will be reluctant to vote on." Chairman Cochran's retort delighted the staff member, a traditionalist who believed in the right of senators to debate legislation: any senator who lost an election because of a vote on a spending bill deserved to lose. "I could have kissed him," the staff member said. Chairman Cochran's argument was less persuasive to Majority Leader Frist. The bills did not go to the floor (Staff Interview E 2012).

Policy makers say that omnibus bills offer an effective way out of these difficulties. First, packaging bills together helps the majority to overcome gridlock because it attracts a broader base of support than a single bill might attract on its own. "It's de facto coalition building," according to former Senate majority leader Tom Daschle. "Putting bills together, you increase the level of investment." This benefit amounts to a siren song for leaders in tough legislative times. "You're getting something done that may only have been accommodated with an omnibus package" (interview with author, February 15, 2012). Less well understood is the second consequence of omnibus bills: they tend to suppress the number of amendments that members offer. In Daschle's account, this is a by-product of consolidating numerous bills that would normally be debated individually into one package. Less time is available to members when they debate omnibus bills and they must choose their battles more carefully than they would when debating a bill individually (interview with author, February 15, 2012). Omnibus bills streamline the process and offer a degree of insulation from troublesome amendments.

Interviews suggest there are two constraints on leaders when making a decision to create an omnibus. One constraint is that powerful members of the Appropriations Committee generally oppose the practice. The subcommittee chairs responsible for the development of each bill retain substantial power and view writing a bill and managing its passage on the floor part of their authority (Staff Interview B 2012).[17] "The Appropriations Committee today is about the only committee in the Senate at least where subcommittees have real roles" (Daschle, interview with author, February 15, 2012). When bills are not brought to the floor, appropriators see their role as being diminished. One staff member explained: "There's no one more disappointed by not taking a bill to the floor than an appropriator.... That's a beautiful world for an appropriator – regular order" (Staff Interview F 2012). In more practical terms, "It's a monstrous pain in the ass" for the committee to create an omnibus bill (Staff Interview B 2012).

The second constraint on the use of omnibus bills is that they are not the preferred strategy of rank-and-file members. The benefit of the regular order from the standpoint of rank-and-file members is "it gives them the greatest latitude to pass legislation focused on particular areas of priority," according to Senator Daschle. "There's more opportunity to provide some meaningful direction to individual bills over anything that is lumped together in an aggregate legislative form" (interview with author, February 15, 2012). Senator Lott observed: "Members don't like

---

[17] Senator Pete Domenici (R-NM), then chair of the Energy and Water subcommittee of the Appropriations Committee, offers a good example of the criticism that the majority party leadership can face from committee members for abandoning the regular order. In 2006, the Energy and Water bill along with seven others did not receive an individual vote. Domenici spoke on the Senate floor in the wake of the Democrats winning the Senate in the midterm elections of that year. "Some media analysts contend that the Senate was afraid to cast votes on appropriations bills, thinking these votes might be used against incumbent Senators in recently held elections. All sorts of reasons emerged that justified laying aside this appropriations bill or that one. Some feared that amendments to the bills might take too long, too much time. Amendments might be painful choices for Senators. Some of the votes might slow down the process and might show up later in campaign commercials or propaganda.... I took this job knowing full well I would have to vote to decide, to choose, and that these decisions would be second-guessed by a whole host of people. So I reject the notion that the Senate saved itself by avoiding so-called hard votes. We ... did not take the votes, did we? And look at the results in November. If it were our Republican approach to save ourselves, we lost ourselves" (*Congressional Record*, December 6, 2006, S11268).

the omnibus process. First of all, it's an admission of failure. Secondly, it's this huge, massive bill that nobody really knows what's in it unless you're the chairman or ranking member.... Members know it's not the way to do business and they generally chafe under that process" (interview with author, March 7, 2012).

The observations of policy makers are consistent with the idea that members weigh a set of costs and benefits when deciding whether to abandon the regular order. One risk of the regular order is that members will be required to vote on amendments that could cause them political harm. In the words of Senator Lott, the regular order "takes courage because members have to vote. Frankly, they don't like it, particularly in an election year" (interview with author, March 7, 2012). Omnibus bills reduce members' exposure to difficult votes at the cost of reducing their overall ability to participate in the process. Omnibus bills make members feel like they are "getting jammed" (Staff Interview A 2012). If individual bills are not brought to the floor, "then there are seventy senators who are basically disenfranchised" (Staff Interview D 2012). Omnibus bills "limit your access to correcting amendments, and so omnibus bills are viewed by most senators as a sort of double-edged sword" Senator Daschle explained. "You've given up a lot in terms of your ability to influence the direction of appropriations and policy" (interview with author, February 15, 2012).

Gridlock in the regular order creates a separate worry for members: the distant but serious risk that the inability to pass a budget will result in a government shutdown that causes severe damage to the reputation of the party that receives the blame. "That's a disaster to us," reported one longtime staff member (Staff Interview F 2012). Being blamed for a government shutdown is a "huge political liability," according to Senator Daschle. While zealous new members occasionally bandy about threats of shutdowns, staff members report that more seasoned members in both parties view them with trepidation and as a real possibility if the parties miscalculate (Staff Interview A 2012). One staff member who recalled the shutdown in the winter of 1995–1996 compared it to Pickett's Charge in the Civil War. "When we closed the government down under Newt, we got slaughtered" (Staff Interview F 2012). Senator Lott, reflecting on the shutdown, concurred:

> Republicans tried that one time under the leadership of Newt Gingrich ....
> He thought we could roll Clinton with a shutdown. So, we had a shut-
> down. We didn't roll Clinton; it burned us very badly. So, Republicans are
> little jumpier about that then they used to be. Also, Democrats understand

that that's playing Russian roulette. You're spinning the cylinder hoping it won't kill you and will shoot the other guy. It's just no way to run a business. It actually unnerves the American people. They don't know quite what's going on, but they don't feel good about it. They worry the monuments are going to be shut down, the parks are going to be closed, the federal employees are going to be laid off. It's just a terrible thing to put the people up against. (Interview with author, March 7, 2012)

Using omnibus bills to overcome gridlock prevents the majority party from suffering damage to its reputation by avoiding a government shutdown.

Given that omnibus bills are said to suppress amending, it would be reasonable to hear complaints from policy makers that the packages are sharply partisan. Interestingly, staff members of both parties and in both chambers observed that there are limits to the ability of the majority party to pursue partisan policy goals in the bills. Some members of each party generally vote against the bills, and so bipartisan support is usually needed for passage. "If you're trying to do it as just one party, it's going to be difficult" (Staff Interview G 2012). Other policy makers were blunter in their assessment: "You've got a great big bill, and if it craters, that's really bad. You can't afford to use it for partisan purposes" (Staff Interview B 2012). Bills perceived as too partisan reach a "tipping point" that will cause them to fail. "Nobody wins in an omnibus generally," the staff member concluded (Staff Interview F 2012).[18]

THE "LIMITED INFLUENCE" THEORY OF THE SENATE

In the last section of this chapter, I draw on all of these findings to describe the "limited influence" theory of majority party power in the Senate appropriations process. My aim is to specify the extent of majority party influence in appropriations and the conditions under which it is likely to be observed. The first proposition of the theory is that the Senate majority party has an important but constrained ability to influence legislative outcomes on the floor. The limited influence theory places the majority party's ability to influence legislative outcomes midway between

---

[18] Language used by senators when describing omnibus packages on the floor routinely fits descriptions of the bills as bipartisan. Senator Patrick Leahy (D-VT) described an omnibus package for fiscal year 2014 as follows: "This is not exactly what I might have written ... what any one of us would have written if we could write it alone. But after many years and years of gridlock on appropriations, we wrote a bill that can pass" (*Congressional Record*, January 16, 2014, S418). The bill passed with seventy-two votes.

the traditional account of the Senate, in which outcomes are determined on the floor, and the revisionist account that grants the majority party strong powers of agenda control. The majority party can ease the passage of a budget and limit amending, but the effect of its influence is to meet electoral goals by protecting its reputation rather than to secure policy goals. The second proposition is that the majority party is likely to use this power when it is in a poor strategic position in the Senate. Members prefer to adopt bills in the regular order because it maximizes their opportunity to participate in lawmaking. They create omnibus bills when the costs of the regular order rise above those of packaging bills together. I address each proposition in turn.

First, the combined effect of abandoning the regular order and creating an omnibus package constitutes an important form of majority party influence. The majority party exercises negative agenda control when it opts not to consider an appropriations bill in the regular order because it limits the opportunity for members to participate in the legislative process and reduces the total number of votes that take place on amendments. Its influence is constrained because it can reduce the number of votes on amendments but rarely eliminates them altogether. The majority party also exercises powers of positive agenda control when it packages bills together because this strategy eases gridlock and helps it to pass a budget. This influence is also properly described as constrained because the majority party generally cannot use omnibus packages to adopt its preferred policies. Instead, the packages are likely to be logrolls that attract large bipartisan coalitions of support in order to ease the passage of the budget.

It is important to note that amending declines in the limited influence theory because the majority party manipulates the opportunity and incentive to offer amendments, not because abandoning the order changes the rules of the Senate. Members retain their right to offer amendments and in theory can filibuster a bill to protect that right. The first reason amending declines in the limited influence theory is that the majority party does not call appropriations bills up for debate in the regular order. A bill that is not debated cannot be amended. When that occurs, amending will decline unless the subsequent debate on an omnibus offers the same practical opportunity to amend as debate on an individual bill in the regular order. There is considerable evidence that it does not. Policy makers and scholars both observe that the last-minute nature of omnibus bills and their unwieldy size reduce the number of amendments that occur relative to the regular order. Amending can be further restricted on omnibus packages if they are brought to the floor as a conference report or if the majority uses a tactic such as filling the amendment tree. Senators can always resist such tactics with a filibuster, but evidence from the case studies presented in this book suggests that filibustering a conference report can be costly and is unlikely to succeed.[19]

The second proposition is that the Senate majority party is likely to abandon the regular order and to create an omnibus package when it is weak and vulnerable to problems on the floor. Members understand that their two major strategies for passing the budget have costs and benefits that vary along with the majority party's strategic position in the chamber. When the majority party is large, unified, and close to the minority, members believe their reelection and policy interests are best served with the credit-claiming and position-taking opportunities that arise through debating individual appropriations bills in the regular order. The costs of the regular order rise as the majority party becomes smaller, more divided, or more distant from the minority. Members weigh their interest in debating bills individually against the risk of damage to their party reputation and reelection goals. An open amendment process may expose members to votes on politically damaging amendments. They may be rolled by the minority party. They may face gridlock caused by internal divisions or minority opposition that puts them at risk of a government shutdown. Members are more likely to accept the limits omnibus bills place on their ability to participate in lawmaking when they believe the costs of the regular order have risen above those of creating an omnibus.

A basic set of expectations flow from this theory that is suitable for testing in the chapters to come. First, there should be evidence that members prefer the regular order. Parties should seek to bring bills to the floor in the regular order first rather than to initially create an omnibus bill. Second, the abandonment of the regular order should be negatively correlated with majority party strength. It is likely to be associated with minority obstruction on the Senate floor, troublesome minority amendments,

---

[19] The majority abandons the regular order to meet electoral rather than policy goals in the limited influence theory. I do not claim that it can systematically meet policy goals by limiting amendments, but rather that it can shield itself from difficult votes. Consistent with that analysis, filibusters may be hard to sustain either because it is costly for a senator to be perceived as blocking a budget bill or because enough members support the final package to secure cloture.

or splits in the majority party. Third, there should be evidence that abandoning the regular order reduces amendments and eases the passage of the budget, and that omnibus bills are generally bipartisan. Fourth, other contextual issues such as elections, the deficit, divided control of Congress, and divided government are likely to be correlated with the creation of omnibus bills as well because they intensify the difficulties faced by a weak majority party.

Finally, the Senate is part of a larger constitutional system that includes the House of Representatives and the president. These actors may at times constrain the Senate majority party's ability to adopt the budget with an omnibus package. They may also seek to create an omnibus package for their own reasons and compel the Senate to go along with their decisions. Although it is empirically less common, the House also abandons the regular order. When it does so, it forces the Senate to consider an alternative way to fund affected agencies. The president's role is not well defined in existing literature, but I show in chapters to come that the president can affect the likelihood that the House and Senate will create an omnibus bill and the contents of the package.

Fortunately for a study of the Senate, the structure of the appropriations process makes it possible to isolate the Senate's role in the budget process. The key is that both chambers generally set out to pass spending bills by following the regular order (Schick 2007). By tradition, the House acts first on appropriations bills and the Senate acts second. On the rare occasions that the House fails to pass a bill in the regular order, the Senate abides by tradition and does not take up that bill either. I leverage these facts for my analysis of the Senate. First, I assume that the Senate majority party decides for itself how to manage the spending bills each year, with the caveat that it will not vote on a spending bill if the House has not passed it first. Second, I assume that the failure of either chamber to pass an appropriations bill in the regular order effectively forces the other to pass an omnibus package. Accordingly, my broad claim is that the Senate majority party's management of the appropriations process may affect either the likelihood or the size of an omnibus package. If the House passes all bills in the regular order, then the Senate's decision to abandon the regular order forces the House to consider an omnibus bill. If the House has not passed all the bills in the regular order, then a decision by the Senate to abandon the regular order for any of the remaining appropriations bills will make the omnibus bill larger.

CONCLUSION

There is an ongoing debate about the extent of the Senate majority party's influence and the circumstances under which it is used. This chapter outlines a challenge to the traditional and revisionist views of party power in the Senate. In the limited influence theory, the majority party can meet electoral goals by manipulating the annual appropriations process. Each year, the majority party must evaluate the legislative landscape and decide how it will manage the passage of a dozen spending bills. Senate norms and the interest of members in receiving the position-taking and credit-claiming benefits that accompany open debate create a strong incentive for the majority party to pass bills in the regular order. Majority parties that are large, unified, and relatively close to the minority generally succeed in adopting the bills with this strategy. Weaker parties find that it leads them into a quagmire in which their internal divisions or fierce opposition from the minority lead to gridlock, or in which they become bogged down in endless votes on politically damaging amendments. They are likely to abandon the regular order as its costs rise. They avoid its pitfalls by cutting short debate and pulling bills from the floor or not debating them on an individual basis at all. Instead, they package spending bills together, a strategy that streamlines debate on the floor by limiting participation and helps the majority party form a bipartisan coalition to pass the budget. The majority party generally cannot meet its policy goals in this way, but it meets the more basic objective of protecting its party reputation by protecting its members from difficult votes and ensuring the passage of the budget.

In the next chapter, I review the legislative history of appropriations bills from 1975 to 2012 and conduct a series of statistical tests to analyze their relationships to standard measures of party power in the House and Senate. Later in the book, I conduct case studies of three different time periods to demonstrate how omnibus bills are a response to the limits on a majority's power. Finally, I review the state of the appropriations process today and the implications of my findings for standard theories of party power.

2

Testing Expectations

How does the majority party's strength or weakness affect its management of the annual appropriations process? What are the consequences of the choices that it makes as it decides how to adopt a dozen major bills? This chapter evaluates three types of quantitative evidence to test the theory of limited influence. First, I use common statistical tools to analyze the legislative history of appropriations bills from 1975 to 2012 and assess the relationship between party power and abandoning the regular order. Second, I investigate patterns in voting on amendments to examine the effect of abandoning the regular order on the opportunity for members to participate in lawmaking. Third, I examine voting patterns on omnibus spending bills to determine whether the bills draw bipartisan support or spark partisan divisions. The findings provide a strong initial validation of the limited influence theory. The data show that the Senate majority party abandons the regular order when it is small, divided, and distant from the minority, and that failing to bring individual bills to a vote correlates with a reduction in amending in the Senate. Omnibus spending bills also tend to attract large bipartisan coalitions.

The findings are encouraging because they are consistent with expectations, but a word of caution is in order. Quantitative data about the appropriations process have some inherent limits. The strength of these data is that they can be analyzed to identify basic patterns and the relationships between variables. Their limit is that they cannot address the questions of causality that are central to the limited influence theory. The findings of this chapter show that the majority party is more likely to abandon the regular order when it is small, divided, and distant from the minority. They cannot explain why. My solution to this problem is to rely on the accumulated weight of quantitative and qualitative evidence to test the theory. I review the historical record of debates on the Senate floor carefully in chapters to come. The answer to the question of "why" in most cases is easily visible in the record: filibuster fights, votes on difficult amendments, feuding within a party. The quantitative and qualitative data together offer compelling support for the limited influence theory.

REGRESSION MODELS

I begin by presenting a series of regression models estimating the relationship of party power to abandoning the regular order in the Senate. The routine nature of the appropriations process is well suited for this style of analysis, and I build on its unique features to gain insights about party power that are difficult to gain by analyzing other categories of legislation. Most studies rely on the record of roll call votes to support arguments about majority party power. The majority party's ability to control the agenda must be surmised indirectly from this record. There is no consistent way to identify bills or amendments that did not receive a vote, and so efforts to analyze negative agenda control typically rely on analyses of majority roll rates. My approach avoids this problem by treating the regular order as a baseline against which the actions of Congress can be compared, coded, and quantified. The widely recognized normal practice in the appropriations process is to give individual debate and a vote to around a dozen regular appropriations bills (Schick 2007). Any deviation from the regular order, such as failing to bring a bill to a vote on an individual basis or putting it into an omnibus package, is easily identifiable in the legislative record. A testable assumption is that such deviations mark instances of the majority party manipulating the legislative agenda. I code whether Congress followed the regular order or deviated from it and then use regression analysis to test whether or not the deviations vary along with majority party power.

A second advantage of the appropriations process is that it follows a predictable sequence. Both chambers start the appropriations process by attempting to pass appropriations bills in the regular order and make the decision whether to adopt an omnibus later in the year. This predictable sequence makes it possible to isolate the role of the Senate majority party and to follow the chain of events that leads to the creation of an omnibus bill. The distinct role of the Senate majority party can be isolated because strong congressional norms dictate that the Senate will not bring a bill to a vote unless the House has passed it first (Schick 2007). The decisions of the Senate majority party can be analyzed independently as long as the prior action of the House of Representatives is taken into account. My approach builds on these norms by treating the appropriations process as a series of sequential steps. The first step is the consideration of bills in the regular order in the House. The second is the Senate's consideration in the regular order of bills that passed the House. The third is the decision made by both chambers to incorporate some or all of the bills into an omnibus package. It is routine to add any bills that the majority party in either chamber did not adopt in the regular order to an omnibus bill, although other bills may be added as well. I estimate the relationship of majority party power in each chamber to the decision to abandon the regular order in the first two stages of the process and to the decision of both chambers to include bills in an omnibus package in the third stage of the process.

The data for the analysis come from an original data set that tracks the legislative history of 485 regular appropriations bills considered between 1975 and 2012. Regular appropriations bills are defined as the primary bill that each subcommittee of the Appropriations Committee is tasked to write on an annual basis, for example, the "Departments of Labor, Health and Human Services, and Education, and Related Agencies" appropriations bill. The data set identifies changes in subcommittee jurisdictions at the beginning and end of the period under study with a long period of stability in jurisdictions in the middle. There is slight variation in the number of bills considered each year. I identify twenty-six separate bill domains used by the House or Senate between 1975 and 2012 based on the name of the bill and relevant subcommittee. I use all bill domains for the purpose of analysis, but, for ease of discussion, I illustrate my findings with the "Core 13" bills. The Core 13 bills are those that were considered each year by Congress during a period of stable subcommittee jurisdictions between 1979 and 2002.

Major variables in the data set include the following.

No Floor Vote. I denote the majority party's decision to abandon the regular order with its failure to vote on a regular appropriations bill. Bills that do not receive a vote may have received some debate on the floor or none at all. Regular appropriations bills that received an initial vote (or UC request) on passage in the regular order are coded 0. Regular appropriations bills that did not receive a vote are coded 1.[1] The

---

[1] In some cases, multiple versions of a bill were considered during a single year. I code a bill as 0 as long as at least one version of the bill was voted on. For example, if the Agriculture bill is adopted by both chambers, vetoed, and a second version of the Agriculture bill is

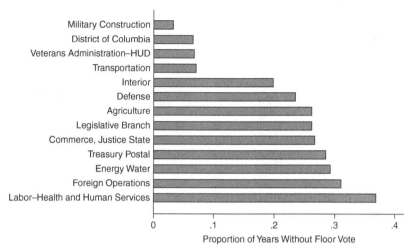

FIGURE 2.1. Abandoning the regular order by bill. U.S. Senate, Core 13 bills.

Senate did not hold a floor vote on 127 bills (26 percent) between 1975 and 2012 and voted on 358 (74 percent). The House did not hold a vote on 60 bills (12 percent) and voted on 425 (88 percent). Virtually all bills that do not receive a vote are included in omnibus spending bills. Five were funded with a continuing resolution (CR) covering just one bill.

There is substantial variation in the data in the number of times the Senate did not call a vote on a particular bill or included it in an omnibus package (Figure 2.1). Some appropriations bills are regarded as more controversial than others because of their subject matter. The Senate did not vote on the Labor–Health and Human Services bill, packed with spending on social services, 37 percent of the time and included it in an omnibus package 55 percent of the time. By contrast, the Senate did not vote on the popular Military Construction bill only once, and it was included in an omnibus package only 10 percent of the time. I account for this group variation by assigning each bill category a fixed effect in my analysis.

In Omnibus. Packages of bills can take a variety of forms. For the purpose of this analysis, I broadly define "omnibus bills" to include any legislative vehicle that substitutes for the passage of two or more regular appropriations bills and provides funding for an entire fiscal year or the remaining portion of one. A regular appropriations bill that is included in or otherwise covered by an omnibus package is coded 1. A bill that is

not voted on in the Senate before being incorporated into an omnibus, I code the bill as 0 because the first version was voted on.

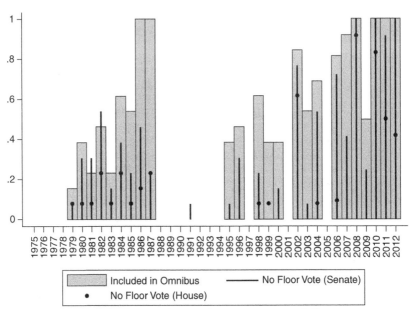

FIGURE 2.2. Consideration of annual appropriations bills. U.S. Congress, 1975–2012.

adopted on an individual basis in the regular order is coded o. A total of 190 bills (39 percent) were included in omnibus packages between 1975 and 2012, while 295 bills (61 percent) passed in the regular order. Sixty-four percent of bills in omnibus packages did not receive an individual vote in the House, Senate, or both chambers. Thirty-six percent were included after receiving a vote in both chambers.

Figure 2.2 illustrates patterns in the consideration of regular appropriations bills over time. There are two waves of activity. The first begins in 1979 and continues until 1987. The second begins in 1995 and continues today. Both waves start with the chambers not bringing a handful of bills to a vote and creating small omnibus packages followed by growth in both variables over time. The overall frequency of not calling votes and the size of packages generally increase from the beginning to the end of the time period in both chambers.

Party power is conceptualized and operationalized in a variety of ways (Aldrich 2011; Binder 1996; Schickler 2000). I operationalize majority party power with its three major elements: majority party homogeneity, majority party margin of control, and the ideological distance between the majority and minority.

Majority Homogeneity. The ideological unity of the majority party is defined in the same manner as Aldrich and Rohde as the standard

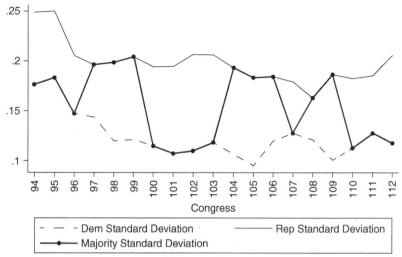

FIGURE 2.3. Democratic, Republican, and majority DW-NOMINATE standard deviation. U.S. Senate, 1975–2012.

deviation of the first dimension DW-NOMINATE score of the majority party divided by the standard deviation of the chamber. The scale of the variable is reversed so that the majority party grows increasingly unified as the variable increases. It ranges from 0.39 to 0.74 in the Senate with a mean of 0.57 (standard deviation 0.12) and 0.35 to 0.72 in the House with a mean of 0.56 (standard deviation 0.13). I rescale the variable from 0 to 1 in my analysis for easier interpretation. I treat homogeneity as a sign of majority party strength because unified majority parties are more likely to meet their goals successfully than divided parties (Smith 2007).

There is substantial variation in majority homogeneity in the Senate because of differences in the unity of the two parties and changes in the control of the chamber over time. Figure 2.3 illustrates the first dimension DW-NOMINATE standard deviations of the Democrats, Republicans, and majority party in the Senate from 1975 to 2012. Senate Democrats were the more unified of the two parties in the nearly four decades under study and had an average first dimension DW-NOMINATE standard deviation of 0.12 compared with 0.20 for Senate Republicans. The average homogeneity of the majority party moves up and down substantially as a result of changes in majority party control.

Margin of Control. The majority party's margin of control is the proportion of seats it controls in the House or Senate based on the records of

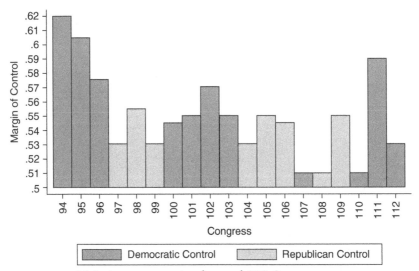

FIGURE 2.4. Majority party margin of control. U.S. Senate, 1975–2012.

the Senate Historical Office.[2] This margin can change over the course of a session because of death or retirement. I use the majority's average margin for the session, rescaled from 0 to 1 for my time period to aid in calculating marginal effects. Prior to rescaling, the margin of control in the Senate ranged from 0.51 to 0.62, with an average of 0.55 (Figure 2.4).[3] The margin of control in the House ranged from 0.51 to 0.67, with an average of 0.58. I treat a large margin of control as a sign of majority party strength because large parties are more likely to have the votes to meet their goals than small parties are (Smith 2007).

Distance. The distance between the two parties is coded as the absolute value of the distance between the median Democrat on the first dimension DW-NOMINATE scale and the median Republican. It ranges from 0.54 to 0.83 in the Senate, with a mean of 0.68 and from 0.52 to 1.07 with a mean of 0.76 in the House. A prominent feature of the variable is that it increases monotonically over time, with the lowest levels of distance at the beginning of the time period and highest at the end (Figure 2.5).

[2] U.S. Senate. 2014. "Party Division in the Senate, 1789–Present." Accessed June 23. http://www.senate.gov/pagelayout/history/one_item_and_teasers/partydiv.htm.

[3] The Senate in the 107th Congress was initially divided fifty-fifty between the parties and under the effective control of the Republicans with the tie-breaking vote of Vice President Dick Cheney. Control shifted to the Democrats when Senator Jim Jeffords of Vermont shifted his affiliation from the Republicans to the Democrats and gave Democrats a one-seat advantage.

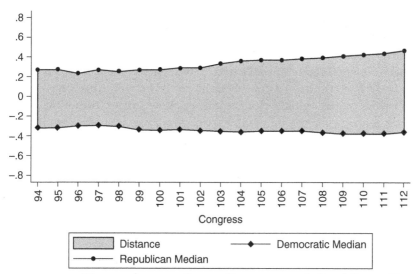

FIGURE 2.5. Distance between Senate Democrats and Republicans. First dimension DW-NOMINATE scores.

I rescale the variable from 0 to 1 for the purpose of analysis and calculating marginal effects. I treat a large distance between the majority and minority as a sign of majority party weakness in the Senate because it is more likely to generate intense minority opposition that makes it more difficult for the majority to meet its goals (Rae and Campbell 2001).

I also employ a series of variables to control for factors that have been found to influence the appropriations process and the likelihood of forming omnibus spending bills. Divided control of Congress may increase the likelihood of omnibus bills because they help to overcome the difficulty of negotiating with a chamber controlled by the other party (Krutz 2000). It is coded 0 if control of Congress is unified under one party and 1 if it is not. Divided government may promote omnibus bills because negotiating over a single package is an effective way for Congress to deal with a president of the opposite party (Sinclair 2012). The variable for divided government is a dummy variable coded 0 if the House, Senate, and presidency were controlled by one party and 1 if they were not. Election years may affect legislative productivity and make it more difficult to pass spending bills (Binder 2003). I code this variable as 1 if it is an election year and 0 if it is not.

Variation in the size of the federal deficit is said to force difficult budgetary choices and enhance partisan conflict (Krutz 2000; Sinclair 2012).

Following Krutz, the deficit variable is coded as the proportion of annual expenditures that exceed revenues using figures from the Congressional Budget Office. The sign is reversed so that the deficit grows as the proportion increases. The variable ranges from −0.13 to 0.40 with a mean of 0.14. Deficit reduction agreements negotiated between Congress and the president may ease budgetary pressures as long as the terms of the agreement remain generally acceptable to major players in the budget process. The Budget Enforcement Act (BEA) of 1990 is widely regarded as the most effective deficit reduction agreement. Testimony from the director of the Congressional Budget Office indicates that members of Congress generally abided by the terms of the BEA from 1990 to 1997, but the return of surpluses in 1998 undermined the act's effectiveness (Holtz-Eakin 2004). I include a dummy variable for the BEA coded as 1 for the years 1990 to 1997 in my analysis.

Finally, both waves of abandoning the regular order show an increase in the proportion of bills that did not receive a vote and that were included in omnibus packages over time. A common observation in interviews was that omnibus bills are beginning to be regarded as routine by members (Staff Interview D 2012). I include a lagged variable of the total number of bills included in an omnibus bill the previous year to control for the possibility that member resistance to omnibus packages declines as they become more common.

Abandoning the Regular Order in the Senate

I turn first to models estimating the relationship between majority party power and abandoning the regular order in the Senate. These models present the first and most important test of the limited influence theory. The theory's key proposition is that members of the majority party make an initial effort to pass bills in the regular order but abandon that effort when it becomes perceived as too costly. The decision not to call a vote on a bill is the "canary in the coal mine" that signals members of the majority party have decided to exercise influence over the legislative process in order to ensure the passage of problematic bills and protect their reputation. Any bill that does not receive a vote and is later included in an omnibus package is included because it must be in order for those government agencies to be funded. Not calling a vote on an appropriations bill should have a strong, negative relationship to the size and homogeneity of the majority party and a positive relationship to its distance from the minority. By contrast, bills may be included in omnibus packages

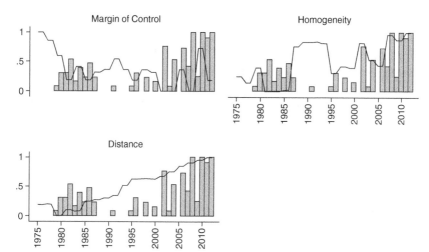

FIGURE 2.6. Party characteristics and failing to call votes. U.S. Senate, 1975–2012.

after they have already successfully cleared both chambers for a wide variety of reasons, such as the fact that they are popular and are likely to build support for the package.

The data on majority party characteristics in the Senate are well suited for regression analysis because they vary substantially over time and are not highly correlated with each other.[4] Figure 2.6 illustrates the relationship between the three party variables and the proportion of bills that did not receive a floor vote each year in the Senate with each variable scaled from 0 to 1. There are several patterns to note. Margin of control fits the data the best and shows a generally negative relationship with the proportion of bills that did not receive a vote. As the majority party's margin of control increases, it is less likely to abandon the regular order. Homogeneity has a negative relationship with the failure to vote on bills in the early years of the data set. The proportion of bills with no vote rises as homogeneity falls and declines as homogeneity rises through 2000. After that the relationship appears to reverse itself and show a positive correlation. The distance between the two parties rises steadily over time. The variable does not appear to vary with the two waves of abandoning the regular order visible in the data, but there is an overall positive correlation because variables both rise over time.

---

[4] See Table 2.4 for correlations among the party characteristic variables in the Senate.

I begin the analysis with a logistic regression model using "No Floor Vote" as the dependent variable and the three measures of party power as independent variables. I exclude control variables in this initial test of the limited influence theory in order to assess the basic relationship of party characteristics to the failure to vote on a bill in the regular order. I control for fixed effects by bill type (Agriculture, Defense, etc.) by including a dummy variable for each category of bill in the analysis to account for variation in the likelihood of a positive outcome in the dependent variable. Standard errors are clustered by year to adjust for contemporaneous correlation. It is common to consider variables to have a statistically significant relationship with the dependent variable when there is a 95 percent level of confidence ($p < 0.05$) that the result is different from zero. I also report levels of significance at $p < 0.10$ to demonstrate strong relationships that are just short of the standard level of significance. Finally, I limit the sample of bills used in the analysis only to bills that received a vote in the House because the Senate will not vote on a bill if the House has not voted on it first. There are a total of 422 bills in the data set that passed the House of Representatives and were eligible to be considered by the Senate in the regular order. Of those bills, 355 (84 percent) were voted on in the regular order and 67 (16 percent) were not voted on.

The important results to examine are the strength and the direction of majority party margin of control, homogeneity, and distance from the minority in each model. Table 2.1 shows that the estimates for all three variables are in the expected direction of the limited influence theory. The majority party's margin of control and homogeneity are negatively correlated with the failure to vote on a bill in the Senate at $p = 0.03$ and $p = 0.08$, respectively. The distance between the majority and minority parties is positively correlated with the failure to vote on a bill at $p = 0.03$. The findings are an initial validation of the limited influence theory. The failure to vote on a spending bill in the regular order is correlated with majority party weakness rather than strength.

Next, I expand the analysis to include control variables. Table 2.2 presents the results of four separate logistic regression models using "No Floor Vote" as the dependent variable. Each model truncates the data set at a different point in time. The first model truncates the data set in 2006, the second in 2008, and so on. Analyzing the model at different points in time provides the opportunity to observe whether the rapid rise in the distance variable has an effect in the fitness of the model over time. As in the earlier model, these models control for fixed effects by bill category and cluster standard errors by year, and I analyze only bills that passed the House of Representatives.

TABLE 2.1. *Party Characteristics and Failing to Call a Vote in the U.S. Senate, Logit Analysis, 1975–2012, Fixed Effects by Bill and Standard Errors Clustered by Year*

Variable	Expected Direction	Coefficient (Standard Error)
Margin of Control	–	−2.12**
		(1.00)
Homogeneity	–	−1.74*
		(1.00)
Distance	+	3.35**
		(1.50)
Constant		−2.04**
		(0.89)
Log Pseudolikelihood		−144.33
Pseudo R²		0.22
N		422

Effects are significantly different from zero at *p < .10; **p < .05; ***p < .01; two tailed test.

The results are consistent with the limited influence theory and show evidence of change over time. Coefficients and 95 percent confidence intervals for each model are illustrated in Figure 2.7. The estimates for all three variables are in the expected direction. Margin of control and homogeneity are both negative, although the magnitude of the coefficients for the two variables has been shrinking since 2008. Distance is positive, and its coefficient is growing over time. Margin of control is statistically significant (p < 0.01) in all four versions of the model. Homogeneity is also statistically significant (p < 0.05) in all four versions. Distance is not significant in the early years of the model but reaches standard levels of significance (p = 0.05) by 2010. Several control variables have statistically significant effects as well. Election years are statistically significant in all models. The BEA is significant and negative in 2008–2012, indicating that not calling a vote on a bill was less likely during years the BEA was effective. Republican control of government is significant and negative in 2008–2012, indicating that Democratic majorities were more likely not to call votes on spending bills. The lagged variable indicating the total number of bills included in omnibus packages the previous year is significant in 2006 and 2008, although in the opposite of the expected direction.

To facilitate interpretation of these coefficients, I estimate the impact of changes in the majority party's margin of control, homogeneity, and

TABLE 2.2. *Party Characteristics and Failing to Call a Vote in the U.S. Senate, Logit Analysis, Year Ending in 2006, 2008, 2010 and 2012, Fixed Effects by Bill and Standard Errors Clustered by Year*

Variable	Expected Direction	2006	2008	2010	2012
Margin of Control	–	−8.24*** (2.49)	−11.19*** (3.19)	−4.72*** (1.21)	−4.31*** (1.16)
Homogeneity	–	−6.60** (3.13)	−10.11*** (3.07)	−5.90*** (2.28)	−5.75** (2.27)
Distance	+	1.63 (2.97)	4.59 (3.13)	6.74** (3.18)	8.18*** (3.08)
Divided Control of Congress	+	0.52 (1.53)	−2.97** (1.46)	−0.60 (0.89)	−0.05 (0.87)
Divided Government	+	−2.73** (1.16)	0.81 (0.93)	0.61 (1.09)	0.91 (1.13)
Republican Control of Senate		0.43 (1.49)	−3.74** (1.65)	−2.00* (1.17)	−2.10* (1.11)
Election Year	+	2.08*** (0.49)	1.77*** (0.43)	1.87*** (0.50)	2.12*** (0.52)
Deficit	+	−4.01 (3.78)	4.40 (3.35)	8.22** (3.48)	9.56*** (3.61)
Budget Enforcement Act	–	−0.63 (0.95)	−3.03*** (0.87)	−2.07*** (0.70)	−2.07*** (0.71)
Proportion of Bills in Omnibus (Lagged)	+	−3.75*** (1.20)	−2.62*** (0.93)	−1.08 (0.84)	−0.87 (0.98)
Constant		2.96 (3.04)	5.69 (3.78)	−1.75 (2.58)	−3.38 (2.36)
Log Pseudo-likelihood		−69.60	−87.20	−100.89	−104.81
Pseudo R²		0.49	0.42	0.38	0.43
N		382	395	409	422

Effects are significantly different from zero at *p < .10; **p < .05; ***p < .01; two tailed test.

distance from the minority by calculating the effect of a one-unit change in each variable on the likelihood that the majority party will not call a vote on an appropriations bill. Each of the variables is scaled from 0 to 1, so a one-unit change moves from the variable's minimum to its maximum. The marginal effects vary by bill and by the conditions specified for the model, such as whether it is an election year. For the purpose of example, I calculated the marginal effects of changes in the three variables with two different settings for the model simulating moderate and difficult

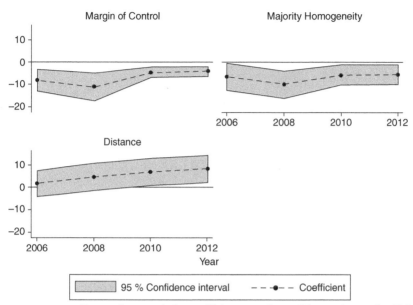

FIGURE 2.7. Party characteristic coefficients and confidence intervals. U.S. Senate, 2006–2012.

floor conditions. In the "moderate" setting, there is unified Republican control of government, it is an election year, and the BEA was not in effect. All other variables are set at their means. The "difficult" setting assumes there is divided government and Democrats control the Senate, and it keeps other values the same.

I illustrate the estimated point values and confidence intervals using the Defense bill and Labor–Health and Human Services bill in Figure 2.8. In the "moderate" setting, increasing the majority's margin of control from its lowest to highest observed value decreases the likelihood that the majority will not vote on the widely supported Defense bill by 12 percent and the more controversial Labor–Health and Human Services bill by 58 percent. A corresponding increase in majority homogeneity results in a 27 percent decrease in the likelihood of not calling a vote on the Defense bill and a 71 percent decrease for the Labor–Health and Human Services bill. Finally, moving from the minimum to the maximum of the distance variable results in a 50 percent increase in the likelihood that the majority will not call a vote on the Defense bill and an 88 percent increase for the Labor–Health and Human Services bill. In the difficult setting, the estimated effects are larger and the confidence intervals are narrower. A one-unit increase in margin of control and homogeneity leads to a 77 and 80 percent decline, respectively, in the likelihood of not calling a vote on the Defense bill, and

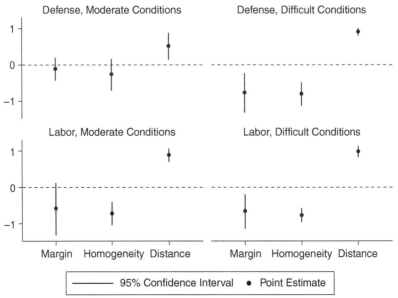

FIGURE 2.8. Marginal effects of change in party power variables. Defense and Labor–Health and Human Services bills.

a 66 and 77 percent decline, respectively, in the likelihood of not voting on the Labor–Health and Human Services bill. A similar change in the distance variable increases the likelihood of not voting on the Defense bill by 90 percent and the Labor–Health and Human Services bill by 98 percent.

Overall, the "No Floor Vote" models offer strong evidence in support of the limited influence theory. The majority party is more likely at statistically significant levels not to call a vote on a bill when it is small, divided, and distant from the minority. The relationship between distance and not voting on a bill appears to be growing stronger as the distance variable has grown larger. The growth in the significance of the distance variable may explain the apparent positive correlation between not calling a vote on a bill and majority party homogeneity in the later years of the data set. Variation in majority homogeneity may have less of an effect on the majority's decision to call a vote when the distance between the two parties is large and gridlock is common.

Abandoning the Regular Order in the House of Representatives

Appropriations bills that do not receive a vote in the regular order in the House of Representatives are interesting for two reasons. First, a decision by the House majority party not to vote on a spending bill has a

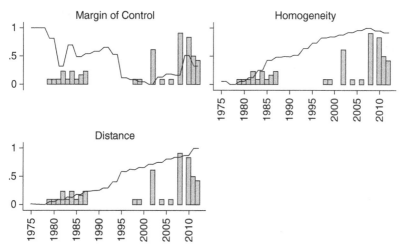

FIGURE 2.9. Party characteristics and failing to call votes. U.S. House of Representatives, 1975–2012.

direct impact on the Senate appropriations process because the Senate will not vote on a bill unless the House does so first. Understanding why the House fails to call votes on spending bills helps to explain events on the Senate floor. Second, party characteristics may have a different effect in the House than they do in the Senate because the rules of the two chambers differ. A reasonable expectation is that the data from the House will better fit the expectations of Conditional Party Government (CPG) than of the limited influence theory. Comparing the two chambers can help to illustrate how each is distinctive.

Analyzing the failure to call votes on bills in the House is a challenge because it is rare, and there is little variation in the data to explain. I illustrate the patterns in the consideration of appropriations bills in the House in Figure 2.9. The House failed to call a vote on only 12 percent of appropriations bills in the last 38 years, or 60 of the 485 bills in the data set. Much of that occurred recently. The House has not voted on forty-two bills since 2000. The characteristics of the House majority party are also all highly correlated with each other at a level of –0.76 or higher (see Table 2.4).[5] The risk of including highly correlated variables in a regression model is that they may inflate standard errors and make coefficient estimates unreliable – a problem known as multicollinearity. A correlation

---

[5] Correlation coefficients range between –1 and 1. A score of –1 is a perfect negative correlation, 1 is a perfect positive correlation, and 0 is no relationship.

TABLE 2.3. *Party Characteristics and Failing to Call a Vote in the House of Representatives, Logit Analysis, 1975–2012, Standard Errors Clustered by Year*

Variable	Expected Direction	Model A	Model B	Model C	Model D
Margin of Control	−	−3.14 (2.37)	−7.40** (3.13)		
Homogeneity	−	1.06 (3.40)		5.67*** (1.86)	
Distance	+	3.17 (4.08)			5.56*** (1.90)
Divided Control of Congress	+	1.47** (0.75)	0.21 (0.69)	1.97*** (0.76)	1.88** (0.77)
Divided Government	+	0.74 (0.77)	0.95 (0.83)	0.70 (0.77)	0.55 (0.68)
Republican Control of House		−2.34** (0.92)	−1.49* (0.82)	−1.79** (0.81)	−2.31** (0.97)
Election Year	+	1.80*** (0.63)	1.76*** (0.56)	1.87*** (0.65)	1.92*** (0.70)
Deficit	+	5.69 (5.12)	13.72** (5.59)	3.31 (2.86)	0.64 (2.68)
Proportion of Bills in Omnibus (Lagged)	+	−0.27 (1.18)	0.28 (1.08)	0.15 (1.04)	−0.11 (1.25)
Constant		−5.56*** (1.43)	−3.25*** (1.08)	−8.31*** (1.74)	−6.54*** (1.37)
Log Pseudolikelihood		−115.03	−210.85	−117.22	−116.49
Pseudo R²		0.34	0.31	0.33	0.33
N		479	479	479	479

Effects are significantly different from zero at *p < .10; **p < .05; ***p < .01; two tailed test.

with a magnitude of 0.80 or higher is often suggested as the level at which such correlation may become problematic (Berry and Feldman 1985). I explain how I address this concern in the following paragraph.

Table 2.3 presents the results of four logistic regression models using the "No Floor Vote" variable from the House of Representatives as the dependent variable. These models do not include fixed effects by bill category because of the lack of variation in the data. The BEA variable is omitted for the same reason. Standard errors are clustered by year to take into account potential annual effects. All years in the data set are included in the analyses. Post-regression tests suggest that the estimated effects of majority margin of control, homogeneity, and distance from the minority in Model A are unreliable because of multicollinearity.[6] Hanushek and Jackson observe that there are few good strategies to address multicollinearity and that "one must either live with imprecise estimates or find more information" (1977, 92). Absent more information, I demonstrate the estimated effects of the variables together and then separately to illustrate the effect of each one. Model B includes only majority party margin of control. Model C includes only majority homogeneity. Model D includes only the majority's distance to the minority. Excluding variables from the model raises the risk of model misspecification, but it is one way to observe the behavior of each variable in isolation from the others.

None of the three party characteristic variables are statistically significant in Model A, but a different pattern emerges when the variables are considered one at a time. Margin of control has a statistically significant and negative relationship with not calling a vote in the House in Model B. Homogeneity and distance each have a statistically significant and positive relationship with failing to vote on a bill in Models C and D. The most interesting finding that emerges from the series of models is that majority party homogeneity has a positive relationship with the dependent variable. Contrary to the expectations of the limited influence theory, the majority party is more likely not to call votes on spending bills as its homogeneity increases. The estimated effects of the control variables are in the expected directions although not always statistically significant. Democratic control of the House of Representatives is associated with abandoning the regular order at $p < 0.05$ in three of four models. Election years are associated with not calling a vote at statistically significant levels in all four models.

Two points about the majority's management of appropriations bills in the House are clear despite the problems caused by multicollinearity. First, the findings taken as a whole do not support the limited influence theory. The theory requires that all three variables have a relationship in the predicted direction with bills that did not receive a vote. The independent effects of distance and homogeneity are hard to estimate

---

[6] I tested for multicollinearity by specifying each of the party characteristic variables in turn as a dependent variable and regressing the remaining two variables on it to evaluate how much of the variation in the dependent variable the other two variables could explain. An R^2 approaching 1 is a sign of multicollinearity. The R^2 for majority party margin of control homogeneity and distance from the minority were 0.66, 0.94, and 0.92, respectively. In contrast, the corresponding scores for the Senate analysis of "No Floor Vote" bills were 0.18, 0.37, and 0.45, respectively.

because of their high correlation, but the clearest evidence from the models is that majority party homogeneity and distance to the minority are positively correlated with bills that did not receive a vote in the House. Second, the fact that the limited influence theory does not fit data from the House supports the argument that the Senate is distinctive and that party power operates in a different way there than it does in the House.

Omnibus Packages

Next I analyze the relationship of party characteristics to the inclusion of a bill in an omnibus package. Omnibus packages consist of appropriations bills that received a vote in both chambers along with a second group of bills that did not. I expect that the relationship between majority party power and the full group of bills in omnibus packages will be weaker than it is for bills that did not receive a vote. In the limited influence theory, the decision not to vote on a bill is likely to be associated with trouble on the floor. Bills that receive a vote in both chambers are by definition less likely to cause the majority party difficulty, and there may be a wide range of reasons for their inclusion in an omnibus package. For example, they might be included in a package because they are popular and will offset unpopular provisions in another bill.

Both the House and the Senate are necessarily involved in the decision about which bills to include in an omnibus package, and models of omnibus bills need to take into account the characteristics of the majority party in both chambers. This requirement raises some difficulties for the analysis because the variables for majority party margin of control, homogeneity, and distance from the minority are all highly correlated in the House. There is also an additional threat of multicollinearity because some House variables are highly correlated with Senate variables. Table 2.4 shows a correlation matrix for all variables from the House and Senate. As earlier, I address this problem by specifying models in which variables are included together and separately and comparing their estimated effects to assess their overall relationship to the inclusion of a bill in an omnibus package.

A final challenge presented by the analysis is that Congress failed to complete the appropriations bills in 2002, 2006, and 2008 before a new Congress was seated. This raises the question of whether to include variables that describe the Congress in which the appropriations process was initiated or the Congress in which it was concluded in the regression

TABLE 2.4. *House and Senate Party Characteristics Correlation Matrix*

	House Margin	House Homo- geneity	House Distance	Senate Margin	Senate Homo- geneity	Senate Distance
House Margin	1					
House Homo- geneity	−0.81	1				
House Distance	−0.76	0.96	1			
Senate Margin	0.81	−0.58	−0.51	1		
Senate Homo- geneity	−0.24	0.61	0.59	−0.22	1	
Senate Distance	−0.68	0.94	0.98	−0.41	0.61	1

analysis. My approach is to use variables describing the Congress in which the process was initiated on the grounds that its actions likely structured the appropriations process for the year. The estimations for the party power variables for the Senate presented in Table 2.5 are substantially the same if the outlier years are excluded from the analysis.

Table 2.5 presents the results from seven models estimating the relationship of party characteristics in the House and Senate to the inclusion of a bill in an omnibus package. Model A includes only the control variables. Model B includes only variables from the Senate. Models C to F estimate the effects of all House variables together, then one at a time. Model G includes variables from both the House and Senate. The results of the models are similar to the major findings from the "No Floor Vote" models of both chambers. The effects of the Senate party variables in Model B are consistent with the limited influence theory. Margin of control is negative and statistically significant ($p < 0.01$). Homogeneity and distance are both in the expected direction at $p = 0.08$ and $p = 0.07$, respectively. Models of the House show the same patterns observed in the analysis of bills that did not receive a vote in that chamber and are not consistent with the limited influence theory. Margin of control is negative and significant in Model D, homogeneity is positive and significant at $p = 0.05$ in Model E, and distance is positive and significant in Model F at $p = 0.05$. In Model G, the Senate's margin of control is negative at $p = 0.13$ and homogeneity negative and significant at $p = 0.01$. Distance is significant at $p < 0.01$, but the sign has reversed and is negative. The distance variable from the House is positive and significant. The House and Senate distance variables are correlated at a level

TABLE 2.5. *Party Characteristics and Inclusion of Bill in Omnibus Package, U.S. House and Senate, Logit Analysis, 1975–2012, Fixed Effects by Bill and Standard Errors Clustered by Year*

Variable	Expected Direction	Model A	Model B	Model C	Model D	Model E	Model F	Model G
Margin of Control (Senate)	−		−5.77*** (1.45)					−11.19 (7.35)
Homogeneity (Senate)	−		−3.61* (2.05)					−18.79** (7.59)
Distance (Senate)	+		4.14* (2.25)					−20.69*** (6.02)
Margin of Control (House)	−			−5.42** (2.48)	−5.69*** (2.19)			−0.03 (5.34)
Homogeneity (House)	−			−1.49 (4.31)		2.80* (1.45)		2.63 (4.67)
Distance (House)	+			2.02 (4.70)			3.32* (1.73)	32.83** (14.49)
Divided Control of Congress	+	0.47 (0.83)	−1.57 (1.04)	−0.35 (1.05)	−0.38 (0.87)	0.82 (0.92)	0.79 (0.95)	−6.49** (2.78)
Divided Government	+	0.84 (0.88)	1.68 (1.13)	1.16 (1.00)	1.13 (1.09)	0.89 (0.93)	1.01 (0.90)	4.19** (1.79)

Republican Control of House		1.51** (0.74)		−0.49 (0.92)	−0.30 (0.79)	0.40 (0.89)	0.19 (0.91)	−2.18 (3.09)
Republican Control of Senate		0.38 (0.61)	−1.03 (1.02)					−8.16*** (2.97)
Election Year	+	1.53** (0.76)	1.33** (0.66)	1.32* (0.70)	1.30* (0.71)	1.44* (0.76)	1.45* (0.74)	1.21* (0.62)
Deficit	+	4.92 (3.81)	9.70*** (3.43)	10.19** (5.20)	10.93** (4.96)	4.84 (3.99)	4.45 (4.10)	17.22*** (6.24)
Budget Enforcement Act	−	−1.63** (0.72)	−2.95*** (0.71)	−2.36*** (0.72)	−2.45*** (0.68)	−1.84*** (0.71)	−1.72** (0.70)	−4.42*** (1.32)
Previous Year in Omnibus	+	2.20 (1.45)	−0.06 (1.39)	0.54 (1.48)	0.48 (1.54)	1.23 (1.57)	1.34 (1.57)	−1.38 (1.52)
Constant		−4.10*** (1.19)	−0.58 (2.17)	−0.87 (2.25)	−0.87 (1.52)	−4.63*** (1.35)	−4.63*** (1.24)	8.14** (4.02)
Log Pseudo-likelihood		−209.71	−184.26	−192.58	−193.03	−201.99	−200.90	−165.11
Pseudo R²		0.35	0.43	0.40	0.40	0.37	0.38	0.49
N		479	479	479	479	479	479	479

Effects are significantly different from zero at *$p < .10$; **$p < .05$; ***$p < .01$; two tailed test.

of 0.98, and the reversal of the sign on the Senate distance variable likely is a consequence of multicollinearity.

Several interesting findings emerge from the control variables. Regular appropriations bills are more likely to be included in omnibus packages in election years at statistically significant levels of $p < 0.10$ or better in all models. In general, large deficits are associated with a higher likelihood of inclusion in an omnibus package (significant in Models B, C, D, and G), but the BEA made it less likely that a bill would be included in an omnibus package during the years that it was effective. It is statistically significant in all models. Finally, it is more likely that bills will be included in omnibus packages when Democrats control the Senate (Model G).

These findings are consistent with the expectations of the limited influence theory. The estimated effects of party variables in each chamber in Models B–F are in the same direction as those from the "No Floor Vote" models, but their statistical significance is weaker, as expected. Party power also appears to operate in a different way in the two chambers. Majority party homogeneity in the Senate is negatively associated with the inclusion of a bill in an omnibus package in Models B and G and positively associated with it in the House in Models E and G. Bills are more likely to be added to an omnibus package when the Senate majority party is divided and when the House majority party is unified.[7]

Discussion of Regression Models

The evidence from the "No Floor Vote" models and omnibus models is consistent with the expectations of the limited influence theory. Not calling votes on regular appropriations bills in the Senate is associated with small margins of control, ideological heterogeneity, and large ideological distances between the majority and minority. The decision not to vote on a bill in the House follows a pattern more consistent with CPG. It is more likely when the majority party is homogenous and distant from the minority. Not calling a vote on a bill in the House is also more likely when the majority party in the chamber is small. The results from models using the "In Omnibus" dependent variable are weaker, as expected, but consistent with those of the "No Floor Vote" models. The

---

[7] As an alternative way to deal with multicollinearity, I estimated a version of Model 2.5G that replaced the three party power measures in each chamber with index variables for the House and Senate. Full results are not reported here. The index variable was created using the formula *majority homogeneity + margin of control + (1–distance)*. Consistent with expectations, the Senate power variable was negative and significant at $p = 0.005$. The House variable was not statistically significant.

coefficients for the characteristics of the majority party in the House and Senate are in the same direction as the "No Floor Vote" models with the exception of the distance variable.

VOTING ON AMENDMENTS

In the limited influence theory, the net number of votes on amendments in the appropriations process should decline as the proportion of "No Floor Vote" bills increases even when taking into account the opportunity to amend an omnibus bill. Amending declines because the majority party imposes a degree of negative agenda control on the legislative process as the amendment-friendly regular order is replaced by the more restrictive omnibus process. Policy makers say that omnibus bills are not conducive to amending because of time constraints and the size of the package. Packages may also be created in conference and closed to amendment.

I test the expectation that amending declines when the majority party abandons the regular order by examining patterns in voting on amendments in the appropriations process between 1981 and 2012. Digital copies of the legislative histories of the bills were retrieved from the Library of Congress's THOMAS database. All votes cast in the Senate related to amendments, including votes on passage and procedural votes such as tabling motions, were tallied electronically to generate a picture of the total amount of legislative activity on each bill.[8] I aggregated this information to identify the total number of amendment-related votes that occurred during the appropriations process each year, defined as all the floor debate that took place on regular and omnibus spending bills for a fiscal year. The Senate cast 6,399 votes between 1981 and 2012 during the appropriations process, including 1,425 roll call votes and 4,974 voice votes. Senators cast an average of 200 votes on amendments per year, ranging from 0 to 415 with a standard deviation of 93. An average of 45 were roll call votes, and an average of 155 were voice votes.

---

[8] The actual counting of amendments was performed by a Yahoo! Pipe. The pipe identified legislative actions dealing with amendments in the Senate by filtering the legislative history of relevant regular and omnibus appropriations bills for the strings "S.AMDT" or "S.UP.AMDT." The selected legislative actions were tallied as a voice vote if they contained the string "voice vote." They were tallied as roll call votes if they contained the strings "yea-nay" or "recorded vote." A check of the data gathered by the Pipe against the legislative history of bills shows that the method misses a few votes related to amendments that do not include the search strings, such as appealing the ruling of the chair, but accurately reflects overall patterns of voting. I did not count non-controversial amendments adopted by unanimous consent.

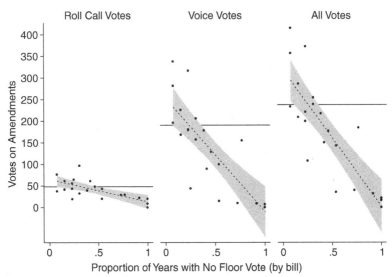

FIGURE 2.10. Abandoning the regular order and voting on amendments. U.S. Senate, 1981–2012.

There is a strong relationship between abandoning the regular order and a decline in the number of votes on amendments in the appropriations process, even when taking into account the opportunity to debate omnibus packages. The proportion of bills that did not receive a vote each year is negatively correlated with the number of roll call votes at a level of −0.61, voice votes at −0.77, and all votes on amendments at −0.79. Figure 2.10 illustrates this relationship using a scatterplot and loess curves with 95 percent confidence intervals shaded in gray. The horizontal gray lines on each plot indicate the average number of votes during years in which all bills were considered in the regular order. There was an average of forty-eight roll call votes per year during years in which all bills passed in the regular order. As the proportion of bills that did not receive a vote increases, the number of roll call votes on amendments declines gradually and approaches zero. The decline in voice votes is far steeper. The number of voice votes declines from an average of 190 in years during which all bills pass in regular order and approaches zero as the proportion of bills that did not receive a vote equals 1. The relationship between the proportion of bills included in omnibus packages and voting on amendments is weaker but in the same direction. It is correlated with the number of roll call votes at a level of −0.46, voice votes at −0.41, and all votes at −0.45.

TABLE 2.6. *Abandoning the Regular Order and Amending in the Appropriations Process, 1981–2012, Negative Binomial Regression Analysis*

	Model A Roll Call	Model B Voice	Model C All	Model D Roll Call	Model E Voice	Model F All
Proportion of Bills	−1.23***	−2.71***	−2.24***	−0.70***	−1.12**	−1.02***
	(0.26)	(0.47)	(0.34)	(0.26)	(0.49)	(0.39)
Constant	4.11	5.65	5.81	4.09	5.49	5.71
	(0.11)	(0.19)	(0.14)	(0.15)	(0.28)	(0.22)
Log Likelihood	−138.88	−183.57	−188.29	−143.46	−191.19	−197.16
Pseudo R²	0.05	0.05	0.06	0.02	0.01	0.02
Incidence Rate Ratio	0.29	0.07	0.11	0.50	0.33	0.36
(Standard Error)	(0.08)	(0.03)	(0.04)	(0.13)	(0.16)	(0.14)
N	32	32	32	32	32	32

Effects are significantly different from zero at *p < .10; **p < .05; ***p < .01; two tailed test.

Another way to estimate the effect of abandoning the regular order on amending is with regression analysis (Table 2.6). I fit a series of six bivariate negative binominal regression models appropriate for count variables using the total number of roll, voice, and all votes as the dependent variables. In Models A–C, the proportion of "No Floor Vote" bills is the independent variable. In Models D–F, the proportion of bills in an omnibus package is the independent variable. The results can be reported as Incidence Rate Ratios that indicate the change in the expected rate of the dependent variable with a one-unit change in the independent variable. Not calling a vote on any of the regular appropriations bills during a year reduces the number of roll call votes to 29 percent of the normal level, voice votes to 7 percent of the normal level, and all votes to 11 percent of the normal level. Simply including a bill in an omnibus package has a weaker and less precisely estimated effect on amending. Including all bills in an omnibus package reduces roll call votes to 49 percent of their usual level, voice votes to 32 percent of their usual level, and all votes to 36 percent of their usual level.

The majority party opts not to call a vote on an appropriations bill in the limited influence theory in part to escape a tide of amendments that bogs down bills and forces the majority party to cast politically risky votes. An expectation consistent with this argument is that the majority party will be

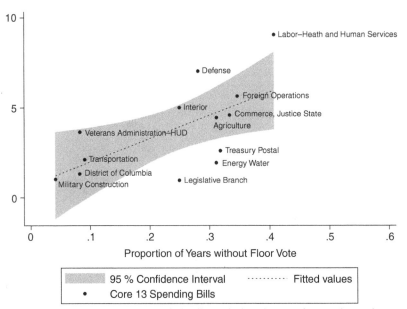

FIGURE 2.11. Frequently amended bills and abandoning the regular order. U.S. Senate, 1981–2012.

more likely not to call votes on spending bills that typically receive a large number of amendments. Figure 2.11 plots each of the Core 13 spending bills by the average number of roll call votes they receive in the Senate during years that they are adopted in the regular order on the vertical axis and the proportion of times a vote was not called on that bill on the horitzontal axis. The results meet expectations. The proportion of times a bill did not receive a vote rises along with the average number of roll call votes on amendments. The two variables are positively correlated at a level of 0.63.

Discussion

Voting patterns on amendments are consistent with the expectations of the limited influence theory. The majority party restricts the opportunity for members to offer amendments when it abandons the regular order even when taking into account later opportunities to debate appropriations bills as part of an omnibus package. The majority is most likely to abandon the regular order on bills that are frequently amended and more likely to cause it trouble. Ironically, the majority party's effort to protect itself from damaging roll call votes sharply curtails noncontroversial voice votes while only partially protecting members from roll call votes. Not voting on all regular appropriations bills reduces the amount of roll call votes to 29 percent of the normal level. Majority party members cast fewer roll call votes when the regular order is abandoned, but they still cast some. The effect on voice votes is far more severe. Amendments that are approved by voice vote are typically broadly supported efforts to improve the underlying bill. The Senate approves an average of 190 amendments to appropriations bills by voice vote in years when all bills are adopted in regular order and less than a tenth of that amount when it fails to vote on all the bills. The majority's effort to avoid roll call votes has the unfortunate side effect of decimating routine legislative tinkering on the floor and demonstrates the cost that abandoning the regular order imposes on members.

VOTING ON OMNIBUS BILLS

In the limited influence theory, the majority party forms an omnibus package as a defensive strategy to help it build a bipartisan coalition to pass the budget. Decisions over policy are more likely to be made by the majority party than on the floor, but the majority's ability to enact its preferred policies is constrained by its need to win minority support. I test this expectation by analyzing votes on omnibus bills using the vote for final passage of the conference report as a benchmark. I adopt *Congressional Quarterly*'s standard that a vote in which at least half of each party votes against the other is a partisan vote to assess the degree to which omnibus bills are partisan. Omnibus bills were passed in twenty-four years of the thirty-eight years under study. There were twenty-four recorded votes on the packages, four voice votes, and one adoption by unanimous consent.[9]

Table 2.7 lists the levels of majority and minority opposition to omnibus packages in every year in which an omnibus bill was considered between 1975 and 2012. Twenty votes on passage for omnibus packages have levels of minority opposition below 50 percent or were not recorded. Only nine votes exceed the threshold of 50 percent minority opposition. On seven occasions, majority opposition actually exceeded minority opposition. These patterns are far more consistent with bills that are generally bipartisan in nature rather than bills that are being used to push policy in the majority's preferred direction.

---

[9] On three occasions, Congress adopted two small packages of appropriations bills instead of a single package.

TABLE 2.7. *Opposition Levels to Omnibus Spending Bills, 1979–2012*

Year	Omnibus Bill	Majority Opposition	Minority Opposition
1979	H.J. Res. 440	0.33	0.29
1980	H.J. Res. 644	0.20	0.68
1981	H.J. Res. 370[a]	0.04 (1)	0.75 (1)
	H.J. Res. 409	0.19 (2)	0.17 (2)
1982	H.J. Res. 631	0.29	0.59
1983	H.J. Res. 413	voice	voice
1984	H.J. Res. 648	0.10	0.15
1985	H.J. Res. 465	voice	voice
1986	H.J. Res. 738	voice	voice
1987	H.J. Res. 395	0.23	0.46
1995	H.R. 3019, S. 1594	0.21	0.00
1996	H.R. 3610 (Defense)[b]	0.27	0.02
1998	H.R. 4328 (Transportation)	0.38	0.22
1999	H.R. 3194 (District of Columbia)	0.22	0.27
2000	H.R. 4577 (Labor)[c]	UC (1)	UC (1)
	H.R. 4635 (VA-HUD)	0.12 (2)	0.05 (2)
2002	H.J. Res. 2[d]	0.02	0.41
2003	H.R. 2673 (Agriculture)	0.08	0.53
2004	H.R. 4818 (Foreign Operations)	0.13	0.51
2006	H.J. Res. 20[d]	0.00	0.31
2007	H.R. 2764[e]	0.06 (1)	0.29 (1)
	(State-Foreign Operations)	0.52 (2)	0.02 (2)
2008	H.R. 2638 (Homeland Security)[c]	0.02	0.23
	H.R. 1105[d]	voice	voice
2009	H.R. 3288 (Transportation-HUD)	0.05	0.91
2010	H.R. 1473	0.08	0.32
2011	H.R. 2112 (Agriculture)[c]	0.00 (1)	0.64 (1)
	H.R. 2055 (Mil-Vets)	0.04 (2)	0.65 (2)
2012	H.R. 933	0.02	0.56

[a] H.J. Res. 370 provided funding through March 31, 1982. H.J. Res. 409 provided funding for the remainder of the fiscal year.

[b] H.R. 3610 was the final omnibus conference report. Prior to its passage by voice vote, the Senate first adopted an identical bill (H.R. 4278) by roll call vote. I report the roll call vote for H.R. 4278 here.

[c] Congress passed two separate packages in 2000, 2008 and 2011.

[d] Passed by the next Congress.

[e] Two separate votes were taken on the omnibus in 2007, one related to war spending and the other on the remainder of the bill.

Bill names (Defense, Labor, etc.) indicate that a regular appropriations bill carried the omnibus package.

ALTERNATIVE ACCOUNTS

There are two major debates about majority party influence in the Senate. The first is whether the Senate majority party has the ability to influence legislative outcomes, or whether outcomes are primarily determined on the floor as described in the traditional account of the Senate. The second debate is about the conditions under which majority party influence is likely to be observed. Is it an outgrowth of majority party strength, weakness, or unrelated to the majority party's characteristics? The last section of this chapter outlines expectations consistent with each approach and how they fit the three major findings from the appropriations process: (1) abandoning the regular order is negatively correlated with majority party power; (2) abandoning the regular order is correlated with an overall decline in amending, even when the opportunity to debate an omnibus is taken into account; and (3) omnibus bills generally receive bipartisan support for passage. Each of these findings fits the expectations of the limited influence theory. I assess alternative frameworks by establishing a set of expectations consistent with each approach and evaluating how well the evidence fits with those expectations.

The Senate majority party lacks the ability to influence legislative outcomes in the traditional view of the Senate (Smith 2005). If this account is correct, the characteristics of the majority party are unlikely to have a systematic relationship with abandoning the regular order, and the majority party should not demonstrate a significant ability to reduce amendments. It is also likely that votes on omnibus packages will be bipartisan since the majority party generally must satisfy the minority to pass legislation. Partisan frameworks of Congress treat abandoning the regular order and packaging bills together as a form of agenda control. In the cartel theory, the majority party can exercise negative agenda control to keep policies off the legislative agenda regardless of its characteristics (Cox and McCubbins 2005).[10] Abandoning the regular order should be uncorrelated with the majority party's characteristics, and there may be an observable reduction in amending. The majority's efforts to exert negative agenda control will not lead to the passage of partisan policies, and so votes on omnibus bills are likely to be bipartisan. In CPG, the majority

[10] I only discuss expectations relating to the use of negative agenda control in the cartel theory. The majority party can also exercise positive agenda control when it is homogeneous in the cartel model, and its expectations overlap with those of CPG in that respect.

TABLE 2.8. *Model Expectations and Results*

	Limited Influence	Traditional Senate	CPG	Cartel	Result
Party Characteristics					
Margin of Control	Negative	No Relationship	No Expectation	No Relationship	**Negative**
Homogeneity	Negative	No Relationship	Positive	No Relationship	**Negative**
Distance	Positive	No Relationship	Positive	No Relationship	**Positive**
Other Findings					
Amending	Declines	No Change	Declines	Declines	**Declines**
Vote on Omnibus	Bipartisan	Bipartisan	Partisan	Bipartisan	**Bipartisan**

party uses its influence to pursue policy goals when it is unified and distant from the minority party (Aldrich and Rohde 2001). Homogeneity and distance should both be positively correlated with abandoning the regular order, but the majority's margin of control is not expected to have a systematic relationship with influence. The consequences of the majority's actions are likely to include a reduction in amending and more partisan votes on the omnibus package as the minority reacts to policy shifting in the direction of the minority.

Table 2.8 compares the findings of the chapter with the expectations of the limited influence theory and its alternatives, and the results do not fit well with the alternative accounts. The sharp decline in amending and the statistically significant relationship of majority party characteristics to abandoning the regular order and forming an omnibus package are strong evidence that these practices are a form of majority party influence. The traditional theory of the Senate offers no easy explanation for these relationships. The cartel theory offers no explanation for the strong negative relationship between abandoning the regular order and party power, and CPG cannot account for the fact that the majority party is more likely to abandon the regular order when it is ideologically divided or that the result of its influence is a bill that wins bipartisan support. In CPG, the majority party would be expected to influence the agenda when it is unified to pursue policy goals. The limited influence theory offers the best fit for these findings.

The majority party has a limited degree of influence that it uses when it is small, divided, and distant from the minority to protect its reputation by reducing the number of amendments and facilitating the passage of the budget.

CONCLUSION

This chapter presents three different types of quantitative evidence to test the limited influence theory. First, regression models that test the relationship of abandoning the regular order to party power show that the majority party is more likely not to call a vote on a bill when it is small, divided, or distant from the minority. Second, the total number of votes related to amendments in the appropriations process declines along with the number of bills that do not receive a vote in the regular order, even when the later opportunity to debate an omnibus is taken into account. Third, votes on final passage for omnibus bills are generally bipartisan. Together, these findings fit the expectations of the limited influence theory that the majority party can exercise a constrained degree of influence over the appropriations process to help it adopt a budget and meet electoral goals.

3

The First Wave (1979–1987)

I turn next to a set of case studies analyzing how the characteristics of the Senate majority party affect its management of the annual appropriations bills. The value of case studies is that they can show whether theories and the findings of quantitative studies meaningfully fit the messy reality of the political world. I evaluate the reasons why the Senate majority party abandons the regular order and judge their consistency with the expectations of the theory using events on the floor of the Senate and the perceptions of important actors as evidence. I do not expect that the weakness of the Senate majority party will be the only factor influencing the creation of omnibus spending bills, but its effect should be plainly visible. I also make a more general assessment of the spirit behind the majority's actions to assess whether the majority party abandons the regular order when it goes on the offense to pursue its policy goals or as a defensive strategy to ensure the passage of the budget when it has difficulty managing the floor.

This chapter analyzes the first term of President Ronald Reagan from 1981 to 1984 when omnibus bills first became a common way to adopt the budget. The evidence from this crucial period fits the expectations of the limited influence theory well. The Republican majority was weak because it had a narrow margin of control and was ideologically divided. Social issues such as abortion and school prayer divided the party. Republican-led filibusters on appropriations bills were common and disrupted the party's ability to adopt regular appropriations bills. The majority's response was to transform temporary continuing resolutions (CRs) into full-year substitutes for regular spending bills it was unable to pass. When these full-year substitutes themselves became routine, the omnibus appropriations bill was born. The evidence suggests that the packages helped the majority party to reduce amendments and ensure passage of the budget but did not lead to systematic policy wins for the party. All of these packages attracted bipartisan support, although at times minority opposition rose above 50 percent of the minority party.

DIVIDED SENATE REPUBLICANS

The power of the majority party in the Senate dropped sharply in 1981 as a consequence of the election of the first Republican majority in the chamber since 1955. Democrats had controlled the Senate for decades, and in the 1970s they enjoyed wide margins of control and relative ideological uniformity compared with Republicans. The Democratic majority of the Senate in the 96th Congress (1979–1980) had fifty-eight members and a first dimension DW-NOMINATE standard deviation of just 0.15 as compared with 0.21 for the minority Republicans. The Republican victory in the 1980 elections propelled the party into control of the Senate with a narrower margin of fifty-three and without changing the comparative diversity of the two parties. The Senate Republican majority in the 97th Congress remained ideologically diverse with a DW-NOMINATE standard deviation of 0.20. Democrats were more unified with a standard deviation of 0.14.

Figure 3.1 compares the two parties as control of the Senate shifted using scatterplots of the ideological positions of their members. The horizontal axis is the first dimension DW-NOMINATE score that is commonly interpreted as the standard left–right ideological spectrum. The vertical axis is the second dimension DW-NOMINATE score. Its meaning has shifted over time. It is thought to represent divisions over slavery prior to the Civil War, divisions over race in the twentieth century, and divisions over social issues today (Poole and Rosenthal 2007). The Democrats are in the upper left corner of each chart, and Republicans are in the lower right. Democrats are more tightly distributed in both charts than Republicans along the horizontal axis, signaling their greater ideological unity. As Republicans took control of the Senate, their narrow and fractious majority faced a large and unified group of Democrats.

Republican senators consisted of liberals such as Charles Mathias (R-MD), Lowell Weicker (R-CT), and Bob Packwood (R-OR). Mathias was reported to "gall his conservative colleagues to a degree wholly unwarranted by his actual influence" and was blocked from assuming

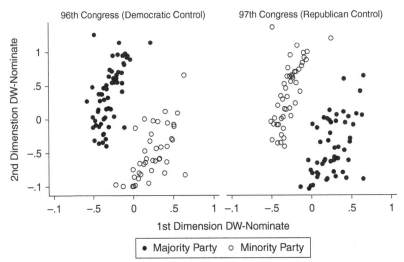

FIGURE 3.1. Transition to Republican control of Senate. 96th and 97th Congresses, 1978–1982.

the chairmanship of the Judiciary Committee by his party.[1] Weicker "elevated righteous indignation to a political art form"[2] and frustrated President Ronald Reagan so much that the president referred to him as a "pompous, no good fathead" in his diaries (Hayward 2009, 227). Packwood was known for his strong views favoring abortion rights and willingness to filibuster to defend them. On the other side of the ideological divide were conservatives such as Senators Jeremiah Denton (R-AL), Steven Symms (R-ID), and Jesse Helms (R-NC). Denton, a navy veteran, former POW, and religious conservative, was firmly antiabortion. Symms was a "veteran of four years of guerilla warfare in the House, where he and allies on the right used demands for roll-call votes, frequent quorum calls and numerous amendments to tie up the Democratic leadership."[3] Helms was regarded as the "apostle of conservatism" and known for a mastery of Senate rules as well as his willingness to stir controversy by proposing amendments on hot-button issues.[4]

[1] "Charles McC. Mathias Jr. (R)" in *Politics in America: Members of Congress in Washington and at Home*, 515 (Washington, DC: Congressional Quarterly Press, 1981).
[2] "Lowell P. Weicker Jr. (R)" in *Politics in America: Members of Congress in Washington and at Home*, 202 (Washington, DC: Congressional Quarterly Press, 1981).
[3] "Steven D. Symms (R)" in *Politics in America: Members of Congress in Washington and at Home*, 311 (Washington, DC: Congressional Quarterly Press, 1981).
[4] "Jesse Helms (R)" in *Politics in America: Members of Congress in Washington and at Home*, 891 (Washington, DC: Congressional Quarterly Press, 1981).

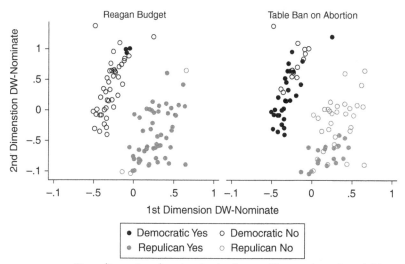

FIGURE 3.2. Two-dimensional voting in the Senate. Economic and social issues.

The divisions among Republicans were particularly evident on social issues such as school prayer and abortion that were becoming common subjects of debate in the appropriations process. Some bills, because of their areas of jurisdiction, were particularly likely to attract challenging amendments. The Commerce, Justice, and State bill drew amendments on school prayer and school integration because of its jurisdiction over the Department of Justice. The Labor–Health and Human Services bill and Treasury-Postal bill attracted amendments on abortion because of their respective jurisdiction over Medicaid and federal employee health plans. These issues sparked filibusters led from within the Republican Party that were difficult to resolve.

Figure 3.2 demonstrates the challenge that social riders created for Republicans using scatterplots of two votes in the Senate in the 97th Congress (1981–1982). The first is the vote to approve President Reagan's Fiscal Year 1983 federal budget.[5] The second is a vote to table a Helms amendment to ban abortion.[6] The second dimension adds little explanatory power to the vote on the budget. The two parties are almost perfectly divided on the horizontal axis. In the case of abortion, the second dimension is salient. Pro-life votes in each party are more heavily concentrated on the positive end of the vertical axis, while pro-choice votes are concentrated on

[5] Roll Call Vote 194, U.S. Senate, 97th Congress, Second Session, June 23, 1982.
[6] Roll Call Vote 344, U.S. Senate, 97th Congress, Second Session, September 15, 1982.

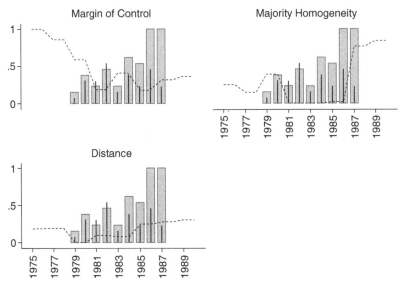

FIGURE 3.3. Party characteristics and abandoning the regular order. U.S. Senate,
1975–1990.

the negative end. It is noteworthy that pro-life and pro-choice voters can be
found in both parties and on both sides of the main first dimension. Similar
patterns are visible on votes for other social issues such as school prayer.

The first wave of omnibus spending bills began in 1979 and lasted until
1987 during a time in which the majority party had particularly small
margins of control and low levels of homogeneity. Figure 3.3 illustrates
the total proportion of regular appropriations bills that did not receive
a vote (solid black lines) and included in omnibus packages (gray bars)
along with the majority party's margin of control, homogeneity, and distance from the minority during this time period. The majority party failed
to vote on 30 percent of spending bills and included 51 percent of them
in omnibus packages between the beginning of the wave and its end. The
size of omnibus packages increased over time and included all regular
appropriations bills in 1986 and 1987. The majority returned to passing
bills in the regular order in 1988 and continued to pass the spending bills
on an individual basis until 1995.

THE OMNIBUS ERA BEGINS

The Congressional Budget and Impoundment Control Act was imple-
mented in 1975 with the drafting of the budget resolution and

appropriations bills for fiscal year 1976. The transparency in spending decisions created by the new law brought with it heightened conflict as congressional conservatives sought to challenge federal spending. Despite these noisy debates, overwhelming Democratic majorities helped the new budget process work smoothly in its opening years. It faced more trouble as conservatives gained momentum following the election of Jimmy Carter. Trade-offs between social welfare and defense programs combined with the need to reduce the federal deficit led to sharp clashes over budget priorities in Carter's last two years and slowed the passage of spending bills in the Senate. The crisis in appropriations deepened with the election of President Ronald Reagan and a narrow Republican majority in the Senate in 1980.

97th Congress (1981–1982)

Ronald Reagan took office with the goal of dramatically reshaping the federal budget by cutting taxes and domestic spending to reduce the size of government. Social conservatives in the party viewed Republican control of the Senate and presidency as an opportunity to pursue long-sought goals on issues such as abortion and school prayer. They drew on a strategy honed during President Carter's last years in office and pursued their goals by offering amendments to appropriations bills. Their efforts sparked a furious backlash by liberal Republicans and Democrats and complicated the passage of individual spending bills in an environment already strained by debates over Reagan's budget program. Under these pressures, Senate Majority Leader Howard Baker (R-TN) was unable to bring some individual bills to a vote. His response was to transform CRs that were traditionally used as temporary extensions of government funding into full-year resolutions that substituted for several spending bills at once.

1981

President Reagan's ambitious budget goals and contentious debates over social riders put a severe strain on the appropriations process in 1981 (Table 3.1). The House of Representatives failed to vote on one bill (Legislative Branch), while the Senate failed to vote on four (Commerce, Justice, and State; Legislative Branch; Labor–Health and Human Services; and Treasury-Postal). Two of the bills – Treasury-Postal and Commerce, Justice, and State – failed to pass because the majority was unable to overcome dissension within its ranks. More limited evidence suggests the

TABLE 3.1. *Legislative History of Appropriations Bills, 1981, First Session, 97th Congress*

Bill	No Floor Vote (House)	No Floor Vote (Senate)	Bill in Omnibus
Agriculture			
Commerce, Justice, and State		✓	✓
District of Columbia			
Defense			
Energy and Water			
Foreign Operations			
Interior			
Labor–Health and Human Services		✓	✓
Legislative Branch	✓	✓	
Military Construction			
Treasury-Postal		✓	✓
Transportation			
Veterans Administration–HUD			
Total	1	4	3

majority opted not to bring the Labor–Health and Human Services bill to the floor to avoid amendments that would have disrupted its passage. Funding for all the bills that were not adopted in the regular order but Legislative Branch ultimately was provided through a CR, H.J. Res. 370.

A major problem in 1981 was the inability of Congress and the president to agree on overall spending levels for the bills. The administration spent the opening months of its first year in office pushing through a budget reconciliation bill that cut spending by $130.6 billion over a three-year period. Pressure from skyrocketing deficit projections that summer led the administration to push for an additional $13 billion in cuts by congressional appropriators. This demand caused the Republican majority in the Senate Appropriations Committee to balk and the normal process of passing spending bills ground to a halt.[7] The delay meant that Congress would not pass the spending bills by the beginning of the new fiscal year on October 1.

Leaders prepared a temporary CR, H.J. Res. 325, to keep the government in operation until November 20 and give Congress additional

---

[7] "Budget and Appropriations 1981: Overview" in *CQ Almanac 1981*, 37th ed., 245–46 (Washington, DC: Congressional Quarterly, 1982.) http://library.cqpress.com/cqalmanac/cqal81-1172382.

time to pass the bills.[8] The extension proved to be insufficient. One bill had been enacted and two were ready for the president's signature as the November 20 deadline drew near, but the remaining ten bills had not cleared Congress. Needing additional time to complete the bills, leaders prepared a new CR, H.J. Res. 357. They also aimed to update funding levels in the CR by basing its spending on the new versions of the spending bills that were still in process in the House and Senate. Majority Leader Baker wanted to pass as many appropriations bills as possible for that reason. Senate-approved bills would put the Senate's positions on record and improve its bargaining position with the House of Representatives. If he failed, the spending levels in the House versions of the bills would be used by default.

Baker's effort to pass the regular appropriations bills was hampered by a series of disputes over social issues that were waiting to emerge when the bills reached the Senate floor. The Treasury-Postal bill was a tinderbox because the House had adopted an amendment restricting federal health plans from covering abortion. The Senate Appropriations Committee voted 14–7 against including it in its version of the bill, but the abortion issue was expected to surface again on the Senate floor.[9] Conflict also was brewing on the Commerce, Justice, and State bill. Conservatives wanted to restrict the Department of Justice from interfering with programs promoting voluntary prayer in public schools. Early in the summer of 1981, the House of Representatives adopted an amendment to its version of the bill to meet that goal. This amendment met with an unfriendly reception in the Senate, where Senator Lowell Weicker (R-CT) was chair of the Commerce, Justice, and State subcommittee of the Appropriations Committee. Weicker was ready with an amendment to strike the House language as soon as the bill was considered on the Senate floor.[10]

Weicker brought the bill to the floor on November 16 under pressure from Baker to adopt it quickly. Instead, his amendment to strike the prayer language sparked a three-day floor debate. The chairman's first obstacle was a motion to table his amendment from the ranking member of the

---

[8] "First Continuing Resolution: Oct. 1–Nov. 20" in *CQ Almanac 1981*, 37th ed., 290–94 (Washington, DC: Congressional Quarterly, 1982). http://library.cqpress.com/cqalmanac/cqal81-1172511. The CR also provided full-year funding for the Legislative Branch appropriations bill in an effort for members of Congress to avoid a direct vote on a congressional pay raise.

[9] Weiss, Laura B. "Senate Panel Recommends Increased Postal Subsidies in $9.8 Billion Funding Bill." *CQ Weekly* (October 3, 1981), 1894.

[10] "$85 Billion Bill Approved for Nation's Social Programs." *CQ Weekly* (November 7, 1981), 2203.

committee, Senator Ernest Hollings (D-SC). It passed 70–12.[11] Weicker responded with new amendment to replace the prayer provision with language stating that Justice would not interfere with "constitutional" programs of voluntary prayer. Senator Jesse Helms (R-NC) successfully tabled this amendment on a vote of 51–34, drawing the votes of eighteen Democrats and losing twelve Republicans.[12]

The back-and-forth on the prayer issue was consuming precious time, and Majority Leader Baker remained determined to pass as many bills as possible. Taking to the floor, he reminded his colleagues: "It is the intention of the leader to ask the Senate to continue consideration of appropriations bills as they are here and available. The reason for that, I think, is obvious; that is, the CR as it is likely to pass in either body will reference perhaps the lower of the House- or Senate-passed version or the conference level so there is still an opportunity for the Senate to make its mark.[13] The debate on Commerce, Justice, and State dragged into another day despite the urgings of the majority leader. Weicker won his first victory on November 17 with an amendment that added the language of the First Amendment to the provision in an effort to demonstrate that the language on prayer provision was unconstitutional. Helms countered with a successful amendment reinforcing the original language.[14]

After this defeat, Weicker took to the floor in frustration. He argued that there was no dispute over money in the bill and that the committee had faithfully discharged its work. "Our job is done. The Senator from South Carolina and the Senator from Connecticut and the members of the Appropriations Subcommittee have done our job. Now it has all gone for naught, while we sit here hung up on a couple of points which should have stood on their own feet, as a matter of their own debate, as a matter of their own legislation. This all is going onto a continuing resolution. All this time will have been lost and nobody regrets it more than I do." He chastised his fellow Republicans for legislating on appropriations bills. "I do not understand how it is that he and some of his conferees here on the Senate floor have managed to take the appropriations process and so convolute it that we cannot get any business done." He noted that the rise of social legislation on appropriations bills had created a situation in which "no appropriations bill can now clear the floor. The net

[11] *Congressional Record*, November 16, 1981, 27489–27490.
[12] Roll Call Vote 377, U.S. Senate, 97th Congress, First Session, November 16, 1981.
[13] *Congressional Record*, November 16, 1981, 27520.
[14] See Roll Call Votes 380 and 393, U.S. Senate, 97th Congress, First Session, November 17 and 18, 1981.

result is that we are now going from continuing resolution to continuing resolution."[15] Chairman Weicker then refused to bring the bill to a vote, and shortly afterwards it was pulled from the floor.

With no immediate opportunity to pass Commerce, Justice, and State and other bills still pending, Majority Leader Baker brought up the CR, H.J. Res. 357. In an extraordinary step, the House had extended the previous year's bills for the remainder of the fiscal year – a step that negated the need to pass the regular bills at all. The full-year extension sparked an uproar in the Senate because it was viewed as handing power to the president and a restriction of the Senate's traditional right to debate and amend legislation. Senator William Proxmire, the ranking Democratic member of the Appropriations Committee, condemned the approach:

> What this basically means is that we are attempting to handle funding for the entire Federal Government for the remainder of the fiscal year in a 26-page resolution covering hundreds of departments, bureaus and agencies and thousands of individual programs. And we are working under an almost unendurable time pressure – we have to complete action on the resolution by midnight on Friday or the entire Government comes to a screeching halt.... We are wrapping up all the days and weeks of debate that normally occur when these bills come to the floor, all the dozens of amendments, all the colloquies and criticisms, all the close questioning and careful examination, in 12 to 18 hours of debate at the very most. It means we are helter-skelter pushing these extraordinarily complex pieces of legislation through Congress from committee through conference in about 3 working days.[16]

The resolution and debate over how to meet the budget cuts demanded by President Reagan led to an intense all-night debate in the Senate. Ultimately, the extension was shortened to six months, and a 4 percent spending cut was agreed to on the morning of November 20. Hours later, Reagan vetoed H.J. Res. 357 on the grounds that it spent too much money, and federal workers were sent home for the day for the first ever broad government shutdown.[17] Congressional leaders scrambled to end the crisis by adopting a new temporary CR that extended the terms of the original CR, H.J. Res. 325, until December 15.[18]

---

[15] *Congressional Record*, November 18, 1981, 27895–27897.

[16] *Congressional Record*, November 18, 1981, 27903.

[17] "2nd Continuing Resolution: 1st Reagan Veto" in *CQ Almanac 1981*, 37th ed., 294–301 (Washington, DC: Congressional Quarterly, 1982). http://library.cqpress.com/cqalmanac/cqal81-1172528.

[18] Donnelly, Harrison. "Weekend Contest Produces 3-Week Funding Accord; Government Shutdown Ends." *CQ Weekly* (November 28, 1981), 2324.

The Senate's refusal to pass a full-year CR put new pressure on Majority Leader Baker to pass the appropriations bills individually, but there were still thorny issues of social policy to decide. Baker called up the Commerce, Justice, and State bill on December 9 in another effort to pass it before the temporary CR expired. The prayer issue proved to be impossible to resolve. Weicker continued to refuse to bring the bill to a vote, and Senator Helms filed a cloture motion to end debate in response.[19] Senate rules did not permit an immediate vote on the motion, so the bill was set aside to make way for other business. Baker also attempted to debate the Treasury-Postal bill, but his unanimous consent request was met with an objection.

Majority Leader Baker turned his full attention to negotiating a new CR with the House and administration. Congress and the president ultimately agreed on a CR (H.J. Res. 370) with a deadline of March 31, 1982, that would provide funds in place of any bill that did not pass in regular order. At the time of drafting, this included all bills except for three: Energy and Water, District of Columbia, and Legislative Branch. The new CR imposed about half of the cuts sought by President Reagan to domestic programs but handed Chairman Weicker a victory: it was silent on the issue of school prayer. It also handed proponents of abortion rights a victory by requiring that federal employee health benefits funded by the Treasury-Postal bill be provided according to the terms of the Senate bill, which permitted coverage of abortion.[20]

The resolution was debated briefly for portions of two legislative days on the Senate floor before being adopted on a partisan vote. Eleven Democrats favored the bill, and thirty-three opposed it. Forty-nine Republicans supported the bill and two opposed it.[21] Despite its breadth – it covered ten separate spending bills – the speed of its consideration and the fact that members still anticipated debating each of the bills individually probably explain why the Senate only voted on eight amendments to the package. The brief debate was particularly consequential for the Labor–Health and Human Services bill because it proved to be the last opportunity for members to offer any amendments related to it. The original bill (H.R. 4560) had been intensely debated in the House, which had voted on twenty-one amendments before passing it, but it was never called up on an individual basis in the Senate.

[19] *Congressional Record*, December 9, 1981, 30126.
[20] Donnelly, Harrison. "Stopgap Funds Bill Cleared; $4 Billion in Cuts Approved." *CQ Weekly* (December 12, 1981), 2428–2429.
[21] Roll Call Vote 482, U.S. Senate, 97th Congress, First Session, December 11, 1981.

Once the CR had been passed, the Senate spent its last days before the Christmas break in an attempt to clear as many of the bills covered by the resolution as possible. As each bill was enacted, it "dropped out" of the CR, and funding was provided for government agencies under the new terms of the enacted legislation. Ultimately, only the Commerce, Justice, and State bill, Treasury-Postal bill, and Labor–Health and Human Services bill failed to clear the chamber. The Commerce, Justice, and State bill was called up shortly after the passage of the CR, but Senator Helms' cloture motion failed when Senator Weicker and fourteen other Republicans joined with twenty Democrats to vote against it.[22] Senate leaders never attempted to debate Labor–Health and Human Services, likely because they would have faced contentious amendments on abortion or spending levels for the bill. They did bring the Treasury-Postal bill to the floor, and it ignited a debate on abortion just as many had feared. Senator Jeremiah Denton (R-AL) offered an amendment to impose the abortion restrictions passed by the House, but Senator Bob Packwood (R-OR) objected repeatedly when Denton tried call a vote.[23] The Senate moved on to other legislation and Treasury-Postal was never passed individually. Observers noted "parliamentary confusion, the controversial nature of the [amendment], and the end-of-session pressure to adjourn" led leadership to pull the bill from the floor.[24] As a result of the Senate's inability to resolve these controversies, a CR intended to provide temporary funding became the primary vehicle for providing funding in place of the regular bills.

When the CR expired in March, it was extended again for the remainder of the fiscal year. Chairman Mark Hatfield (R-OR) noted his displeasure with the process: "I would much rather have the Senate consider the three bills which this continuing resolution covers, but because of the problems of Senate scheduling, threat of legislative riders and our inability to make final budgetary decisions … this goal seems less and less likely." Hatfield explained that he would oppose any amendments to the bill. "I do not believe that we can risk the opening of Pandora's box with the acceptance of any amendment on the continuing resolution, because once we do that, all Senators have equal rights and we will be getting into abortion, school prayer, busing, and all the other things that have traditionally been loaded [on]."[25]

---

[22] Roll Call Vote 483, U.S. Senate, 97th Congress, First Session, December 11, 1981.

[23] *Congressional Record*, December 14, 1981, 31101.

[24] Weiss, Laura B. "Treasury and Post Office Appropriation Bill Entangled in Employee Abortion Issue." *CQ Weekly* (January 9, 1982), 48.

[25] *Congressional Record*, March 29, 1982, 5634.

The path to a three-bill CR in 1981 is consistent with the argument that omnibus packages arise out of the failure of a weak majority party to control the floor.[26] Fierce debates over President Reagan's budget cuts initially deadlocked Congress, but most of the spending bills survived this turmoil and passed individually. The fates of the three bills that did not are well explained by the politics of the Senate floor. Conflict among Senate Republicans blocked the Commerce, Justice, and State bill and the Treasury-Postal bill from clearing the Senate floor after both had passed the House. The indirect evidence available on the Labor–Health and Human Services bill suggests that the majority imposed a degree of negative agenda control and limited the difficult amendments it faced by debating the social welfare bill only in the context of a CR. It is noteworthy H.J. Res. 370 did not resolve disputes over social policies in favor of the more conservative positions on school prayer and abortion preferred by the House and most Senate Republicans. On the other hand, the CR cut spending below the initial levels adopted by the House and Senate in committee and moved the budget in a more conservative direction. This fact likely accounts for the partisan nature of the vote for the resolution.

Overall, the appropriations process in 1981 illustrates how Congress shifted from the regular order toward the unorthodox process of creating omnibus bills through a process of trial, error, and adaptation to changing circumstances. The Senate majority did not set out to create a three-bill omnibus package. Instead, a routine practice of adopting temporary CRs was adapted to provide funding for an entire year when passing three bills on the Senate floor proved to be too difficult for the majority.

1982

The tentative first steps that Congress took toward omnibus bills in 1981 paved the way for the consolidation of the unorthodox new process in 1982. The Senate did not vote on seven bills in 1982, and six were ultimately included in a yearlong CR (Table 3.2). In contrast to 1981, when Senator Baker attempted to debate most appropriations bills on the floor but was unable to bring them to a final vote, the majority did not bring six bills to the floor on an individual basis for debate at all in 1982. Nor did it repeat its earlier fight over the time period covered by the CR. Instead, it substituted debate on a single yearlong CR for individual debate on the bills it contained.

[26] The Legislative Branch bill, driven by politics of its own, passed by an earlier CR in an effort by Congress to shield members of both chambers from a tough vote on a pay raise.

TABLE 3.2. *Legislative History of Appropriations Bills, 1982, Second Session, 97th Congress*

Bill	No Floor Vote (House)	No Floor Vote (Senate)	Bill in Omnibus
Agriculture			
Commerce, Justice, and State		✓	✓
District of Columbia			
Defense		✓	✓
Energy and Water	✓	✓	✓
Foreign Operations	✓	✓	✓
Interior			
Labor–Health and Human Services		✓	✓
Legislative Branch	✓	✓	
Military Construction			
Treasury-Postal		✓	✓
Transportation			
Veterans Administration–HUD			
Total	3	7	6

The absence of a floor debate on the bills that did not receive votes prevents a bill-by-bill examination of the record, but the overall pattern of the session is consistent with the argument that difficulty managing the Senate floor contributes to the abandonment of the regular order. The Senate floor was a treacherous arena for the majority in 1982 because of its inability to overcome policy disputes between liberal and conservative Republicans. The session was marred by rising numbers of filibusters, including one that consumed five critical weeks just before the start of the new fiscal year. A *CQ Almanac* summary of the session noted that because of frustration over frequent filibusters, "When adjournment finally came in December, senators left town tired and bitter, with many of them muttering about the need for changes in Senate rules."[27] In this context, the Senate abandoned its effort to pass spending bills individually in favor of packaging them together.

When the 97th Congress returned to session in early 1982, it was presented with new proposals from the Reagan administration to cut

[27] "Congress and Government 1982: Overview," in *CQ Almanac 1982*, 38th ed., 507–508 (Washington, DC: Congressional Quarterly, 1983). http://library.cqpress.com/cqalmanac/cqal82-1163331.

entitlement spending and discretionary programs in the fiscal year 1983 budget. Facing an election year and exhausted by the previous year's budget debate, Congress balked. Rather than accept President Reagan's proposed cuts, congressional leaders negotiated modest cuts in the defense budget and $98.3 billion in new taxes. By the time a budget resolution finally passed Congress on June 23, the negotiations had consumed five months and Congress was six weeks past its statutory deadline for passing a budget. This meant a late start for the House Appropriations Committee, which traditionally wrote its bills early in the year and presented them to the Senate at the beginning of summer. The new fiscal year was just a month away when the House began to pass the spending bills in September.

The Senate had to act quickly to pass the spending bills before the deadline of the new fiscal year on October 1, but it was bogged down in a contentious debate on social issues. A must-pass bill to raise the limit on the national debt had been brought to the floor on August 16 and was immediately beset by conservative senators with riders on abortion and school prayer. Liberals led by Senator Bob Packwood (R-OR) took to the floor to filibuster the bill in response. Senator Packwood filibustered the bill the old-fashioned way and read at length from a history of abortion in the United States. For five long weeks, a coalition of Republicans and Democrats prevented conservative amendments from coming to a vote.[28] Nineteen Republicans joined with twenty-five Democrats to sustain the filibuster on a key cloture vote on a Helms amendment to restrict abortion.[29] Finally, the conservatives admitted defeat and the debt limit bill was passed without any social riders on September 23.[30]

The debt ceiling debate had consumed an enormous amount of time at a critical point in the year. Funding for government agencies would expire in just one week on October 1, and Congress had passed only one of the thirteen spending bills. A temporary CR was inevitable and needed to provide a substantial extension of time given the desire of members to return home for the fall campaign. In response to these pressures, leaders drafted a CR (H.J. Res. 599) to give Congress until December 17, 1982, to adopt the regular spending bills. It was brought to the Senate floor

---

[28] "Senate Kills Abortion, School Prayer Riders" in *CQ Almanac 1982*, 38th ed., 403–5. (Washington, DC: Congressional Quarterly, 1983). http://o-library.cqpress.com.bianca. penlib.du.edu/cqalmanac/cqal82-1164771.

[29] Roll Call Vote 343, U.S. Senate, 97th Congress, Second Session, September 15, 1982.

[30] "Debt Limit Increases," in *CQ Almanac 1982*, 38th ed., 44–45 (Washington, DC: Congressional Quarterly, 1983). http://library.cqpress.com/cqalmanac/cqal82-1163541.

for a hurried but lively debate on September 29 in which senators cast thirty-six votes on amendments to the bill. The resolution received an initial vote of approval of 72–26 in the Senate with majority support by both parties.[31] Congress passed the final version with little controversy on October 1 and immediately adjourned. President Reagan signed it the next day.

The task of passing remaining spending bills was urgent when Congress reconvened for a lame-duck session on November 30. The 97th Congress was ending and all unfinished legislative action would expire with it when the 98th Congress was seated in January. This meant that the Senate Appropriations Committee's work that year to write and report the bills would be lost and members would have to rewrite any bills they failed to pass from scratch.

There were a few success stories. In early December, the Senate debated and passed the District of Columbia, Interior, and Transportation bills. It also gave final passage to the Agriculture conference report that had cleared both chambers in September. Other bills risked reigniting the same debates on abortion and prayer that had consumed the Senate on the debt ceiling extension. The House had adopted its usual limitations in the Commerce, Justice, and State bill on the involvement of the Department of Justice in school prayer cases and prohibited federal health insurance policies from covering abortion in the Treasury-Postal bill. Both provisions had caused problems on the floor the previous year. Neither bill was brought to the Senate floor in 1982.

Instead, the Senate continued with its pattern of innovation. A new CR (H.J. Res. 631) was brought to the floor on December 16 that incorporated by reference the texts of the individual bills that had been approved by committee and lasted for the entire remaining fiscal year. This step allowed the Senate to adopt all the remaining individual bills simultaneously instead of extending the previous year's legislation with new dollar amounts as it had done in years past. Appropriations Committee member Senator Ted Stevens (R-AK) explained: "We will be passing 10 bills in one bill on this occasion. It is not like the old way of just folding in the numbers. We folded in the limitations not only in the bills but in the reports that accompany the bill."[32]

The CR included ten bills, but as a practical matter it would apply to only six. Four bills that were near completion in the regular order would

[31] Senate Roll Call Vote 373, September 29, 1982.
[32] *Congressional Record*, December 16, 1982, 31317.

drop out of the CR once they were passed. The remaining six had not
been debated on the Senate floor and would remain in the package. The
fact that they would only be debated as a group rather than individually
broke new ground in the Senate. The temporary CR was set to expire in
a day, and the limited time available to review the massive bill rankled
members. Senator David Pryor (D-AR) complained,

> We will be, in effect, passing six bills in one bill in about 25 hours with
> only a few minutes to debate this time tomorrow night on each amend-
> ment.... Where has the appropriations process gone and where has the
> opportunity gone to look at each one of these measures and discuss it on
> the floor of the Senate? Has it disappeared from the face of the Earth?...
> Now the Senate knows as well as I do, that 24 hours from right now we
> are going to be talking about closing down the Government. We are going
> to be talking about cutting off social security checks. We are going to be
> encouraging people to limit their debate to 2 or 3 minutes on a side. It is
> going to happen. It happened in the past, and it is going to happen tomor-
> row night.[33]

Chairman Hatfield agreed with his critics that the CR was "not the way
to do business." Instead, "What we are trying to do ... is consider 1983
a lost cause" and to start the next fiscal year with a clean slate.[34] He
maintained that the CR had been forced on the Senate by budgetary constraints, the tight timeline imposed by delays in the passage of the budget
resolution, and debates over riders:

> Beyond the procedural impediments of the congressional budget process
> is still another serious and growing obstruction to the timely enactment of
> appropriations bills – this is the wide acceptance of the use of appropria-
> tions bills as a vehicle for legislative "riders." The inability of the normal
> authorizing and legislative process to provide an adequate forum in which
> to address these issues has led to increasing pressure on appropriations
> measures which must be enacted on a regular basis. The subjects of these
> legislative riders range from the divisive subject of abortion to the regula-
> tion of used car sales, and now include almost every major concern facing
> the Congress.... Not only must the committee grapple with issues and pro-
> visions outside its area of expertise, it must frequently endure the prolonged
> debate and consideration surrounding controversial issues....Such delays
> are the reason that continuing resolutions are necessary, despite the ineffi-
> ciencies they engender in the management and operation of Government
> programs.[35]

[33] *Congressional Record*, December 16, 1982, 31317.
[34] *Congressional Record*, December 16, 1982, 31316.
[35] *Congressional Record*, December 16, 1982, 31313–31314.

Hatfield urged his colleagues to pass the bill quickly. Majority Leader Howard Baker endorsed his call for brevity as well, noting that the Appropriations Committee had taken only four hours to approve the CR and that this was a good model for all senators to follow on the floor.[36]

Senators completed their work under the shadow of an impending government shutdown at midnight on December 17. They debated the CR through the night of December 16 and all day on December 17. The prayer issue was never brought up, but the House prohibition on the coverage of abortion by federal health plans was one of the first issues to be raised. Both sides agreed to limit the abortion debate to twenty minutes, and the House provision was defeated on a vote of 49–48.[37] The bill was still not complete when government funding expired at midnight, but an immediate shutdown was averted because it was a Friday and government offices had closed for the weekend.

It took the remainder of the weekend to finalize the bill. In all, Senators cast seventy-one votes on amendments before passing the new CR on a vote of 63–31 with a majority of votes in both parties.[38] Six Senate Democrats later abandoned their support for the bill after funding for a jobs program was dropped in conference because of a veto threat from President Reagan. The conference report passed the Senate on Monday, December 20, by a vote of 55–41. Twenty-six of the forty-four Democrats opposed the bill. The government was technically out of funds on Monday, but a shutdown was avoided when President Reagan indicated he would sign the bill and the executive branch ordered all employees to remain at work.[39]

The history of the appropriations process in 1982 is consistent with expectations. The majority party's grip on the floor was tenuous. Some of the time constraints it faced were out of its control (such as the late start of the House writing the bills), but others, such as the lengthy debate over the debt ceiling bill, were a result of the politics of the Senate floor. The majority's decision to create a yearlong CR was not a reflection of

---

[36] *Congressional Record*, December 16, 1982, 31313.

[37] *Congressional Record*, December 16, 1982, 31390–31397.

[38] "2nd 1983 Continuing Resolution: $379 Billion," in *CQ Almanac 1982*, 38th ed., 238–242 (Washington, DC: Congressional Quarterly, 1983). http://library.cqpress.com/cqalmanac/cqal82-1164141.

[39] Tate, Dale. "$379 Billion Stopgap Funding Bill Cleared." *CQ Weekly* (December 25, 1982), 3092–3094.

its strength but its assessment that the bills were a "lost cause" and its
need to pass a budget. The CR was actively amended, but the process
was relatively disciplined as the twenty-minute time agreement to debate
the normally explosive abortion issue demonstrates. Finally, the final
bill received support from both sides, consistent with the argument that
omnibus bills are not heavily partisan.

98th Congress (1983–1984)

1983

The 1982 midterm elections led to some limited gains for Democrats
in Congress. Democrats picked up twenty-six seats in the House of
Representatives, while the party balance was unchanged in the Senate.
Observers at the time declared the end of the Reagan era as the Senate's
"moderate Republican bloc" took hold of power in Congress.[40] President
Reagan's first budget sent to the new Congress was declared dead on
arrival, and Republicans and Democrats scrambled to write their own.[41]

The Senate failed to vote on only two bills in 1983: Foreign Operations
and Treasury-Postal (Table 3.3). Both bills were included in a full-year CR
(H.J. Res. 413) along with the Agriculture bill. The majority's reasons for
abandoning the regular order are clearly identifiable in the record. The
Foreign Operations bill was historically unpopular because it provided
foreign aid, and the House of Representatives did not produce a bill. The
Treasury-Postal bill remained troubled by controversy over abortion, and
Majority Leader Baker was blocked in his effort to call it up for individual debate. Finally, both chambers approved the Agriculture bill, but a
dispute with President Reagan forced it into the CR.

The year began relatively smoothly. Congress completed action on
more appropriations bills by the start of the fiscal year on October 1
than for any year since 1978. Four bills had been signed into law and two
more were waiting for the president's signature. Seven bills still needed to
be passed, and so Congress passed a CR giving itself until November 10
to complete its work. While most bills were moving smoothly through
the chambers, the Treasury-Postal bill was caught up in a debate over
abortion. The House Appropriations Committee again passed the bill

---

[40] *Politics in America: Members of Congress in Washington and at Home* (Washington,
DC: Congressional Quarterly Press, 1983).

[41] "Economic Policy, 1983 Overview" in *CQ Almanac 1983*, 39th ed., 217–18 (Washington,
DC: Congressional Quarterly, 1984). http://library.cqpress.com/cqalmanac/cqal83-
1198703.

TABLE 3.3. *Legislative History of Appropriations Bills, 1983, First Session, 98th Congress*

Bill	No Floor Vote (House)	No Floor Vote (Senate)	Bill in Omnibus
Agriculture			✓
Commerce, Justice, and State			
District of Columbia			
Defense			
Energy and Water			
Foreign Operations	✓	✓	✓
Interior			
Labor–Health and Human Services			
Legislative Branch			
Military Construction			
Treasury-Postal		✓	✓
Transportation			
Veterans Administration–HUD			
Total	1	2	3

with a rider prohibiting federal employee health plans from covering abortion. The bill initially failed on the House floor on June 8 when a coalition of conservatives objecting to spending and liberals objecting to the abortion rider combined to oppose it. A slightly trimmed second version of the bill, still containing the abortion rider, passed on a voice vote on October 27 after leaders pled with members to send the issue to the Senate.[42] Meanwhile, the Senate Appropriations Committee followed its past practice by keeping its version of the bill free of abortion restrictions.[43]

The fate of the Treasury-Postal bill in the Senate came to a head that November as Congress approached the expiration date for the first CR. Five bills remained to be passed. Both the House and Senate Appropriations Committees had prepared their own versions of a CR to provide funding for the remainder of the fiscal year with the understanding that they would continue to try to pass as many individual bills as possible. As in previous years, bills would "drop out" of the CR once

[42] Rothman, Robert. "House Approves Treasury, Postal Service Bill." *CQ Weekly* (October 29, 1983), 2269–2270.
[43] Rothman, Robert. "New Funding Bill Reported for Treasury, Postal Service." *CQ Weekly* (October 22, 1983), 2174.

they were enacted in regular order.[44] The problem facing Majority Leader
Baker was that the Treasury-Postal bill was likely to generate a heated
debate when it was called up.

In order to debate the Treasury-Postal bill, Majority Leader Baker
needed to ask unanimous consent for the Senate to adopt a motion
to proceed to it. This proved to be impossible. Senator Don Nickles
(R-OK) warned that a filibuster was certain if the Senate turned to
the bill, burning up valuable working time as the Senate was racing
to adjourn for the year.[45] Sure enough, Baker reported that after hours
of negotiation, he was unable to reach an agreement to proceed to the
bill.[46] That meant the bill would have to be covered by the CR and that
the ground for the abortion debate would shift from the individual bill
to the full-year CR. The resolution providing funding for government
operations expired at midnight the next day, and the Senate did not
have long to act.

Majority Leader Baker called up the Senate version of the CR, S.J.
Res. 194. It contained no provision on abortion, but Senator Jeremiah
Denton soon offered an amendment to prohibit federal employee health
plans from covering abortion.[47] Senators Weicker and Packwood led the
opposition and argued that the controversial amendment threatened the
passage of the CR. "The current continuing resolution expires at midnight tomorrow night," Weicker noted. "If ever there was an argument
for keeping what should be as simple continuing resolution clean, we
have one now."[48] Weicker's move to table the amendment failed 44–51,
and so Packwood began to filibuster the amendment by reading once
again from his book on the history of abortion in America, picking up
from where he had left off during the debate on the debt ceiling with the
year 1842.[49]

With the Senate deadlocked on abortion, the House of Representatives
passed its own version of the CR, H.J. Res. 413 with the usual House

---

[44] See, for example, the comments of Chairman Hatfield: "The Senate passed a Defense
appropriations bill. They expect to go to conference very shortly. Of course, when that
conference is completed, we will vote on that conference report; and if we adopt the conference report and the President signs the measure, this whole matter drops out from the
CR" (*Congressional Record*, November 10, 1983, 31949).

[45] *Congressional Record*, November 9, 1983, 31661.

[46] Ibid, 31664.

[47] Ibid, 31669.

[48] Ibid, 31671.

[49] Ibid, 31675. Also, see Roll Call Vote 345, U.S. Senate, 98th Congress, First Session,
November 9, 1983.

language restricting the coverage of abortion in federal employee health plans. The next morning, with the current CR set to expire that night and the Senate hung up on Denton's abortion amendment, Baker shifted gears and called up the House version of the CR. The House language shifted the ground in favor of antiabortion senators. The abortion language was now in the bill, and the only option of Packwood and Weicker was to offer an amendment to strike the language. Such an amendment would almost certainly fail, and then the only remaining option would be to filibuster the entire CR. This was a far more dangerous strategy than filibustering an amendment since the delay in the CR's passage would appear to be their responsibility rather than Denton's.

The debate was brought to a close when Appropriations chairman Mark Hatfield offered an amendment to strike the rider. Hatfield opposed abortion, but he also believed it was inappropriate to micromanage the coverage of employee health plans. He and Majority Leader Baker voted in favor of striking the abortion language along with Weicker and Packwood. Their effort narrowly failed, 43–44.[50] The only option left for Weicker and Packwood was to filibuster the entire CR with funding for the government set to expire in just hours. Baker and Hatfield took to the floor to plead with the pair to let the debate on the CR move forward. "It is time to move now to other things. I urge Senators to consider that we have to finish this bill tonight, and do so, if possible, before 12 o'clock," Baker told the chamber.[51]

Weicker and Packwood abandoned the fight. They had blocked the provision from being attached to the Treasury-Postal bill in 1981 and 1982 and had filibustered abortion restrictions on the debt ceiling bill for weeks and won their fight. Faced with the prospect of shutting down the government, they ended their filibuster and conceded defeat.[52] The Senate approved the House CR on November 11 after a vigorous debate and dozens of votes and approved the conference report the following day. Both votes were conducted by voice, and so the breakdown in partisan support cannot be measured. As expected, the Commerce, Justice, and State and Defense portions of the CR dropped out of the bill when Congress passed each bill in regular order. Three bills were not passed individually and were covered by the CR for the remainder of the year.

[50] Roll Call Vote 349, U.S. Senate, 98th Congress, First Session, November 10, 1983.
[51] *Congressional Record*, November 10, 1983, 31949.
[52] *Congressional Record*, November 10, 1983, 31949.

TABLE 3.4. *Legislative History of Appropriations Bills, 1984, Second Session, 98th Congress*

Bill	No Floor Vote (House)	No Floor Vote (Senate)	Bill in Omnibus
Agriculture			✓
Commerce, Justice, and State			
District of Columbia			✓
Defense	✓	✓	✓
Energy and Water			
Foreign Operations	✓	✓	✓
Interior		✓	✓
Labor–Health and Human Services			
Legislative Branch			
Military Construction		✓	✓
Treasury-Postal			✓
Transportation	✓	✓	✓
Veterans Administration–HUD			
Total	3	5	8

The path of spending bills in 1983 demonstrates the range of circumstances that led to the abandonment of the regular order. The failure of the House to act on the Foreign Operations bill and President Reagan's objections to Agriculture account for the inclusion of both bills in the final package. The inclusion of the Treasury-Postal bill is attributable to the fact that Senate leaders could not overcome objections and bring the bill to the floor on an individual basis. The abortion debate still broke out on the CR itself, with interesting results. Members were sensitive to the risk of being blamed for holding up the CR, and abortion rights proponents gave up their fight when it became clear their only option was to filibuster the resolution.

1984

The vulnerability of the Republican majority to delaying tactics made possible by the Senate's individualistic rules was powerfully demonstrated in 1984. In the last year of President Reagan's first term, an initially smooth year for appropriations bills was disrupted when Senate Democrats filibustered a budget waiver required to proceed to the Agriculture bill. Their efforts delayed the Senate's effort to consider all bills in regular order, leading the Senate not to call votes on five bills and to create an omnibus containing eight regular spending bills (Table 3.4).

The first sign that 1984 would be challenging occurred when the House and Senate failed to approve a joint budget resolution to set spending ceilings for the year. The failure was problematic for two reasons. First, it meant the House and Senate Appropriations Committee would be working with different spending ceilings as they wrote their bills, forcing them to be reconciled at a later date. Second, it meant that any appropriations bill brought to the floor would be in violation of the Budget Act and subject to a point of order that could block its consideration. The House handled the need for a budget waiver easily and passed a blanket waiver for all its bills. The Senate did not adopt a similar mass waiver. Instead, senators would have to adopt a waiver on a bill-by-bill basis or vote on whether to sustain any point of order made by an individual senator. This motion was debatable and subject to a potential filibuster, and it left the bills vulnerable to being delayed.

The appropriations season got off to a solid start despite this uncertainty. The House voted on eight bills by the end of June and the Senate on five, putting both chambers in a strong position to complete most of the bills in regular order. Then as August approached, Senate Democrats, frustrated with the lack of a budget, derailed the train. On August 1, Senator Lawton Chiles (D-FL) objected to Majority Leader Baker's unanimous consent request for a budget waiver for the Agriculture bill. "Since the leadership has done about all it can to waive the Budget Act all year long, I think it is time we put a halt to that fast footwork ... [W]e need a budget resolution before we proceed with these appropriations bills any further."[53] Senator Chiles and his allies filibustered the bill for a full week, beating back one attempt to impose cloture before the majority leader finally secured it on August 8.[54]

The Senate passed the Agriculture bill after a two-day debate on August 10, but Senator Chiles was not finished. Majority Leader Baker next sought to call up the District of Columbia appropriations bill. It would also require a waiver, and Senator Chiles made clear that his price for granting it was a high-level summit between House and Senate leaders to establish an overall figure for defense spending and provide guidance on other spending levels. With little choice if he wanted to avoid another extended debate, Senator Baker agreed. The exchange between the two of them remarkably demonstrates the dependence of the majority on the cooperation of individual members. Senator Baker noted that

[53] *Congressional Record,* August 1, 1984, 21785.
[54] *Congressional Record,* August 8, 1984, 22721.

it would not be possible to convene the summit before Labor Day and found himself in the humbling position of asking permission to pass the District of Columbia appropriations bill immediately since it was ready to be debated. "Would it be possible just for this one appropriations bill to go forward," he asked, recognizing that the remaining six bills would have to wait. "I certainly would honor the majority leader's request that we take up the DC appropriations bill," Senator Chiles replied. "I appreciate his saying we are going to try to keep the budget process, we are not trying to push all the bills through at this time ... and I certainly will not object." With the path for the District bill now clear, Baker replied, "I thank the Senator. I am most grateful."[55]

The timing of the summit complicated the ability of the Senate to adopt the remaining bills in the regular order. House and Senate leaders did not reach agreement on spending levels until September 20 when the new fiscal year was eleven days away. The upcoming election further complicated matters since members wanted to hit the campaign trail as soon as possible. Under pressure, the Senate managed to pass one bill (Labor–Health and Human Services) and then proceeded to package together the bills that had not yet cleared Congress into a full-year CR.[56]

Despite the Senate's action on the Labor bill, it was nearly adopted as part of the CR because of thorny debates over abortion and school prayer. Senator Weicker now chaired the Labor–Health and Human Services subcommittee and was using his power as chairman to target two provisions in the bill that had been routinely adopted for several years at the urging of the House. The first was a provision that restricted Medicaid funding for abortion to circumstances in which the mother's life was at risk. Senator Weicker wanted to broaden the list of exceptional circumstances to include rape and incest. The second prohibited the Department of Education from interfering with programs promoting voluntary prayer in the classroom. Weicker's version of the bill dropped this provision.

Conservative senators were ready to challenge Weicker and felt they had the advantage. The House had won debates in previous years with the Senate over the two provisions, and conservatives believed it was unlikely Weicker's position would survive conference. Moreover, the House and Senate versions of the CR covered the Labor bill as a precaution. They

---

[55] *Congressional Record*, August 10, 1984, 23736.
[56] "Stopgap Measure Was Biggest, Most Complex." *CQ Weekly* (October 20, 1984), 2732. http://library.cqpress.com/cqweekly/WR098403791.

followed the standard practice of extending the terms of the previous year's bill and included the restrictions.[57] If there was a deadlock on the regular Labor bill, Weicker would still have to find a way to remove the abortion and prayer provisions from the CR.

The first decision of the conservatives was to avoid a direct challenge to Weicker on the Senate floor. They announced that they would accept his provision on abortion and that their position would be sustained either in conference or on the CR.[58] The dispute over school prayer was not resolved as easily. Senator Jesse Helms offered an amendment to reinstate the prohibition on interference with school prayer. Weicker reacted furiously, threatening to sink the bill and opt for a CR instead:

> Do I want to see a year's work go down the drain? No; but this issue, too, is important. The shame of putting it on this bill, No. 1, that is not my shame. I have just sent word to the Appropriations Committee which is reviewing the continuing resolution to incorporate all that has been done so far by the committee and by the Senate into the continuing resolution. I realize it will probably be postponed by a day or two because probably the same group will try to put a prayer amendment on the continuing resolution, and I will have to fight that.[59]

Senator Helms was unruffled by the threat. Noting that the House concurred with his position and that the Senate had agreed to it in the past, he offered to accept changes Weicker had proposed to weaken his amendment. "I do not believe I am giving away the store with this modification. I think I know what is going to happen in conference."[60] The Senate then approved the revised amendment by voice vote. With major areas of controversy settled for the day, the full bill was approved hours later.

As the House and Senate began their conference negotiations on the Labor bill, Majority Leader Howard Baker called up for debate H.J. Res. 648, the massive new CR. The date was September 27, 1984, and in just a few days government funding would expire with the new fiscal year. Chairman Hatfield opened the debate with a plea to members to refrain from offering amendments. He warned that the new tradition of legislating on appropriations bills was doing violence to the spending process and the Senate as an institution.

---

[57] Tate, Dale. "Congress Loads Up Emergency Funding Bill." *CQ Weekly* (September 29, 1984), 2355–58. http://library.cqpress.com/cqweekly/WR098403570.

[58] *Congressional Record*, September 25, 1984, 26669.

[59] *Congressional Record*, September 25, 1984, 26685.

[60] *Congressional Record*, September 25, 1984, 26688.

I do not want to revive the whole history, but I stood in this same position in 1981 and said ... when we put an abortion amendment on the first appropriation bill we were going to ask for trouble down the road, and this is the result. Now we are going to end up here with all the legislative matters that we have not been able to resolve on this CR, and I can tell you it is going to go down – if the CR ever survived in the conference it is going to be vetoed by the President. Then we are going to be back here next week, or going to be here at a time when some should be out, because of these riders when we should have done our business in a reasonable time. So let us be aware of what we are asking for down the road from this point when we begin to hang all of these matters on the CR. The Government and its operations on which our constituents depend, will be shut down.[61]

Hatfield's warning went unheeded. Over the next few days, members proceeded to load up the resolution with new water projects, an omnibus crime bill, and dozens of other measures. Sensing a political opportunity in the midst of his presidential campaign, President Reagan indicated he would veto the bill as it was developing. For good measure, he also ordered the shutdown of eight cabinet agencies and sent 500,000 federal employees home for half a day when Congress failed to pass a short-term CR to keep the government running while it debated the yearlong resolution. Appearing at a campaign rally, he laid responsibility for the shutdown at the feet of House Democrats.[62]

With the CR now fodder in the presidential campaign and under pressure to adjourn, Congress abandoned most of the add-ons that had been tacked onto the bill in favor of the core components of the spending bills. Two issues that remained to be resolved were abortion and school prayer. The conference on the regular Labor–Health and Human Services appropriations bill was deadlocked on the two issues and unlikely to produce a conference report anytime soon. Meanwhile, the CR extended the restrictive language on both provisions from the previous year and appeared certain to pass. The question was whether Weicker and his allies could succeed in a last-ditch effort to amend the CR to ease the restrictions. Weicker's first move was to propose an amendment to the CR to add a rape and incest exception to the ban on funding for abortions, but Majority Leader Baker successfully tabled it on a vote of 55–44.[63] Unable to remove the abortion language from the bill and facing the same likely fate on the prayer issue, Weicker's only remaining option was to filibuster

---

[61] *Congressional Record*, September 27, 1984, 27457.

[62] Weisman, Steven R. "Reagan Calls for Election of 'Our Team' in Congress." *The New York Times* (October 5, 1984).

[63] Roll Call Vote 274, U.S. Senate, 98th Congress, Second Session, October 3, 1984.

the CR. Instead, days after threatening to torpedo his own bill, he stood down. His choice was either to accept the restrictions in a CR that would fail to incorporate most of his committee's work for the year or accept them as part of his regular bill. He opted for the latter. The conference deadlock on the bill was broken, and Congress passed the Labor bill in regular order.[64] The CR was passed as well by a vote of 78–11, with opposition split between both sides. It ultimately provided funding for eight bills that were not adopted in regular order.

Overall, the creation of the omnibus package in 1984 powerfully illustrates how the bills do not arise out of a carefully planned majority strategy. Instead, they are a product of a weak majority struggling to maintain control of the floor. In 1984, the majority's plan to pass as many individual spending bills as possible was thwarted by a filibuster that delayed passage of nearly half of the bills. With little other choice given the time pressures, they opted to package the bills together into an omnibus package. The omnibus also eased the resolution of the typically challenging debates on abortion and school prayer that split the Republican Party.

CONCLUSION

The history of the appropriations process in the first term of President Ronald Reagan (1981–1984) demonstrates how omnibus spending bills arose when the routine act of passing temporary CRs was transformed by using the resolutions to provide funding in place of groups of unpassed bills for the entire year. The problems facing the Republican majority are consistent with the relative weakness of the party at this time. Divisions within its membership led to serious policy disputes over issues such as school prayer and abortion. Republican-led filibusters prevented the passage of some spending bills on an individual basis and made it difficult for the Senate leadership to meet budgetary deadlines. In other cases, Democrats took advantage of their procedural rights to disrupt the passage of spending bills to pursue other legislative goals. In this troubled context, Senate leaders packaged together groups of bills into a CR as a way to ensure passage of the budget.

The omnibus bills they produced have the appearance of bipartisan logrolls. The bills always received at least some bipartisan support,

---

[64] "$104 Billion Bill Clears for Labor, Health and Human Services Departments," in *CQ Almanac 1984*, 40th ed., 421–425 (Washington, DC: Congressional Quarterly, 1985). http://library.cqpress.com/cqalmanac/cqal84-1151655.

although opposition at times climbed to more than 50 percent of the Democratic caucus. The resolution to disputes over abortion and school prayer did not systematically favor one side or the other. While the influence of factors such as divided power in Congress, presidential preferences, and election years are visible on the decision to create omnibus bills, problems arising from the weakness of the majority party are a clear and consistent signal during these years.

The case studies from the early 1980s offer a broad set of lessons about the influence that party leaders wield as they manage the appropriations process. Majority Leader Howard Baker was not captive to events on the Senate floor, nor did he dominate them. Instead, he was a savvy manager of the chamber who responded to problems as they arose and adjusted his tactics as necessary to meet the broad goal of adopting the budget. The limits to Baker's power are clear. He could not eliminate dissension within his party, nor could he force an end to filibusters that made it impossible to pass some bills in the regular order. Nor did Baker take an obvious side in the disputes that divided his party. Instead, he brought up troublesome bills in the context of full-year CRs that attracted broadbased support, defused bitter debates, and often reduced the opportunity to offer amendments. That Baker was able to overcome the many obstacles in the appropriations process and pass a budget despite having so few formal powers is impressive. His record effectively illustrates the important yet constrained nature of majority party influence in the Senate.

4

Back to the Regular Order

In the early 1980s, the struggles of a weak Senate majority party helped to establish the new practice of packaging regular appropriations bills together as omnibus bills. This contentious practice gained momentum as President Ronald Reagan entered his second term. Congress packaged all thirteen bills together for passage in 1986 and 1987, leading to complaints from members and from the president himself. Then, in an abrupt shift, Congress abandoned omnibus legislating. Each appropriations bill was passed in the regular order from 1988 to 1994. Omnibus bills did not return until April of 1996 when the passage of a five-bill package signaled the end of a budget crisis that tarnished Newt Gingrich's "Republican Revolution" and breathed political life back into Bill Clinton's presidency.

Chapter 4 explores the abandonment and resumption of omnibus legislating and the seven-year period of regular order between them. I test whether the patterns of this time fit the expectations of the limited influence theory. The first section of the chapter reviews changes in the political landscape and Senate majority power that commenced with the Democratic takeover of the Senate in 1986. The second section presents the results of brief case studies of the Senate's consideration of spending bills, including the resumption of the regular order at the end of President Reagan's administration and the return of omnibus bills in the Clinton era. The chapter concludes with an investigation of the relationship between executive–legislative conflict and the creation of omnibus spending bills.

The findings support the expectations of the limited influence theory and add a wrinkle to it by describing the effects of shocks to the political system. The first wave of omnibus legislating ended when President Reagan threatened to veto further omnibus bills in his State of the Union address, and the second wave began when Speaker Newt Gingrich chose to confront President Bill Clinton on the budget using spending bills as his vehicles. These kinds of strategic choices take place outside the limited influence theory, and I treat them as exogenous. Within that context, the expected patterns are visible and help to explain the enduring nature of the changes that each shock created. Throughout this period, the likelihood, size, and contents of omnibus bills are heavily influenced by the strength of the Senate majority party. Congress returned to the regular order when the strength of the majority party spiked sharply as a result of the replacement of the small, fractious Republican majority in the Senate with a larger, more unified Democratic majority in the 1986 elections. The new Democratic majority faced fewer problems than its predecessor did managing spending bills on the floor and passed them in the regular order. Omnibus bills returned to stay when a comparatively weaker Republican majority was elected in 1994 that lacked its predecessor's ability to dominate the Senate floor.

The new wave of omnibus bills that began in 1996 included an important procedural innovation. The majority began to create omnibus packages in conference proceedings by adding bills that had not been passed onto an appropriations bill that was already in conference. This technique protected the packages from being amended on the floor. Power of this kind could theoretically be used to shift policy outcomes toward the majority median, but voting patterns suggest that omnibus packages remained bipartisan. They drew majority support from both parties, and opposition levels were at times higher within the Republican majority than the Democratic minority.

This era is a particularly good illustration of how presidents can affect the likelihood of omnibus bills by influencing events on the Senate floor. I leverage this fact to describe a new theory of presidential involvement in the appropriations process that I call "opportunistic bargaining." Past research has found that presidents have little ability to shape the format in which appropriations bills arrive on their desk and that omnibus packages give a negotiating advantage to Congress. I show that presidents have some capacity to shape the likelihood of an omnibus bill and individualized views on whether the practice helps or hurts their negotiating position.

Ronald Reagan, George H. W. Bush, and Bill Clinton each faced a Congress controlled by the other party but had sharply different views on the effect of omnibus packages on bargaining between the branches. Ronald Reagan worked to end omnibus bills in his last two years in office because he felt they disadvantaged the president in negotiations. George H. W. Bush worked with Congress to pass spending bills in the regular order and issued narrowly targeted veto threats to rid them of policies that were objectionable to Republicans. Bill Clinton conspired with the Democratic minority in the Senate to slow down the passage of individual spending bills and force the creation of omnibus packages because he felt they gave him a negotiating advantage with Republicans. I describe these presidents as opportunistic bargainers because they did not follow a set strategy in the appropriations process but seized opportunities as they arose to improve their bargaining positions.

PARTY POWER IN THE SENATE FROM 1986–1996

In 1986, Senate Republicans lost the majority they had held since Ronald Reagan's landslide win in 1980. The outgoing Republicans were far different from the incoming Democrats (Table 4.1). The Republican majority was fractious, divided between liberal and conservative factions, and without a commanding margin of control. They held fifty-three of the Senate's seats and had a relatively high DW-NOMINATE standard deviation of 0.20. The new Democratic majority was larger and more unified. Democrats had a DW-NOMINATE standard deviation of 0.11 and a margin of control of that began at fifty-five in the 100th Congress and grew as high as fifty-seven in the 103rd Congress. A combination of Democratic retirements and an Election Day wipeout in 1994 brought the Republicans back to power in the 104th Congress with a fifty-three-seat majority. The new majority was led by Senator Robert Dole (R-KS) and made up of old guard moderates such as Ted Stevens (R-AK), a few left-leaning senators such as future party switchers Jim Jeffords (R-VT) and Arlen Specter (R-PA), and a new generation of conservatives such as Rick Santorum (R-PA). The ideological diversity of this group is reflected in its high DW-NOMINATE standard deviation of 0.19. Republicans were back in control, but their narrow majority and high ideological diversity meant their hold on the Senate floor was more tenuous than the Democrats they had replaced.

Figure 4.1 uses scatterplots to show the distribution of Republicans and Democrats in the Senate during the period in which control shifted between the parties. Democrats, in the upper left-hand portion of each scatterplot, are tightly concentrated regardless of whether they are in the minority or majority. Republicans, by contrast, are more broadly

TABLE 4.1. *Majority Size and Homogeneity, U.S. Senate, 1985–1996*

Congress	Majority Homogeneity	Initial Majority	Majority Party
99	0.20	53	Republicans
100	0.11	55	Democrats
101	0.11	55	Democrats
102	0.11	56	Democrats
103	0.12	57	Democrats
104	0.19	53	Republicans

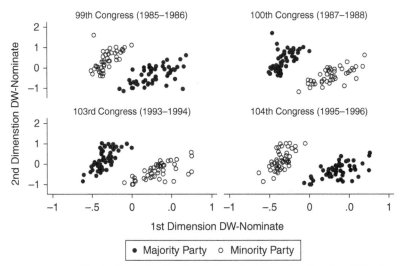

FIGURE 4.1. Ideological distribution of majority and minority. U.S. Senate, 1985–1996.

distributed in the scatterplots. This basic difference between the two parties in this time period put the Republicans at a disadvantage. When they were in the majority, their ideological divisions made it difficult to agree on and pursue policy goals, and their narrow margin of control left them open to obstruction and unfriendly amendments. When they were in the minority, they lacked the cohesion to present an effective opposition to the Democrats. As this chapter will demonstrate, many of their members frequently voted with Democrats on key votes and contributed to the relative ease with which Democrats managed the Senate floor.

Figure 4.2 illustrates the major characteristics of the majority party and patterns in the passage of appropriations bills. The Senate typically adopted bills in the regular order during this era and created omnibus bills

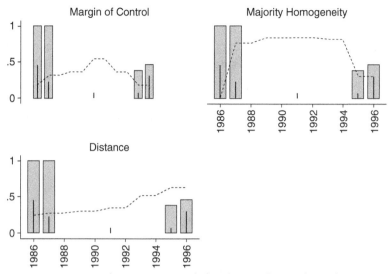

FIGURE 4.2. Party characteristics and abandoning the regular order. U.S. Senate, 1986–1996.

only at its beginning and end. The gap in the creation of omnibus bills is intriguing and provides some important leverage to understand what factors led to the abandonment of the regular order. It is noteworthy that the return to the regular order overlaps with increases in the majority's margin of control and homogeneity. The distance between the two parties also steadily increases during this time, although it does not reach the highs recorded in later years of the data set. Next, I turn to a set of case studies to investigate each part of the period and assess the effect of party characteristics in the management of the appropriations bills.

TRANSITIONING TO REGULAR ORDER

The first wave of omnibus bills came to an end at the conclusion of Ronald Reagan's presidency. In 1987, Democrats took control of the Senate for the first time since 1980, and President Reagan faced a unified Democratic Congress. The transition to Democratic control was smooth, and over the summer the new Congress successfully passed all but three appropriations bills individually through each chamber. Despite that progress, none had reached the president's desk by the beginning of the fiscal year. Democrats were in disagreement with the president about overall spending levels for the bills and how best to reduce the federal deficit. A stock market crash on October 19 gave both sides incentive to meet in a budget summit to negotiate a deficit reduction agreement. In the wake of that summit, Democrats followed what had become common practice and packaged all thirteen spending bills into a single yearlong continuing resolution (CR), H.J. Res. 395.[1]

The Reagan administration's response to the bill was a striking departure from its routine acceptance of omnibus bills in past years. It issued a Statement of Administration Policy (SAP)[2] that threatened a veto in part on the grounds of the following:

> The Administration opposes the current Congressional practice of funding the entire government in one omnibus continuing resolution. The appropriations process allows both the legislative and the executive branches the opportunity to consider funding in thirteen separate and distinct appropriations bills. An omnibus continuing resolution ... denies the President the opportunity to make decisions on a bill-by-bill basis.[3]

Reagan did not follow through on the veto threat. Contemporary reports indicate that the administration received virtually everything it wanted in the package, although final vote totals for the bill suggest it was a bipartisan compromise.[4] Support for the bill was about evenly split between the parties in the House, with a slight majority of Republicans favoring the bill and slight majority of Democrats opposing it. It won the support of most Democrats and a narrow majority of Republicans in the Senate.

Nonetheless, the president was ready to take a stand against omnibus legislating in his final year in office. The following January, in his final State of the Union address, Reagan dramatically dropped H.J. Res. 395 on his lectern and threatened to veto another such bill. His demand: "13 individual bills, on time and fully reviewed by Congress."[5] Thirty-four senators and forty-nine House members (virtually all Republican) supported the president in letters to the leadership of Congress in which they

---

[1] "Appropriations 1987: Overview," in *CQ Almanac 1987*, 43rd ed., 401 (Washington, DC: Congressional Quarterly, 1988). http://library.cqpress.com/cqalmanac/cqal87-1145333.

[2] A SAP is a policy document issued by the Office of Management and Budget (OMB) stating the administration's support for or objections to a particular piece of legislation.

[3] Statement of Administration Policy. H.J. Res. 395: FY1988 Omnibus Full-Year Continuing Resolution, 1987. 100th Congress (Kernell).

[4] "$603.9 Billion Omnibus Funding Bill Clears," in *CQ Almanac 1987*, 43rd ed., 480–488 (Washington, DC: Congressional Quarterly, 1988). http://library.cqpress.com/cqalmanac/cqal87-1145568.

[5] Woolley, John T. and Gerhard Peters, *The American Presidency Project* [online]. Santa Barbara, CA: University of California (hosted), Gerhard Peters (database). http://www.presidency.ucsb.edu/ws/?pid=36035. Accessed February 8, 2008.

vowed to oppose future omnibus bills because the bills made "virtually impossible thoughtful analysis of appropriations bills by individual members."[6] The president's action and its support by a significant portion of members of Congress sparked a remarkable change: that fall, for the first time since 1976, Congress passed all bills in regular order before the October 1 deadline of the new fiscal year.

President Reagan's action ushered in a new period of passing appropriations bills in the regular order and may have broken a practice that was starting to become habitual. Policy makers interviewed for this book note that the longer Congress uses omnibus bills, the more routine the practice becomes. Congress returned to passing bills in the regular order for the next six years in the wake of Reagan's address. The key question is why the shift to the regular order endured after the shock to the system from his veto threat faded. One reason is that the Democratic majority in the Senate was strong enough to adopt the bills in the regular order without disruption and had no need to create an omnibus package.

THE BUSH ADMINISTRATION

George H. W. Bush succeeded Ronald Reagan in office after a hard-fought campaign in which he defeated Governor Michael Dukakis of Massachusetts. Providing an account of the appropriations process during the Bush administration is challenging because of the inherent difficulty of explaining why something did not happen: in this case, why Congress did not abandon the regular order. My approach is to identify conflicts similar to those that disrupted passage of bills in earlier eras and to trace the flow of events on the floor. Just as a weak majority abandons the regular order when the floor begins to slip out of its control, a strong majority should be able to overcome obstruction or avoid being rolled by unfriendly amendments. Both trends are visible in 1989 and 1990. The Republican minority did not attempt to obstruct the process of passing spending bills, noting at times that it lacked the votes to do so. The Democratic majority took tough votes on amendments, but it typically defeated them with ease and with the support of considerable numbers of Republicans. Interestingly, the smooth passage of appropriations bills may have been aided by veto threats from President Bush. Republicans often lacked the votes to defeat or obstruct the Democratic majority, but they also declined to challenge the Democrats at

[6] Kenworthy, Tom, "Senators Join Protest over Catchall Spending; 33 Republicans, 1 Democrat Say 'Enough,'" *Washington Post*, February 9, 1988.

times on the grounds that President Bush was meeting their policy goals through his use of the veto.

1989

George H. W. Bush's first year in office cemented the sea change that took place in the appropriations process in 1988. The political context was favorable for the smooth passage of the spending bills. Overall spending levels for the year had been set by the 1987 deficit reduction agreement negotiated between congressional Democrats and President Reagan, removing one dimension of dispute from the appropriations process. Congress was unified under the control of one party, limiting the likelihood of serious disputes between the chambers. The usual hot-button issues did not derail the passage of spending bills on the Senate floor as they had in years past. Even an end-of-year time crunch did not spur Congress to package the bills together. It passed eight individual bills on November 20 just as a CR was about to expire, and President Bush signed them all separately.[7]

The relative lack of conflict on the Senate floor in 1989 is striking after years of intense disputes over abortion, school prayer, and other controversial issues. Accounts of appropriations bills from the 101st Congress are notable for the list of controversies that were resolved and compromises that were reached. The fate of long-standing disagreements over abortion illustrates how the Senate had changed from the early 1980s. The first area of concern was the long-standing restriction in the Labor–Health and Human Services bill on the use of federal funds for abortion unless the life of the mother was at risk. Democrats wanted to broaden the exemption to include instances of rape and incest. The District of Columbia bill was similarly embroiled in controversy about the conditions under which locally raised tax dollars could be used to fund abortions. Neither dispute led to a filibuster on the Senate floor. Senator Gordon Humphrey (R-NH) explained why antiabortion senators chose not to fight as they had in the past: "We don't have the votes. Why should we pretend?"[8] Humphrey's assessment was likely correct. Two years earlier, in 1987, a

---

[7] Calmes, Jackie, "APPROPRIATIONS: Bush Signs Last Eight Bills in Final Hours of Session," *CQ Weekly*, November 25, 1989, 3226. http://library.cqpress.com/cqweekly/WR101407997.

[8] "Bill for Labor, Health and Human Services Vetoed over Abortion," in *CQ Almanac 1989*, 45th ed., 707–714 (Washington, DC: Congressional Quarterly, 1990). http://library.cqpress.com/cqalmanac/cqal89-1137852.

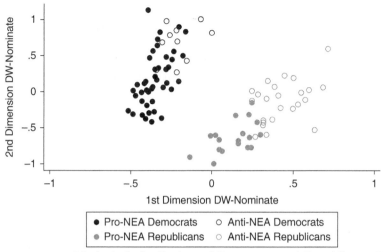

FIGURE 4.3. Ideological distribution of Democrats and Republicans. Helms Amendment on National Endowment of the Arts.

similar amendment to restrict abortion on the District of Columbia bill had been tabled with sixty votes. Democrats were growing more united on the issue, but it continued to divide Republicans. Seventeen percent of Senate Democrats had voted with Republicans to restrict abortion, while 35 percent of Republicans had joined the Democrats to loosen the restrictions.[9] Antiabortion senators also viewed a floor fight as unnecessary since President Bush had threatened to veto both bills unless they included the restrictive language on abortion he preferred.[10] This assessment was correct as well. The president vetoed the two bills, his language was restored, and the bills were adopted in regular order with the abortion restrictions attached.

The Democratic majority also sidestepped a potential obstacle to the passage of the Interior bill. Senator Jesse Helms (R-NC) offered an amendment to the bill to restrict funding to works of art that might be deemed obscene. It was turned back on a vote of 62–35, with nineteen Republicans joining forty-three Democrats to defeat the bill.[11] Figure 4.3 shows the ideological distribution of the voting coalition behind the

[9] Senate Roll Call Vote 289, September 30, 1987.
[10] See *Congressional Record*, September 21, 1989, 21247, for discussion of the Labor-Health and Human Services bill and *Congressional Record*, September 14, 1989, 20495, for discussion of the District of Columbia bill.
[11] Senate Roll Call Vote 242, October 7, 1989.

defeat of the amendment. The sizable coalition of liberal Democrats and Republicans was sufficiently strong to overcome a filibuster had Helms chosen to pursue one. Instead, Senator Helms was left to nurse his wounds and wait for another day: "Old Helms has been beat before," the senator remarked on the Senate floor. "But old Helms does not quit. If the Senate does not approve the amendment today, the Senate will vote on it again and again, on bill after bill, month after month, year after year, until government subsidies for 'artistic' perversion are prohibited once and for all."[12] Given the magnitude of Helms's defeat, it would take some time before his assessment was likely to come true. The Interior bill became law without this provision.

The most serious disputes on appropriations bills in 1989 did not take place on the Senate floor. They came in the form of veto threats from President George Bush. The Office of Management and Budget (OMB) issued veto threats against the Foreign Operations and Transportation bills when they were debated in the Senate. The administration also issued SAPs against the District of Columbia, Foreign Operations, and Labor–Health and Human Services bills when they were in conference and vetoed the three bills when Congress ignored the administration's demands.[13] In each case, the policies that had led to the veto were removed, and the bills passed in regular order.

1990

By the second year of the Bush administration, the political context had grown more complicated. The deficit reduction agreement President Reagan had reached with congressional Democrats in 1987 was expiring, and the need to establish a new long-term deficit reduction plan complicated Democratic efforts to pass a budget resolution. Democrats were divided on the proper mix of domestic versus defense spending cuts, and Republicans wanted a new budget summit with the president. In response, President Bush invited congressional leaders to the White House in May to begin budget talks. The talks consumed the next five months and resulted in the president breaking his famous "Read my lips: no new taxes" pledge. The agreement that ultimately took shape was a combination of tax hikes and spending cuts. It also

---

[12] *Congressional Record*, October 7, 1989, 23905.
[13] Davis, Zeo, *Presidential Vetoes, 1989–2000. Office of the Secretary of the Senate* (Washington, DC: Government Printing Office, 2001).

included a set of changes to the budget process that were incorporated into the Budget Enforcement Act (BEA) of 1990 – the most effective deficit reduction measure in the period under study. It set caps on discretionary spending through fiscal year 1995 and required that new mandatory spending be paid for through tax increases or spending cuts elsewhere.[14]

The lengthy negotiations over the budget and uncertainty over final spending levels delayed the passage of the appropriations bills until well after the beginning of the new fiscal year. Five CRs were needed to provide the additional time needed to reach a final agreement.[15] Despite these delays, the appropriations bills all passed in regular order. The House and Senate each moved the bills through committee, debated the normal array of hot-button issues on the floor of each chamber, and worked through nine veto threats from the administration. There were debates on abortion on the Labor–Health and Human Services bill and the District of Columbia bill.[16] The Interior bill triggered another debate on obscenity and the National Endowment of the Arts.[17] All of these debates were resolved without significant delays in the passage of the bills. Congress moved quickly on each of the bills and adopted twelve of the thirteen during a single week in late October.[18]

What accounts for the enduring nature of the shift to the regular order in 1989 and 1990? Three major variables changed in comparison with the Reagan administration. First, power in Congress was no longer divided, and so disputes between the two chambers were less likely to slow down the passage of spending bills. Second, the deficit reduction agreement meant that there was an overall consensus on total spending

[14] "New Budget Process for Congress, President," in *CQ Almanac 1990*, 46th ed., 173–178 (Washington, DC: Congressional Quarterly, 1991). http://library.cqpress.com/cqalmanac/cqal90-1112347.

[15] "Budget Adopted after Long Battle," in *CQ Almanac 1990*, 46th ed., 111–166 (Washington, DC: Congressional Quarterly, 1991). http://library.cqpress.com/cqalmanac/cqal90-1112280.

[16] See "Abortion-Free D.C. Bill OK'd by Senate," in *CQ Almanac 1990*, 46th ed., 891–893 (Washington, DC: Congressional Quarterly, 1991). http://library.cqpress.com/cqalmanac/cqal90-1112043; "$188.2 Billion for Labor, Education, and Health and Human Services," in *CQ Almanac 1990*, 46th ed., 847–853 (Washington, DC: Congressional Quarterly, 1991). http://library.cqpress.com/cqalmanac/cqal90-1111908.

[17] "Art, Owls, Oil Drilling Argued in Interior Bill," in *CQ Almanac 1990*, 46th ed., 870–876 (Washington, DC: Congressional Quarterly, 1991). http://library.cqpress.com/cqalmanac/cqal90-1111974.

[18] "13 Spending Bills OK'd in Final Days," in *CQ Almanac 1990*, 46th ed., 811 (Washington, DC: Congressional Quarterly, 1991). http://library.cqpress.com/cqalmanac/cqal90-1111809.

levels in the appropriations process. Third, the majority party in the Senate was substantially stronger than it had been when the Senate was under Republican control. Issues that had paralyzed the Senate in the early 1980s were resolved with little apparent problem in 1989 and 1990. The budget disputes and late passage of appropriations bills associated with omnibus bills in the early 1980s did not lead to the creation of an omnibus in 1990. Instead, the Senate acted with dispatch when it had to pass a dozen spending bills in a single week.

THE CLINTON ADMINISTRATION (1995–1996)

The spending bills continued to be passed in regular order for the remainder of the Bush administration and for the first two years of unified government under President Bill Clinton. Matters changed swiftly after the Republican takeover of Congress in the 1994 midterm elections. The Republican landslide in the midterm elections of 1994 transformed Congress. Republicans gained fifty-four seats in the House of Representatives and eight in the Senate, giving the party a majority in each chamber. It was the first time Republicans had controlled both chambers of Congress since 1955. In the House of Representatives, Speaker Newt Gingrich centralized power within the Republican leadership and appointed party loyalist Representative Bob Livingston to be the new chairman of the Appropriations Committee. In the Senate, Senator Bob Dole (R-KS) was promoted from minority leader to majority leader.

The two leaders differed substantially in style. Gingrich was fiery and confrontational. Dole was a classic deal maker in the traditional mold of the Senate. Both agreed that Clinton's weakness and Republican control of Congress created the perfect opportunity to pursue long-sought Republican goals such as reducing federal spending and loosening federal regulations. Gingrich took the lead in setting the party's strategy and worked with the House Appropriations Committee to draft a set of spending bills that sharply reduced spending levels and included policy riders targeted at Republican nemeses such as the Environmental Protection Agency. This decision marks the second shock to the system discussed in this chapter. Gingrich's decision sparked two government shutdowns that were resolved by the passage of the first omnibus bill since 1987. The shutdowns weakened Republicans and helped to transform a fifteen-point favorability advantage over Democrats with the public in the wake of the 1994 election into an eleven-point deficit.[19] It also inaugurated a second wave of omnibus appropriating that continues today.

1995

The full story of the government shutdown has been well told elsewhere (Brady and Volden 2006; LeLoup 2005). I focus my attention on a narrower question: what factors explain why some bills were included in the omnibus package that ended the shutdown and others were not? The first shutdown lasted six days and began on November 14, 1995, when Clinton vetoed a CR (H.J. Res. 115) laden with policy riders. Almost 800,000 federal workers were ordered home, and government services such as the processing of Social Security checks were suspended. It ended when Congress passed a clean CR (H.J. Res. 122), extending government funding until December 15 in an effort to give Clinton and congressional Republicans time to reach an agreement on a seven-year plan to balance the budget. When no such agreement was reached, frustrated House Republicans raised the pressure on Clinton by refusing to pass a new CR and letting the government shut down once again over the objections of Dole and Senate Republicans. The second shutdown lasted twenty-one days and ended as a public relations disaster for Republicans. A *Washington Post–ABC News* poll found that most Americans blamed Republicans for the shutdown, and that 57 percent supported the president's budget plan compared with just 36 percent for the Republicans.[20] Support for the strategy collapsed in the House and Senate, and both passed a new CR restoring funding on January 5.[21] The final resolution to the impasse was reached on April 26 when Congress adopted an omnibus bill that incorporated the remaining appropriations bills. The package passed with bipartisan support, but voting patterns suggest at least some Republicans viewed it as a defeat.[22]

---

[19] Sadd, Lydia, "Republican Post-Election Image Less Positive Than in 1994," Gallup News Service, November 21, 1998.

[20] Balz, Dan and Richard Morin. "In This Debate, Voters May Have Last Word." *Washington Post* (January 10, 1996), A01.

[21] "Government Shuts Down Twice Due to Lack of Funding," in *CQ Almanac 1995*, 51st ed., 113–116 (Washington, DC: Congressional Quarterly, 1996). http://library.cqpress.com/cqalmanac/cqal95-1099661.

[22] "Omnibus FY96 Bill Ties Loose Ends," In *CQ Almanac 1996*, 52nd ed., 105–116 (Washington, DC: Congressional Quarterly, 1997). http://library.cqpress.com/cqalmanac/cqal96-841-24596-1091488.

TABLE 4.2. *Legislative History of Appropriations Bills, 1995, First Session, 104th Congress*

Bill	No Floor Vote (House)	No Floor Vote (Senate)	Bill in Omnibus
Agriculture			
Commerce, Justice, and State			✓
District of Columbia			✓
Defense			
Energy Water			
Foreign Operations			
Interior			✓
Labor–Health and Human Services		✓	✓
Legislative Branch			
Military Construction			
Treasury-Postal			
Transportation			
Veterans Administration–HUD			✓
Total	0	1	5

The size and contents of the omnibus package were determined by conflict between the president and Congress over spending levels and the inability of the Senate majority party to overcome opposition to some bills on the floor. In 1995, seven bills were passed in regular order, one (Foreign Aid) was attached to a temporary CR and the remaining five were combined in an omnibus package (Table 4.2). Three of the five bills in the package (Interior; Commerce, Justice, and State; and Veterans Administration–HUD) passed both chambers but were vetoed by President Clinton. Two could not clear the Senate. The Senate initially passed the District of Columbia bill, but its conference report was filibustered by Democrats who objected to a House provision authorizing school vouchers that was adopted in conference. Senate Democrats also blocked a motion to proceed to the Labor–Health and Human Services bill and prevented it from being debated in the regular order.

The fates of the Labor–Health and Human Services bill and the District of Columbia bill illustrate how weakness leads the majority party to abandon the regular order. The primary issue on the Labor bill was a provision that overturned a ban President Clinton had imposed on the federal government doing business with corporations that replaced striking workers. Ironically, the rider did not have the support of the subcommittee's chairman, Senator Arlen Specter (R-PA). It had been added to the bill by the full Appropriations Committee over Specter's objections: "It is my view that it is not appropriate to deal with this matter on an appropriations bills.... And it is unlikely that there are sufficient votes to terminate a filibuster."[23] Specter was right, although the Senate never voted directly on cloture on the bill. Instead, under the terms of a unanimous consent agreement that the two parties had negotiated, sixty members of the Senate had to support a motion to proceed on the bill in order to debate it. In two separate party-line votes on September 28, the Republicans could only muster fifty-four in favor of debating the bill.[24] The Republican leadership was unable to break the deadlock and never tried to move the bill on its own again.

The issue that triggered a deadlock in the Senate on the District of Columbia bill was a provision inserted by House Republicans to establish a program of government-funded school vouchers in the city. The history of the bill was tumultuous. The House wrote two separate bills. The first was so filled with policy riders that Speaker Gingrich stepped in and had the committee draft a second version more acceptable to city officials. This version contained fewer riders but still legislated on issues ranging from abortion to adoption by same-sex couples. When it arrived on the House floor, members voted to attach a provision to authorize $3,000 vouchers for District schoolchildren that could be used for tuition at private or religious schools. This step caused considerable consternation in the Senate, which had approved a comparatively clean version of the bill. The two chambers initially deadlocked on the issue in conference, but the rider was ultimately kept in the conference report that was brought back to the Senate for final approval.[25] There, it met a wall of opposition from Senate Democrats. Republican leaders held four separate cloture votes in an effort to pass the bill and ultimately failed to end the debate.[26] Instead, it was included in the omnibus package.

The two bills were packaged together with the three that had been vetoed into a final omnibus package in the spring of 1996. The House and Senate Appropriations Committees each drafted a version of the omnibus, and it was debated and passed on the floor of each chamber.

---

[23] *Congressional Record*, September 28, 1995, 26770.

[24] Senate Roll Call Votes 471 and 472, September 28, 1995.

[25] "School Voucher Dispute Stalls D.C. Bill," in *CQ Almanac 1995*, 51st ed., 113–133 (Washington, DC: Congressional Quarterly, 1996). http://library.cqpress.com/cqalmanac/ cqal95-1099715.

[26] Senate Roll Call Votes 20, 21, 23, and 25.

The final version was negotiated in conference with officials from the Clinton administration and leaned substantially in the president's direction. Most of the riders objectionable to Democrats were stripped from the bill, including the vouchers program. The worker replacement provision in the Labor bill had become moot as a result of a separate court order that nullified it. The major loss for the Democrats came in the form of spending cuts. They were not as steep as Republicans had demanded, but the bills were about $22 billion below the previous year's amount.[27] Still, voting patterns suggest that the final version of the bill satisfied most Democratic concerns while leaving some Republicans unhappy. The initial draft of the omnibus had been opposed by 184 Democrats and 21 Republicans in the House, while the final draft was opposed by 5 Democrats and 20 Republicans. On the Senate side, the initial bill had been opposed by a coalition of seven liberal Democrats, such as Senator Barbara Boxer (D-CA), and fourteen conservative Republicans, such as Senator James Inhofe (R-OK). When the Senate considered the final version of the bill, all Democrats voted in favor of it and eleven conservative Republicans opposed it.[28]

1996

The shutdown was a disaster for Republicans. As one Republican interviewed for this book put it, "We got slaughtered" (Staff Interview F 2012). The appropriations season that followed was difficult for Senate Republicans. Majority Leader Bob Dole (R-KS) resigned his Senate seat to challenge Clinton for the presidency and incoming Majority Leader Trent Lott (R-MS) took over the leadership of a dispirited and ideologically fractured Republican conference with a narrow margin of control over their Democratic rivals. Meanwhile, President Clinton sought to capitalize on his victory over Republicans in the shutdown debacle by restoring some of the spending cuts he had just given up in the new spending bills for fiscal year 1997.

The president's success negotiating the fiscal year 1996 omnibus bill persuaded the administration that it had the upper hand when negotiating packages of spending bills with Congress. The size of omnibus packages made it likely that administration officials would be sitting across

---

[27] "Omnibus FY96 Bill Ties Loose Ends," in *CQ Almanac 1996*, 52nd ed., 105–106 (Washington, DC: Congressional Quarterly, 1997). http://library.cqpress.com/cqalmanac/cqal96-841-24596-1091488.

[28] See House Roll Call Votes 55 and 135, and Senate Roll Call Votes 42 and 89.

TABLE 4.3. *Legislative History of Appropriations Bills, 1996, Second Session, 104th Congress*

Bill	No Floor Vote (House)	No Floor Vote (Senate)	Bill in Omnibus
Agriculture			
Commerce, Justice, and State		✓	✓
District of Columbia			
Defense			✓
Energy Water			
Foreign Operations			✓
Interior		✓	✓
Labor–Health and Human Services		✓	✓
Legislative Branch			
Military Construction			
Treasury-Postal		✓	✓
Transportation			
Veterans Administration–HUD			
Total		4	6

the table from congressional leaders to negotiate the terms of the legislation. Clinton also judged that Republicans would be leery of a second budget confrontation with the administration. If the president could lead Congress to create another package, the administration would be in a favorable position to meet its budget goals. A staff member familiar with the thinking inside Clinton's OMB recalled that when Congress began to move a new set of appropriations bills in the summer of 1996, the president conspired with Senate Democrats to slow the passage of the bills and force the creation of an omnibus. Intense opposition from Democrats forced the Republican majority in the Senate to abandon the regular order on four spending bills and create a six-bill omnibus package for the year (Table 4.3). Fearful of being blamed for another government shutdown, Republicans gave in to the administration's demands. "We really manipulated the process," the staff member recalled. "We got to the point where we were dictating to them hundreds of things" (Staff Interview D 2012).

Democrats held their fire on the spending bills during the summer months. By July, eight had cleared the Senate. Democrats waited until early September when adjournment and the election were near to press their advantage on Republicans. Five bills were still pending, and Republicans were determined to avoid a repeat of the government shutdown that might further harm their standing with the public. "I am going to be one-dimensional here for the next three weeks: appropriations bills," Senator Lott announced. "That's the best message we send the American people: we get our work done."[29] Lott understood the danger that Democrats might sabotage the process: "I have a sneaking suspicion there is a slow-rolling process already being planned," he noted.[30] Lott's instincts were correct. A Democratic ambush was waiting for him.

The first target for the Democrats was the Treasury-Postal bill. It was brought to the floor on Tuesday, September 10. Over the next three days, the Senate cast fifty-four amendment-related votes on guns, terrorism, health care, and drugs, many aimed at scoring "preelection" points.[31] By Thursday, Lott's frustration was building. "I'm beginning to, you know, get concerned about [whether] the Democrats really do want to ... allow the process to work the way it's supposed to."[32] With no sign that debate was ending, Majority Leader Lott took to the floor later that day and said that he was pulling the bill from the floor and returning it to the calendar. "We have been on this bill 25 hours and 38 minutes," he announced. "I think perhaps we are tired and we need to see if we can go on to something else.... I just do not see how we can get through extended debate tonight and a lot of votes."[33] Off the floor, he was less diplomatic: "It was pure politics. I've been trying to do serious legislative business, and they've been politically positioning. So I'm not going to put up with that."[34]

Meanwhile, Democrats were awaiting the arrival of the Labor–Health and Human Services bill on the floor to make a major push on education spending. They announced on September 13 that they were seeking to add more than $3 billion to the bill to restore cuts the GOP had proposed and to meet President Clinton's spending requests. Republican leaders

[29] Dewar, Helen and Eric Pianin. "Hill Leaders Opt for Early Trip Home; Appropriations Bills, Campaign Push GOP Tax Cut Off the Agenda." *Washington Post* (September 5, 1996), A06.

[30] Abrams, Jim. "Congress Already Talking About Another Government Shutdown." Associated Press (September 5, 1996).

[31] Barr, Stephen and Eric Pianin. "Treasury Appropriations Bill Is Put Aside in Divided Senate." *Washington Post* (September 13, 1996), A20.

[32] "Senate Majority Leader Holds Regular News Briefing." NBC – Professional (September 12, 1996).

[33] *Congressional Record*, September 12, 1996, 23009.

[34] "Clinton Add-Ons Fatten Treasury Bill," in *CQ Almanac 1996*, 52nd ed., 108–184 (Washington, DC: Congressional Quarterly, 1997). http://library.cqpress.com/cqalmanac/cqal96-841-24596-1091676.

were reluctant to bring the bill to the floor for that reason. It would force them into a debate over education that they didn't want to have shortly before an election.[35] Democrats responded by offering their amendment to the next available target: the Interior bill.

The Democratic attack came on Tuesday, September 17, with the proposal of an amendment to increase education funding by $3.2 billion. The topic was not germane to the Interior bill, which dealt with public lands and parks, and the cost of the amendment swamped the relatively small $12 billion bill. Unwilling to let the Senate debate an issue on which Democrats held an advantage so close to the election, Lott pulled the Interior bill after Daschle sought consent to call up the amendment.[36] Off the floor, Lott accused Democrats of seeking to dump their "political garbage" on the spending bills. "If they think I'm going to stand by and let them do their political agenda on the appropriations bills … it's not going to happen that way."[37] Nonetheless, Republicans were on the defense and answered the call for additional education funding with a proposal of their own, raising spending by $2.3 billion. "We can either get our brains beat out politically or we can get in there and mix it up with them," Lott explained.[38]

With both sides maneuvering for advantage, Daschle announced the Democrats would keep up the pressure on education spending. "The majority leader has indicated he doesn't want to give us the opportunity to offer an amendment and so we will have to find ways with which to get this done.… We'll take whatever appropriations measures we can. We may even take another vehicle. Be we're going to get a vote on this legislation sooner or later."[39] In response, Republicans announced they would no longer seek to bring bills to the floor individually and instead would seek to negotiate an omnibus bill.

---

[35] "Education Gets Big Spending Boost," in *CQ Almanac 1996*, 52nd ed., 159–166 (Washington, DC: Congressional Quarterly, 1997). http://library.cqpress.com/cqalmanac/cqal96-841-24596-1091627.

[36] "Interior Bill Sidesteps Controversy," in *CQ Almanac 1996*, 52nd ed., 154–158 (Washington, DC: Congressional Quarterly, 1997). http://library.cqpress.com/cqalmanac/cqal96-841-24596-1091617.

[37] Dewar, Helen and Eric Pianin. "GOP Restores $2.3 Billion It cut in Education Funds; Republicans Want to Avoid Preelection Gridlock." *Washington Post* (September 18, 1996), A01.

[38] Ibid.

[39] "News Conference with Senators Edward M. Kennedy (D-MA) and John Kerry (D-MA) and Senate Minority Leader Tom Daschle (D-SD)." Federal News Service (September 19, 1996).

Majority Leader Lott and Speaker Gingrich explained their decision in a joint press release on September 19:

> It is clear that Senate Democrats are using delaying tactics and political stunts designed more for the upcoming elections than for the completion of the people's business. We have approached the consideration of these bills in good faith, but we have been met at every turn by Democrat gridlock apparently coordinated by the White House. We refuse to be part of this game. We believe Congress should complete its business and adjourn.
>
> Given the Democrat strategy to tie up the Senate floor, House and Senate leaders have decided that the defense appropriations conference report will be the vehicle for final consideration of all uncompleted appropriations issues. The remaining issues will be resolved through bipartisan negotiations between congressional leaders and the White House.[40]

The Republicans had shifted to plan B. They were abandoning their effort to pass bills individually and instead would negotiate a single package directly with the administration and congressional Democrats. One benefit of their strategy is that it would protect the party from being forced to vote on future Democratic amendments since the omnibus would be part of a nonamendable conference report. This limitation particularly affected the opportunity to debate the Commerce and Labor bills. Neither had been brought to the Senate floor, and the chamber would have no direct opportunity to make changes to the bills. Asked about the procedure at a daily press conference, Daschle indicated his opposition: "There is no way we can accept putting something of this consequence on a conference report. Obviously I understand the luxury of not having amendments when you come to the Senate floor, but ... we're not going to let something of the magnitude and importance of this issue come to the floor without the opportunity to amend and debate."[41]

Anxious to get out of town and knowing that the end of the fiscal year was just days away, Republican negotiators announced even before sitting down with the administration that they intended to give the president much of what he wanted in the bill.[42] The final bill provided an additional $6.5 billion in spending sought by Democrats, including the education spending they had proposed. Daschle noted, "In the last 48

---

[40] "Leaders Set Out Appropriations Strategy." Congressional Press Releases (September 19, 1996).

[41] "Regular Briefing with Senate Minority Leader Senator Tom Daschle (D-SD)." Federal News Service (September 20, 1996).

[42] "Senate to Put All but VA-HUD Bill in Omnibus Package." *National Journal's Congress Daily* (September 19, 1996).

hours, the Republicans have responded to our requests in a way I would not have thought possible."[43]

The only remaining question was how the package would come before Congress. Daschle and Lott negotiated inconclusively about the extent to which amendments would be allowed in the days leading up to the deal. Lott's goal was to limit amendments in order to ensure the completion of the bill. "If they want amendments, fine, we'll have amendments. If they want to have a debate, great, we'll have it on what we have. But here's the key. There must be a way to get to the end."[44] Daschle did not want to set a precedent of bringing packages that could not be amended to the floor. "We think it's important to protect the process," Daschle said. "Obviously … on a bill of this magnitude … to amend is something we believe is critical to the legislative process and to our rights as senators. And so we want to protect that, but we certainly don't want to abuse it."[45] On the other, the deal was a good one for Democrats and he did not want to risk delaying or unraveling the deal. He compromised with Republicans by arranging for an amendable version of the bill to come to the floor while simultaneously urging his fellow Democrats not to offer amendments.[46]

The package was adopted with considerable grumbling by members anxious to go home and start campaigning for the November elections.[47] "This is not the way to handle appropriations bills," said Senator Ted Stevens (R-AK), the incoming chair of the Appropriations Committee. "We must find a way to … assure that … each bill is considered on its own merits and it goes to the President in a way that expresses the will of Congress."[48] Senator James Inhofe (R-OK), one of the Senate's most conservative members, was blunt in his criticism: "We on the majority side are somewhat held hostage.… All of this goes back to this horrible fear that – if we do not do this … the government will stop at the end of

---

[43] Sands, David R. "House Approves Compromise Spending Bill; Democrats Hail 'U-turn' by GOP." *Washington Times* (September 29, 1996), A1.

[44] "News Conference with Senate Majority Leader Senator Trent Lott (R-MS)." Federal News Service (September 25, 1996).

[45] "Press Conference with Senate Democratic Leaders Regarding FY 1997 Spending." Federal News Service (September 28, 1996).

[46] "Senate Democrats to decide this afternoon on spending bill amendment strategy; may offer no amendments." *White House Bulletin* (September 30, 1996).

[47] "Clinton Signs GOP's Fortified Bill," in *CQ Almanac 1996*, 52nd ed., 133–139 (Washington, DC: Congressional Quarterly, 1997). http://library.cqpress.com/cqalmanac/cqal96-841-24596-1091561.

[48] *Congressional Record*, September 30, 1996, S11819.

the fiscal year ... and that the Republicans would be responsible for it."[49] Brushing Inhofe's objections aside, the Senate adopted the bill 84–15. All but one of forty-seven Democrats supported the bill, while fourteen of the fifty-two Republicans voting opposed it. The Republican opponents of the bill were on average far more conservative than the supporters were, with an average DW-NOMINATE score of 0.49 compared with 0.33 of supporters. President Clinton signed the bill that night.

Overall, 1996 is a clear illustration of the limited influence theory. In the House of Representatives, a strong majority passed each spending bill individually. In the Senate, a weak majority fell victim to Democratic tactics aimed at making Republicans take tough votes on amendments and at slowing the passage of the bills to force the creation of an omnibus package. Unlike President Reagan, President Clinton believed that an omnibus bill turned the tables in his favor and took advantage of the Republican majority's weaknesses. Republicans, in turn, created an omnibus package as a second choice strategy when it became clear that the strategy of passing bills in the regular order was too costly. Their decision to create the omnibus as part of the Defense conference report helped to shield them from additional amendments when the bill was returned to the floor, but the bill itself was a bipartisan compromise that leaned in the direction of the president.

PRESIDENTIAL STRATEGY IN THE APPROPRIATIONS PROCESS

The time period covered in this chapter is particularly interesting because of the distinct negotiating strategies adopted by Ronald Reagan, George H. W. Bush, and Bill Clinton to meet their goals in the appropriations process. The last section of this chapter investigates the role of the president in more detail and describes a new theory of presidential involvement in appropriations called "opportunistic bargaining." The few studies that have been conducted on the effect of omnibus bills on negotiations between the president and Congress conclude that they undermine the president's bargaining position. The case studies in this chapter show that this characterization fails to capture the flexibility and success shown by presidents in the appropriations process. Presidents are opportunistic bargainers who aggressively pursue their budget goals using different strategies at different times.

---

[49] *Congressional Record*, September 30, 1996, S11835.

Richard Neustadt (1990) famously observed that a president's power in a system of separated institutions sharing power arises from the ability to bargain. Presidents have no formal means to require that Congress adopts their preferred policies, but they do have direct and indirect ways to influence the legislative process (Jones 2005). Brady and Volden (2006) note that presidents can set the legislative agenda, influence the preferences of legislators, and compromise with pivotal legislators. The strongest form of influence wielded by the president is the veto. Veto threats can contribute to a stalemate in which nothing is passed or push policies closer to the president's preference.

Omnibus bills are generally thought to weaken the president's ability to bargain effectively because the bills are costly to veto (Krutz 2000; Wlezien 1996). Standard models of Congress simplify the legislative environment by describing a single dimension along which a policy and major legislative players such as the president can be placed. The likelihood of a veto depends on the relative proximity of the president's preference on this line to the status quo and the proposed new policy. Omnibus bills violate this model's assumptions because they are multidimensional and package together odd policy bedfellows. Presidents may be reluctant to veto packages that mix together provisions the president supports and opposes. Sinclair describes how congressional Democrats in the 1980s packaged legislative provisions opposed by President Reagan with those he supported in an effort to avoid his veto (2012, 154–155). Krutz concludes that omnibus bills give Congress the upper hand compared with bargaining over bills on an individual basis, and that Congress is more likely to satisfy its policy goals on omnibus bills than the president is (Krutz 2001a, 125).

The theory of opportunistic bargaining modifies models of bargaining by incorporating the unique features of the appropriations process. First, it assumes that both the president and Congress agree that funding for the government must be provided even if there are intense disagreements over the details. Second, it treats the appropriations process as an extended bargaining session in which there are multiple paths that lead to the shared goal of funding the government. Appropriations bills can be passed in the regular order or as a package. Temporary CRs can put additional time on the clock to allow further negotiations to take place. These facts lower the cost of a presidential veto. A veto or veto threat at any stage of the process is not an attempt to kill legislation permanently. It is a form of "sequential veto bargaining" – a demand that Congress continue to bargain with the president to produce a bill closer to the president's liking (Cameron and McCarty 2004). The only question presidents must answer is whether the costs of a veto are outweighed by the benefits of continued negotiation. Third, it assumes that presidents are opportunistic and pursue their interests in different ways at different times. As a group, they do not have well-established preferences between the regular order and omnibus bills but look for opportunities to bargain to meet their goals.

The last point is central to understanding the role of presidents in the management of appropriations bills. The study of the presidency has been described as a combination of "the personal and the institutional" because the judgments of individual presidents shape the administration's actions (Jones 2005, 24). Presidents bargain to meet their goals, but "presidential participation in lawmaking is not formulaic" (ibid., 221). Consistent with that argument, presidents do not systematically favor negotiating over appropriations bills individually in the regular order or as a package. By the end of his term, President Reagan took the position that negotiating over individual appropriations bills was preferable. He explained his reasoning in a weekly radio address in September 1987:

> Now, when Congress passes one of these continuing resolutions it puts appropriated federal funding into a huge lump, and when one of these massive continuing resolutions comes to my desk, it's a take it or leave it proposition. Sign the bill, and with it, accept the inability to get wasteful spending under some level of control or reject it and watch the United States Government run out of money and grind to a halt.[50]

In Reagan's view, omnibus bills took power away from the president by raising the cost of a veto to unacceptable levels. Longtime Senate Appropriations Committee chair Senator Robert Byrd (D-WV) made the opposite claim: "Omnibus bills bring the White House to the table and put them in charge.... Omnibus bills allow the White House to set arbitrary ceilings on spending. Omnibus bills preclude Members' rights to debate significant issues."[51] In Senator Byrd's view, omnibus bills gave a negotiating advantage to the president.

A fascinating history of the appropriations process from 1993–2001 compiled by the OMB at the end of the Clinton administration provides good evidence that the administration viewed the appropriations season as an extended negotiation and saw vetoes as ways to improve the

---

[50] "President Reagan's Weekly Radio Text." Associated Press (September 19, 1987).
[51] *Congressional Record*, November 20, 2004, S11742.

bills.[52] Under the heading "A Typical Appropriations Season," the memo describes the administration's effort to influence appropriations bills as a months-long process. The season began with the submission of the budget and testimony by administration officials before Congress and continued with the transmittal of SAPs outlining the administration's position on spending bills. OMB officials provided nightly updates to White House staff on the status of appropriations bills. The memo notes that the omnibus bills negotiated between the administration and Congress resulted in "some of the President's most significant legislative victories" and that "following vetoes and veto threats, these negotiations were also used to overcome prior Congressional funding decisions" (18–19). While the memo was written in part to establish a historical legacy for President Clinton, its description of the appropriations process does not fit with one in which vetoes are costly and omnibus bills put the president at a disadvantage. President Clinton instead appears to be an opportunistic bargainer using all the tools at his disposal to meet his goals in the appropriations process.

A full test of the theory of opportunistic bargaining will have to wait for future research, but several issues can be profitably addressed here. It is well understood that presidents can use vetoes and veto threats to shape policy outcomes. Do vetoes also have an effect on whether Congress passes bills in the regular order or as an omnibus package? To answer that question, I first estimated a variant of the "In Omnibus" models described in Table 2.5 that replaces the divided government variable with a new variable indicating whether the president vetoed a bill. I identified twenty-two vetoes of appropriations bills using reports complied by the Secretary of the Senate supplemented by other sources. The model also includes the "No Floor Vote" variable for the Senate as an independent variable. The Senate will not vote on any bill that the House did not vote on, so this variable effectively measures whether a bill was added to an omnibus package because the House or Senate opted to abandon the regular order. The model includes fixed effects by bill category and clusters standard errors by year.

Table 4.4 presents the results from a logit regression using the "In Omnibus" dependent variable described in Chapter 2. Three variables

---

[52] "A History of the U.S. Office of Management and Budget during the Clinton Administration, 1993–2001." 2000. Office of Management and Budget. Electronic version available from the William Jefferson Clinton Presidential Library Digital Library. http://www.clintonlibrary.gov/nec-omb.html#Office%20of%20Management%20 and%20Budget. Accessed May 25, 2013.

TABLE 4.4. *Inclusion of Bill in Omnibus Package After Veto, Logit Analysis, Fixed Effects by Bill Category and Standard Errors Clustered by Year*

Variable	Model A
No Floor Vote in House or Senate	6.66***
	(1.47)
Divided Control of Congress	0.31
	(0.88)
Veto	2.60***
	(0.71)
Republican Control of House	0.18
	(1.05)
Republican Control of Senate	1.20
	(0.80)
Election Year	0.69
	(0.79)
Deficit	-0.36
	(2.81)
Budget Enforcement Act	−0.78
	(0.79)
Previous Year in Omnibus	3.12**
	(1.41)
Constant	−3.93***
	(1.23)
Log Pseudolikelihood	−126.11
Pseudo R^2	0.61
N	479

Effects are significantly different from zero at $*p < .10$; $**p < .05$; $***p < .01$; two tailed test.

are statistically significant in the model. As expected, "No Floor Vote" is positively correlated with the inclusion of a bill in an omnibus package and significant at a level of $p < 0.01$. A presidential veto of a bill is also positively correlated with the inclusion of a bill in an omnibus package at a statistically significant level of $p < 0.01$. The marginal effect of a veto on the likelihood a bill is included in an omnibus may be significant. Assuming both chambers voted on the bill, Democratic control of the House, Republican control of the Senate, it is an election year, the BEA is not in effect, and all other variables are at their means, a veto increases the likelihood that the Defense bill will be included in an omnibus by 23 percent and the Labor–Health and Human Services bill by 62 percent.[53] These findings are good evidence that presidents can influence the selection of bills that are included in omnibus packages by vetoing a bill. They also fit with the broader argument that negotiating over an omnibus bill does not necessarily place the president at a disadvantage. Presidents are likely to be aware that vetoing a bill raises the chances that it will be placed in an omnibus package, and they opt for another round of bargaining with Congress even though that is the case.

In the remainder of this chapter, I test whether veto threats against a bill make it more likely that the majority will abandon the regular order for that bill. Evidence from case studies on this point is mixed. George H. W. Bush appeared to ease the passage of bills in the regular order with his veto threats by reducing the incentive of the Senate minority to delay them, but that result could be the consequence of the powerful Democratic majority at the time. On the other hand, SAPs and actual vetoes both appear to be elements of Bill Clinton's successful strategy to force the creation of an omnibus package in 1996, but the weakness of the Republican majority may actually be to blame.

Analyzing veto threats offers three benefits. First, it will offer evidence on whether Congress or the president has a systematic advantage negotiating over bills in the regular order or as part of a package. If either Congress or the president is systematically advantaged by the omnibus process, then – all things being otherwise equal – both houses of Congress should respond the same way to veto threats. For example, both might have an incentive to hold a floor vote on the bill in order to put the chambers on record in advance of the showdown with the president. Alternatively, both might skip consideration of the bill in the regular order and put it immediately into an omnibus bill in order to maximize their advantage with the president. Second, it offers a way to test the theory of limited influence. In the limited influence theory, the Senate majority party is more likely to abandon the regular order when bills are controversial because it lacks the power to adopt them. The House is more likely to adopt the bills regardless of their level of controversy because of its strong tools of majority party control. SAPs by definition indicate that bills are controversial, and evidence that the Senate, but not

[53] Variants of this model that replace the "No Floor Vote" variable with the party power variables from the House and Senate have similar results to those presented in Table 2.5 and estimate a statistically significant relationship between vetoes and including a bill in an omnibus at a level of $p < 0.05$.

TABLE 4.5. *Frequency of SAPs, 1985–2004*

Year	House	Senate	Conference
1985	0	1	0
1986	1	2	0
1987	1	1	0
1988	9	5	0
1989	3	2	3
1990	3	5	0
1991	7	4	0
1992	17	9	0
1993	0	0	0
1994	0	0	0
1995	12	7	11
1996	8	2	0
1997	19	10	0
1998	14	5	0
1999	6	5	0
2000	10	8	0
2001	3	4	0
2002	1	1	0
2003	5	6	0
2004	6	1	0
Total	125	78	14

the House, is more likely to abandon the regular order when a SAP is issued would be consistent with the limited influence theory. Third, it will indicate whether or not SAPs have any effect at all on the path a bill takes through Congress. The question here is simply whether presidents have the capacity to affect whether a bill is considered in the regular order by issuing a veto threat.

The data to test these expectations come from a collection of SAPs developed by Samuel Kernell.[54] Kernell's collection includes only SAPs in which the administration issued a veto threat to Congress. The collection includes a total of 937 SAPs issued between 1985 and 2004, of which 217 are targeted to appropriations bills. Fifty-eight percent of SAPs (125) were sent to the House, 36 percent (78) to the Senate, and 6 percent to conferees in both chambers (14). Table 4.5 presents the total number of

[54] Data from U.S. Management and Budget Office; Samuel Kernell, 2007, "Replication data for: Presidential Veto Threats in Statements of Administration Policy: 1985–2004," http://hdl.handle.net/1902.1/10199. Samuel Kernell (Distributor) V1 (Version).

TABLE 4.6. *SAPs and the Failure to Call a Vote in the House and Senate, 1985–2004, Logit Analysis, Standard Errors Clustered by Year*

Variable	Model A	Model B	Model C	Model D
SAPs		0.92**		−0.35
		(0.43)		(0.61)
Margin of Control	−13.88*	−12.90*	−101.65***	−99.93***
	(7.67)	(7.34)	(36.55)	(35.00)
Homogeneity	−28.02**	−24.60***	27.79	31.15
	(11.72)	(9.25)	(55.64)	(55.71)
Distance	10.50	9.53	−32.33	−36.39
	(10.34)	(8.74)	(57.50)	(57.72)
No Vote in House	6.29***	6.69***		
	(1.78)	(1.70)		
Divided Control of Congress	−6.90**	−5.84**	−6.14**	−6.17**
	(2.96)	(2.66)	(2.76)	(2.76)
Republican Control of Chamber	−13.92**	−12.00**	−38.50**	−37.16**
	(6.63)	(5.31)	(17.98)	(17.00)
Election Year	1.98***	2.21***	0.77	0.80
	(0.39)	(0.45)	(0.55)	(0.52)
Deficit	1.92	3.15	31.22***	30.91***
	(4.84)	(4.39)	(10.70)	(10.43)
Budget Enforcement Act	−4.18**	−3.58**		
	(1.69)	(1.39)		
Proportion of Bills in Omnibus (Lagged)	−2.85**	−2.56*	1.11	0.98
	(1.40)	(1.41)	(2.74)	(2.73)
Constant	20.31**	16.57**	39.96	38.61
	(9.19)	(8.28)	(27.45)	(26.45)
Log Pseudolikelihood	−55.63	−54.39	−44.34	−44.19
Pseudo R²	0.50	0.51	0.29	0.30
N	259	259	259	259

Standard errors in parentheses.
*p < 0.10, **p < 0.05, ***p < 0.01.

SAPs sent to each chamber and to conferees by year. SAPs are always directed toward particular bills. The data set identifies the number of SAPs directed against each regular appropriations bill by year during its consideration by the House, Senate, and in conference.

Table 4.6 presents the results of four logistic regressions similar to those presented in Chapter 2. The dependent variable in Models A and B is the "No Floor Vote" variable from Senate. The dependent variable in Models C and D is the "No Floor Vote" variable from the House. Models A and C do not include the SAP variable. Models B and D include the number of SAPs issued against each bill in the data set in the Senate and House, respectively. All models exclude the "divided government" variable used in earlier models since SAPs directly measure conflict between the executive and legislative branches. The data set is limited to the years 1985–2004 when data on SAPs are available. This fact limits the amount of variation in the party characteristics variables and raises the level of collinearity among the House variables. Estimates of the effects of party characteristics in the House are unreliable for that reason. The models also do not include fixed effects by bill because the lack of variation leads to a substantial number of dropped cases. Models C and D exclude the BEA variable for similar reasons.

The results are consistent with the expectations of the limited influence theory and the opportunistic bargaining theory. The Senate majority party is more likely to abandon the regular order on an appropriations bill when the president has issued a SAP against it at statistically significant levels in Model B ($p = 0.03$). There is no statistically significant effect associated with the president issuing a SAP against an appropriations bill in the House ($p = 0.57$). The party characteristic variables in the Senate remain in the predicted directions, although their significance has changed from the models presented in Chapter 2 because of the more limited variation in the data during this time period. As noted earlier, the estimates for party characteristics in the House are unreliable because of multicollinearity.

Consistent with the fact that Congress is primarily responsible for determining how to pass appropriations bills, the marginal effect of the president issuing a SAP against a bill is not terribly large. The majority party is 22 percent more likely to abandon the regular order on a bill when the president issues a SAP against it, assuming the model is set to the "difficult" floor setting described in Chapter 2.[55] The marginal effect falls to zero in the "moderate" floor setting. The relatively small effect is not surprising given the findings of the case studies. George H. W. Bush issued numerous SAPs against spending bills, but the bills were adopted in the regular order consistently during his administration. Nonetheless, the findings are consistent with the argument that the president can exercise some influence over whether bills are considered in the regular order or as an omnibus package and that this effect is attributable in part to the fact that presidents add a layer of controversy to bills in the Senate when they issue a SAP. SAPs make it harder for the majority party to pass bills

[55] The marginal effect is the difference in the likelihood of failing to vote on a bill based on a change from zero to one in the SAP variable. The SAP variable is a count variable, so the marginal effect measures the effect of the president issuing a single SAP against a bill.

in the regular order on the Senate floor and more likely that the majority will opt not to bring a bill to a vote.

CONCLUSION

Chapter 4 reviews a key period in which Congress abandoned the passage of omnibus spending bills for seven years and then returned to omnibus legislating. Several characteristics make this time period particularly noteworthy. First, it demonstrates how shocks to the political system can influence the likelihood of omnibus legislating. In 1988, President Reagan used his State of the Union address to end the first wave of omnibus legislating by threatening to veto another such bill. In 1995, Speaker Newt Gingrich used the appropriations bills to challenge President Bill Clinton on the budget, and the subsequent crisis ended when both sides negotiated an omnibus package to finalize a new budget. The influence of each of those events highlights a larger question: why did the change they sparked endure? Congress returned to the regular order in 1988 after Reagan's veto threat and continued to follow it through 1994, and Congress has adopted omnibus bills on a regular basis since the government shutdown of 1995–1996. The evidence suggests that the strength of the Senate majority party played an important role in each case. From 1988 to 1994, the Senate majority was remarkably strong as a result of a large Democratic margin of control and high degree of ideological unity. The Democratic majority faced challenges on the floor but routinely outvoted its opponents. After 1994, the power of the majority fell when a smaller and more ideologically mixed group of Republicans took control of the chamber. The comparatively weaker Republican majority was unable to pass spending bills individually as a result of a barrage of Democratic amendments and delaying tactics coordinated with President Clinton. Republican leaders responded by pulling individual spending bills from the floor and negotiating an omnibus bill with President Clinton. The resulting compromise package received support from a majority of both parties, but the opposition of conservative Republicans and accounts from the time suggest it leaned in a Democratic direction.

These findings offer further evidence for the limited influence theory. The lack of omnibus bills from 1988 to 1994 is a consequence of the strong Democratic majority not needing them to adopt a budget. During the government shutdown, the addition of the Labor–Health and Human Services bill and the District of Columbia bill to the omnibus package was a consequence of neither being able to clear the Senate floor. And in

1996, the primary reason for the creation of the omnibus package was the inability of the majority to overcome Democratic obstruction and pass bills individually. In response, they negotiated the creation of an omnibus package that would protect the party in the Senate by limiting amending and ensuring passage of the budget.

Finally, this chapter sheds important light on the role of the president. Presidents vary in their assessment of whether omnibus bills are a useful way to help them meet their goals. Some, such as President Reagan, viewed the packages as undermining the role of the president and opposed them. Others, such as President Clinton, believed that omnibus bills gave them a negotiating advantage and worked with congressional allies to create them. Omnibus bills are primarily created as a response to problems the majority faces passing legislation in Congress, but presidents can influence the degree of legislative conflict on the Senate floor and indirectly encourage or discourage the creation of omnibus bills.

5

The Second Wave (1995–2012)

Infighting within the Republican Senate majority during the 1980s helped to transform temporary continuing resolutions (CRs) into year-long measures to fund the federal government. The first wave of omnibus appropriating continued until 1988, when Congress returned to passing appropriations bills on an individual basis. The period of regular order ended with the Republican takeover of Congress in 1995, and omnibus bills again were routinely used by Congress to fund the government. In Chapter 5, I investigate the second wave of omnibus appropriating with a study of the administration of President George W. Bush from 2001 to 2004.

Evidence from this era fits in major respects with the expectations of the limited influence theory. The Senate majority party was weak because of extraordinarily narrow margins of control. The chamber was so closely divided that control over it shifted twice in two years. Each party also had a handful of moderates whose votes could be won by the other side. The risk of defection meant the majority risked being embarrassed or rolled in key votes by the minority when it brought the bills to the floor. The rising ideological gulf between Republicans and Democrats also intensified minority opposition to legislation and raised the risk of disruptive filibusters. These problems made it difficult and politically dangerous for the majority to pass spending bills on an individual basis. Abandoning the regular order helped the majority party to overcome these problems by shielding it from tough votes and ensuring passage of the budget.

While omnibus packages typically won support from both parties during this period, slightly more than 50 percent of the minority party opposed the bills at times. The packages also overturned a number of decisions made on the floors of both the House and the Senate. These findings come closer to matching the predictions of models of majority party control than those presented in earlier chapters, but there are some important problems with that interpretation. Many of the overturned policies passed the Senate with mostly Democratic support, but others had the backing of prominent Republicans. The decisive factor in the policy direction of the bills appears to be the influence of President George W. Bush, who bargained intensely and used veto threats to push policy in a direction he favored. Together, the Clinton and Bush eras suggest that presidents can effectively pursue their preferred policies by negotiating over omnibus packages. The presidential tilt to the packages appears to come at the cost of some votes from the minority, but the bills still won bipartisan support.

NARROW MARGINS, SHARP DIFFERENCES

Figure 5.1 illustrates the characteristics of the majority party and the pattern of omnibus legislating during this era. The majority party abandoned the regular order with increasing frequency during this period. Omnibus packages were relatively small in the beginning of the period but grew

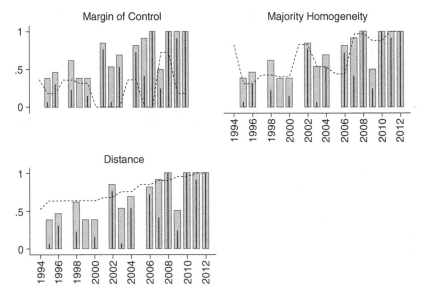

FIGURE 5.1. Party characteristics and abandoning the regular order. U.S. Senate, 1994–2012.

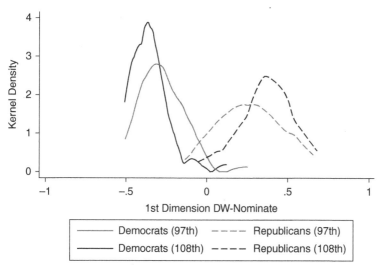

FIGURE 5.2. Ideological distribution of Democrats and Republicans. U.S. Senate, 97th and 108th Congresses.

to include all bills by the end. Similarly, the majority party brought most bills to a vote on an individual basis at the beginning of the period and regularly failed to vote on most of them by the end. Party characteristics show some interesting differences from previous years. The majority's margin of control is generally low at this time with the exception of the 111th Congress, when Democrats controlled sixty seats in the Senate. On the other hand, the majority is relatively homogenous and distant from the minority. Homogeneity appears to be positively correlated with abandoning the regular order in a break from past patterns. The majority party's distance from the minority is also at the highest levels recorded in the period under study.

The large distance between the majority and the minority suggests that the policy differences between the two parties had grown sharper and that the threat from intense minority opposition or filibusters was more serious than in years past. Figure 5.2 illustrates the ideological distribution of Democrats and Republicans in the Senate in the 97th Congress (1981–1982) as compared with the 108th Congress (2003–2004) using kernel densities of their DW-NOMINATE scores. Interestingly, Republicans remained more ideologically diverse than Democrats. In the 97th Congress, the median DW-NOMINATE score for Democrats was –0.30 (standard deviation 0.14) as compared with a median of 0.27 (standard deviation 0.20) for Republicans. By the 108th Congress, the comparable

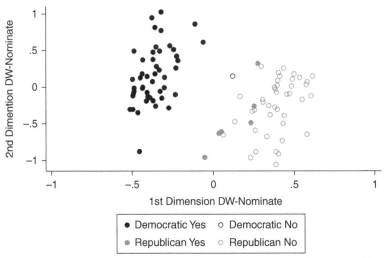

FIGURE 5.3. A Democratic roll: Overturning limits on overtime wages. Roll Call 334, U.S. Senate, 2003.

scores were a median of −0.37 (standard deviation 0.12) for Democrats and a median of 0.39 (standard deviation 0.16) for Republicans.

Razor-thin margins of control during these years left each party vulnerable to being rolled when it was in the majority if a small number of its moderates defected. As discussed later in the chapter, Democrats successfully rolled the Republican majority in the 108th Congress with a series of amendments to appropriations bills designed to unify their caucus and draw moderate Republicans. Figure 5.3 illustrates a typical roll of the majority using a vote on a Democratic amendment to overturn Bush administration limits on overtime pay in 2003. With the chamber divided 51–49 in favor of Republicans, Democrats won the vote by picking up the support of six liberal Republicans while only losing the support of one conservative Democrat. Voting on amendments in the Senate could lead to embarrassing political defeats for the majority.

The early 2000s also brought change to the historically stable structure of the Appropriations Committee. Congress restructured government agencies in the wake of the terrorist attacks of September 11, 2001, and each chamber spent several years experimenting with new jurisdictions for the subcommittees before settling on a new structure in the 110th Congress (Table 5.1). This chapter covers only the 107th and 108th Congresses just as that change was beginning. The 108th Congress created a subcommittee for the new Department of Homeland Security

TABLE 5.1. *Evolution of Appropriations Subcommittee Structure, 107th–110th Congresses*

107th	108th	House 109th	Senate 109th	110th
Agriculture	Agriculture	Agriculture	Agriculture	Agriculture
Commerce, Justice, and State	Commerce, Justice, and State	Defense	Commerce, Justice, Science	Commerce, Justice, Science
Defense	Defense	Energy and Water	Defense	Defense
District of Columbia	District of Columbia	Foreign Operations	District of Columbia	Energy and Water
Energy and Water	Energy and Water	Homeland Security	Energy and Water	Financial Services
Foreign Operations	Foreign Operations	Interior-Environment	Homeland Security	Homeland Security
Interior	Homeland Security	Labor–Health and Human Services	Interior	Interior-Environment
Labor–Health and Human Services	Interior	Military Quality of Life–Veterans Affairs	Labor–Health and Human Services	Labor–Health and Human Services
Legislative Branch	Labor–Health and Human Services	Science, State, Justice, and Commerce	Legislative Branch	Legislative Branch
Military Construction	Legislative Branch	Transportation, Treasury, Judiciary, HUD, and DC	Military Construction and Veterans Affairs	Military Construction and Veterans Affairs
Transportation	Military Construction		State and Foreign Operations	State and Foreign Operations
Treasury-Postal	Transportation-Treasury		Transportation, Treasury, the Judiciary, and HUD	Transportation-HUD
Veterans Admin–HUD	Veterans Admin–HUD			

135

and abolished the Treasury-Postal subcommittee by merging its functions with those of other subcommittees. The 109th Congress continued the evolution of subcommittee jurisdictions in different ways in the House and Senate. The number of subcommittees dropped to ten in the House of Representatives, while the number of Senate subcommittees dropped to twelve. The structures of the two chambers were reconciled in the 110th Congress when Democrats took back control of the House and Senate. Both chambers established twelve subcommittees. Their jurisdictions were identical, but they had evolved substantially beyond those that existed in the 1980s and 1990s.

Next, I turn to a year-by-year analysis of the appropriations process during the first term of President George W. Bush, from 2001 and 2004. The evidence is consistent with the expectation that the majority party abandons the regular order when it is faced with a challenging floor environment in the Senate. Congress failed to pass a budget resolution twice during these years and once failed to pass the spending bills entirely, deferring them for an incoming Congress to deal with. The case studies reveal strong disagreement between the parties on overall spending levels and the routine legislative "riders" attached to the bills. Debates on issues such as trade with Cuba, overtime pay standards, and other matters occur annually for periods of time. Faced with filibusters and the risk of losing important policy disputes on the floor, leaders skipped floor debates on individual spending bills and used conference procedures to create nonamendable, must-pass packages.

107th Congress (2001–2002)

The extraordinary setting of the 107th Congress is without precedent. A heated presidential race between Governor George W. Bush of Texas and Vice President Al Gore resulted in a tie in the Electoral College because of disputed election results in the state of Florida. The Supreme Court resolved the conflict in favor of Governor Bush by stopping a recount of votes in the state. Republicans held on to a thin majority in the House of Representatives, but the parties were tied in the Senate at fifty seats each. Vice President Dick Cheney's tie-breaking vote put control of the Senate in the hands of Republicans as the new Congress was seated, but the defection of Senator Jim Jeffords (R-VT) to the Democrats shifted control to the Democrats by the summer of 2001. Rising partisan rancor in Congress came to an unexpected halt as a result of the terrorist attacks of September 11. Anxiety in Washington deepened when a letter containing anthrax was opened in the office of Senator Daschle on October 15, leading to the temporary closure of the Hart Senate Office Building and a serious disruption in the ability of Congress to carry out its duties. By that winter, American troops were deployed in Afghanistan and an invasion of Iraq was being debated. The nation shifted from peace to war and grappled with serious questions about how to improve security and prevent future terrorist attacks. These events initially suppressed the usual partisan debates over the budget during 2001 and led to an unusually smooth year for appropriations. By 2002, partisan wrangling returned, and the Senate resumed its practice of abandoning the regular order in favor of packaging spending bills into an omnibus package.

2001

The 107th Congress faced several major questions as it considered the budget for fiscal year 2002. The nation had a budget surplus for the first time in decades, and Congress had to determine whether the windfall would be used to finance tax cuts or Social Security and Medicare. Democrats maintained that the budget resolution adopted when Republicans controlled the chamber avoided the trade-off by taking an unappealing third route: shortchanging the amount of money provided for the regular appropriations bills. The defection of Senator Jim Jeffords to the Democrats gave the party the leverage it needed to press for additional funds. Democrats took control of the Senate on June 4 and, among other priorities, vowed to find more money for the spending bills.[1]

The new Democratic majority was initially successful in moving spending bills given the transition in power and uncertainty over final spending levels. Five bills passed before August recess, and only one faced substantial difficulty. The normally placid Transportation bill consumed two weeks of floor time in late July over the issue of whether long-haul trucks from Mexico should be allowed to drive to destinations in the United States as agreed to in the North American Free Trade Agreement (NAFTA). The version of the bill from the Republican-controlled House of Representatives banned truck traffic from Mexico altogether. The

[1] Parks, Daniel J., "Appropriations Season Heats Up as Democrats Say Bush Tax Cut Will Force Raiding of Trust Funds," *CQ Weekly*, July 7, 2001, 1646–1646. http://library.cqpress.com/cqweekly/weeklyreport107-000000277631.

Senate took a milder approach. Senator Patty Murray (D-WA), the chair of the Transportation subcommittee, attached an amendment to the bill that added substantial safety requirements in place of a ban. Both amendments were opposed by the Bush administration, which threatened a veto, and by Republicans senators such as John McCain (R-AZ), Pete Domenici (R-NM), and Phil Gramm (R-TX), who were from border states and favored increased trade.

The bill was held up repeatedly on the Senate floor by its opponents filing amendments.[2] The key moment of the debate occurred when Senator McCain and his allies, having lost every vote in their attempt to modify Senator Murray's safety rules, filibustered the entire bill and successfully blocked a cloture motion with a vote of 57–27.[3] The bill ultimately cleared the Senate by voice vote after Majority Leader Daschle reached an agreement with Senator McCain that no members of the conference committee would be appointed until after the August recess, during which time McCain hoped to be able to gain more support for his position. The delay was only expected to be a temporary respite from the debate. As Senator McCain noted, "We are not moving on. We have the opportunity to have three more cloture votes on this issue. We intend to fight every single one of those when we return in September."[4]

By August, none of the spending bills had gone to conference, and a "major showdown" was expected between Senate Democrats and Republicans over total spending levels for the bills.[5] Instead, the attacks of September 11 occurred, partisan squabbling fell out of favor, and concerns about spending caps were set aside as emergency bills to respond to the disaster were passed. The artificial calm produced by the attacks appears to have suppressed conflict over proposed legislative riders in virtually every field of policy. Controversial riders were quietly dropped or ignored. On the Agriculture and Treasury-Postal bills, debates on opening U.S. trade with Cuba were widely expected but did not emerge. Democrats offered an amendment to the Labor–Health and Human Services bill granting emergency workers the right to unionize but dropped it after

[2] Benton, James C., "Mexican Truck Safety Provision Holds Up Transportation Bill," *CQ Weekly*, July 28, 2001, 1860–1861. http://library.cqpress.com/cqweekly/ weeklyreport107-000000290948.

[3] Roll Call 259, U.S. Senate, 107th Congress, Second Session, July 27, 2001.

[4] *Congressional Record*, August 1, 2001, 15284.

[5] "Spending Fights Put on Hold," in *CQ Almanac 2001*, 57th ed., 2–3 (Washington, DC: Congressional Quarterly, 2002). http://library.cqpress.com/cqalmanac/cqal01-106-6382-328405.

losing a cloture vote. On the Transportation bill, Congress adopted a weakened version of the Murray language that was acceptable to the Bush administration.[6] For the first time in years, each of the appropriations bills received an individual vote in the House and Senate and was passed in regular order.

The smooth passage of the spending bills in 2001 is noteworthy. It is consistent with the idea that members of the majority view the regular order as the preferred, standard procedure and only abandon it when they face difficulty passing individual spending bills. When conflict was artificially suppressed by the national unity that emerged in the wake of terrorist attacks, the process succeeded and Congress passed bills in the regular order.

2002

Politics as usual returned to Washington in 2002, and Congress created an eleven-bill omnibus package (Table 5.2). Problems for the budget process began early in the year when President Bush proposed a $759 billion limit on domestic discretionary spending. The House endorsed this approach in its budget resolution, but Senate Democrats were unable to agree on spending levels and failed to bring a budget resolution to the floor. Complicating matters was the fact that members of the Appropriations Committee in both the House and the Senate viewed the administration's $759 billion limit as insufficient to fund all thirteen appropriations bills. In the House of Representatives, progress on the bills stopped when it became apparent that Speaker Hastert could not muster the support on the floor to pass them without adding more money. In the Senate, Democratic leaders made more money available for the bills, and they were passed from committee with bipartisan support. But with House leaders and President Bush both unwilling to compromise with Democrats on spending levels, the House and Senate passed only three bills (Defense, Military Construction, and Legislative Branch) before progress on the rest stalled in August.[7]

One of the few bills that passed the House was the Interior appropriations bill, but it created an intractable conflict when it was brought to the Senate floor. The cause of the delay was a dispute over forest

---

[6] *CQ Almanac* (Washington, DC: Congressional Quarterly, 2001), 2–46.

[7] "Eleven Spending Bills Postponed," in *CQ Almanac 2002*, 58th ed., 2–3 (Washington, DC: Congressional Quarterly, 2003). http://library.cqpress.com/cqalmanac/cqal02-236-10373-664275.

TABLE 5.2. *Legislative History of Appropriations Bills, 2002, Second Session, 107th Congress*

Bill	No Floor Vote (House)	No Floor Vote (Senate)	Bill in Omnibus*
Agriculture	✓	✓	✓
Commerce, Justice, and State	✓	✓	✓
District of Columbia	✓	✓	✓
Defense			
Energy Water	✓	✓	✓
Foreign Operations	✓	✓	✓
Interior		✓	✓
Labor–Health and Human Services	✓	✓	✓
Legislative Branch			✓
Military Construction			
Treasury-Postal		✓	✓
Transportation	✓	✓	✓
Veterans Administration–HUD	✓	✓	✓
Total	8	10	11

* Omnibus approved by 108th Congress.

fire prevention. Over the course of the 1990s, increasingly severe wild-fires in the West led to calls to reduce the risk of fire by loosening environmental reviews so that timber harvesting to thin forests could take place more quickly. Conservative western senators such as Larry Craig (R-ID) and Conrad Burns (R-MT) championed this strategy in Congress and proposed an amendment to the Interior bill to give the Forest Service broad new authority to log forests in the name of fire prevention.[8] This amendment was strongly opposed by environmental interests and was aimed in part to embarrass Majority Leader Daschle, whose past efforts to reduce forest fire risks in his home state of South Dakota were regularly cited by Republicans as an inspiration for their amendment. Fearing the amendment would pass if it came to a vote, Democratic leaders sought to block it by filing cloture on an under-lying amendment that provided additional funding for fighting forest fires. For parliamentary reasons, cloture would cause the Craig amendment to fall without a vote.

[8] See Senate Amendment 4518, 107th Congress, Second Session.

The result of the conflict was a stalemate that ended any chance of passing the Interior bill on an individual basis.[9] Between September 10, when Senator Craig proposed his amendment, and September 25, when the bill was pulled from the floor, the Senate held three separate cloture votes in an effort to bring debate on the bill to a close. All of them failed to secure the necessary sixty votes.[10] Instead, the two parties traded accusations over which party was responsible for delaying the Interior bill. Republicans framed their position as defending the traditional right to open debate in the Senate. Senator Don Nickles (R-OK) took the floor to chastise the Democrats: "For whatever reason, some people are afraid to vote on the Craig amendment.... We are entitled to a vote. You can file cloture all you want, but we are going to have a vote.... We are not going to finish this bill until we get a vote."[11] For their part, Democrats accused Republicans of filibustering the Interior bill and delaying needed aid. "They can say all they want that they are not filibustering this bill," said Senator Harry Reid (D-NV). "This is the fourth week we are on the bill. If they want to get disaster aid to the farmers, they should allow us to go forward on this legislation.... Those people are waiting for relief as we speak. They should go ahead and allow us to pass the bill. In the meantime, the farmers get nothing."[12] When the third cloture vote failed on September 25, Majority Leader Daschle pulled the bill from the floor with the stalemate unresolved. Senator Lott, reflecting back on the Interior debate months later, noted: "They refused to let us have a direct vote because they didn't want their people to have to vote on how we deal with fire prevention and with fires in America, and so they just let the whole bill die."[13]

With the spending bills stalled, Congress adopted a CR extending funding for the government and recessed for the midterm elections in an atmosphere of heated debate about the proposed invasion of Iraq. The results that November toppled the Democrats' one-seat majority and put Republicans back in control of the chamber. Demoralized Democrats reconvened the Senate for a lame-duck session after the elections and

---

[9] Adams, Rebecca, "Logging Debate Holding Up Interior Bill." *CQ Weekly Online* (September 28, 2002): 2526–2526. http://library.cqpress.com/cqweekly/weeklyreport107-000000514672 (accessed April 26, 2010).

[10] See Roll Call 217, U.S. Senate, September 17, 2002; Roll Call 221, U.S. Senate, September 23, 2002; Roll Call 224, U.S. Senate, September 25, 2002.

[11] *Congressional Record*, September 25, 2002, S9185.

[12] *Congressional Record*, September 25, 2002, S9185.

[13] "Media Availability with Senate Minority Leader Trent Lott (R-MS)." Federal News Service (November 20, 2002).

found the Republicans emboldened and President Bush less willing to compromise than he had been before. In his first news conference following the election, Senator Daschle announced that his preference was to use the lame-duck session to pass spending bills in regular order. "I recognize that may be very difficult to do. I guess my second preference would be to do ... a number of bills in omnibus form. And, failing those two options, then you have nothing left but the CR."[14] Instead, Republican leader Trent Lott and Speaker Dennis Hastert of the House agreed the House would move a CR extending funding until the new Congress was seated in January and reconsider the appropriations bills then in order to maximize Republican influence over the bills.[15] With little other choice, Senate Democrats brought the CR to the floor and deferred the bills until the next Congress when the new Republican majority was in place.

Completing the unfinished appropriations bills was the first order of business of the 108th Congress. Republican leaders announced they would package the eleven remaining bills together for quick passage. Senator Ted Stevens (R-AK), the new chairman of the Appropriations Committee, noted that he would have preferred to deal with each of the bills individually, but that the need to clear the decks for the upcoming year was too pressing to go any route but that of an omnibus package. "We cannot get there if we pass these bills separately," he noted. "As I said before, we will face the prospect of disagreement with the House and endless conferences on 11 bills, and possibilities of vetoes and motions to override, and all the time it will take."[16] The bill was brought to the floor by the Republican leadership in January 2003 without a chance for the Democrats, now in the minority, to see a copy of it in advance.[17] The omnibus was open to amendment in accordance with the standing rules of the Senate, but the time available to debate the massive bill was brief. After spending four weeks debating the $19 billion Interior bill, the Senate spent a total of six days debating the 1,052-page, $385 billion omnibus spending bill.[18] The Senate voted on more than 100 amendments before approving the bill 69–29. A majority of the Democratic

---

[14] "Senate Democratic Leader Tom Daschle (D-SD) Post-Election News Conference." Federal News Service (November 8, 2002).

[15] *Congressional Quarterly Daily Monitor* (November 12, 2002).

[16] *Congressional Record*, January 15, 2003, S349.

[17] *Congressional Record*, January 15, 2003, S340.

[18] "Omnibus Clears Up Fiscal 2003" in CQ *Almanac 2003*, 59th ed., 2-5-2-7 (Washington, DC: Congressional Quarterly, 2004). http://library.cqpress.com/cqalmanac/cqal03-835-24336-1083885.

caucus opposed the bill, with all but one of the "no" votes coming from the minority.[19]

The next step was to negotiate a final conference report. Some Democrats complained that the conference negotiations – controlled entirely by Republicans – pushed policy in a more conservative direction. Senator Robert Byrd (D-WV), now the ranking minority member of the Appropriations Committee, complained that the process for writing the bills had been bipartisan until it reached conference:

> Today's headline in *The Washington Post* reads, "GOP Wraps Up Spending Package." There is some truth to that statement. Behind closed doors, the Senate Majority Leader, the Speaker of the House of Representatives, and the Chairmen of the House and Senate Appropriations Committees met and settled on a number of the big issues. Vice President Cheney provided the administration's views.

> At these partisan meetings, decisions were made on such issues as the overall top line total of the omnibus appropriations legislation, the size of the across-the-board cut, the matter of environmental riders and the substance of the $3.1 billion drought package, along with the offsets from the previously enacted farm bill that were included at the insistence of the White House. These farm bill offsets because necessary when the White House refused to raise the top line by $3.1 billion to accommodate the mandatory spending in the drought package.[20]

A sore spot for Democrats was Senator Craig's controversial amendment on forest fires. The omnibus bill considered on the Senate floor had lacked the provision, and it had never been raised as part of the floor debate. Instead, the omnibus was modified in conference to meet Craig's goals by substantially expanding logging through an existing Forest Service program.[21]

When debate on the final version of the bill opened on February 13, the amendment's opponents could do little but vent their frustration. Senator Barbara Boxer (D-CA) opened her floor remarks by apologizing for the crudeness of the charts she had brought with her, noting that she had had only a few hours' notice about the provision's existence before the conference report was due to be debated. Boxer explained that she was powerless to do anything about the environmental deficiencies she saw in the conference report because it was not amendable. "There is nothing I

[19] Roll Call 28, U.S. Senate, 108th Congress, First Session, January 23, 2003.

[20] *Congressional Record*, February 13, 2003, S2431.

[21] "Making Further Continuing Appropriations for the Fiscal Year 2003, and for Other Purposes," House Report 108–110, 108th Congress, First Session, February 13, 2003, 1031.

can do here except take a few minutes to call this to the attention of my colleagues and the American people because ... we cannot amend this report. It is up or down. That is what makes it so egregious to me."[22]

Voting patterns suggest that the bill was more bipartisan than Boxer's remarks would indicate. The Senate approved the package on a vote of seventy-six to twenty. That was more support than the pre-conference version received when it passed the Senate in January and included the votes of over half of the Democratic caucus.[23] The growth in Democratic support after a Republican-controlled conference casts doubt about whether the bill was as partisan as its critics claimed. Indeed, Senator Byrd voted in favor of the bill on both occasions. An analysis of DW-NOMINATE scores shows that the sixteen Democrats who voted against both the initial Senate version of the bill and the conference report were the party's liberals, such as Senator Teddy Kennedy (D-MA), with an average score of –0.52. Those who supported it both times were the party's most conservative members, such as Senator Ben Nelson (D-NE), with an average score of –0.28. The nine Democrats who switched their votes from "no" to "yes" were on average more conservative than consistent opponents of the bill were, with an average DW-NOMINATE score of –0.43. These patterns suggest that the bill was largely acceptable to the center-right wing of the Democratic party, and that opposition was confined to the party's liberals.

The appropriations process in the 107th Congress is noteworthy for the extraordinarily unusual circumstances of the time, including the attacks of September 11, the mid-session switch in control of the Senate, and the fact that an omnibus bill was created by a new Congress after the previous one had failed to pass the bills. Within this context, some familiar patterns are visible. In 2001, Congress set aside normal disputes over the bills in the wake of the terrorist attacks and passed them in regular order just as expected when the Senate floor is easy for the majority party to manage. Before that artificial calm took hold, the Senate had deadlocked on the Transportation-Treasury bill because of filibusters over Mexican trucking in a manner consistent with expectations. In 2002, the decision by the House majority not to bring most bills to the floor prevented the Senate from taking action on them independently. Nonetheless, one of the few bills that passed the House of Representatives could not clear the Senate because of minority obstruction on a forestry amendment.

---

[22] *Congressional Record*, February 13, 2003, S2427.
[23] Roll Call 34, U.S. Senate, 108th Congress, First Session, February 13, 2003.

The ability of the Senate majority party to manage the floor reduced the likelihood of an omnibus in 2001 and shaped the nature of the package in 2002.

108th Congress (2003–2004)

The 108th Congress inaugurated a new, uninterrupted period of unified government for the first time since Democrats had won control of Congress and the White House in 1992. The House remained under narrow Republican control, and President George W. Bush was president. Republicans controlled the Senate with fifty-one seats. The slim margin of control made the floor a dangerous environment for the Republican majority in the Senate because of the possibility of minority obstruction and the risk of being rolled by the Democrats on amendments. In 2003, it was repeatedly embarrassed by amendments that passed primarily with the support of Democrats or that were opposed by the president. In 2004, Republicans avoided a similar fate by choosing not to bring many of the bills to the floor individually. In both years, Republican leaders in Congress drafted an omnibus bill in conference and brought it to the floor as a nonamendable conference report. Both bills overturned policy decisions made in committee or on the floors of both chambers in favor of positions supported by the president. They were opposed by a narrow majority of Democrats while still winning substantial support from the center and right wing of the party.

2003
Congress created a seven-bill omnibus package in 2003 (Table 5.3). The 2003 appropriations cycle began when President Bush proposed a budget that members of the Appropriations Committee of both parties in the House and Senate viewed as too tight to provide enough funding for the appropriations bills to pass on the floor. Over the course of the summer of 2003, the creative use of supplemental spending bills relieved some of this pressure, and the House of Representatives passed all its spending bills in regular order by September. In the Senate, four bills passed over the course of the summer, but most were not brought to the floor until fall was approaching.[24]

---

[24] "Busy Year for Appropriators," in *CQ Almanac 2003*, 59th ed., 23–24 (Washington, DC: Congressional Quarterly, 2004). http://library.cqpress.com/cqalmanac/cqal03-835-24336-1083879.

TABLE 5.3. *Legislative History of Appropriations Bills, 2003, First Session, 108th Congress*

Bill	No Floor Vote (House)	No Floor Vote (Senate)	Bill in Omnibus
Agriculture			✓
Commerce, Justice, and State		✓	✓
District of Columbia			✓
Defense			
Energy Water			
Foreign Operations			✓
Interior			
Labor–Health and Human Services			✓
Legislative Branch			
Military Construction			
Veterans Administration–HUD			✓
Homeland Security			
Transportation-Treasury			✓
Total	0	1	7

Republican leaders in the Senate aimed to bring all bills to the floor in regular order.[25] Chairman Ted Stevens (R-AK), following the tradition of the Appropriations Committee, insisted that "each spending bill be considered separately ... because he promised Appropriations Committee members they would have the opportunity to debate controversial topics and offer amendments to the spending bills."[26] Stevens's position was in keeping with the Senate's tradition of freely amending legislation and protected the prerogatives of committee members. It also played into the hands of Democrats who saw the bills as an opportunity to force Republicans to take difficult votes and to win some policy battles now that they were in the minority.

One focus of debate centered on the Labor–Health and Human Services bill, which reached the floor in early September. Democrats viewed it as a

[25] Schatz, Joseph J. "GOP Vows No Winter Meltdown in This Year's Spending Debate." *CQ Weekly* (August 30, 2003): 2086–89. http://library.cqpress.com/cqweekly/weeklyreport108-000000807490.

[26] Taylor, Andrew and Joseph J. Schatz. "Stevens' Promise Maintains 'Regular Order' on Spending Bills, For Now." *Congressional Quarterly Daily Monitor* (November 4, 2003).

vehicle to block a proposal by the Bush administration to limit overtime pay compensation for workers, and they had the backing of Senator Arlen Specter (R-PA), the chairman of the Labor–Health and Human Services subcommittee. The ban on implementing the administration's overtime rules was offered as an amendment by Senator Tom Harkin (D-IA), the ranking member of the subcommittee, on September 5. Senator Harry Reid (D-NV) opened the debate by daring the Republican leadership to pull the bill from the floor: "They may want to pull this bill and say we are not going to allow the Congress of the United States to have a vote on this. If they do that, we know that there are other appropriations bills and other issues that come up that maybe this amendment will not be in order, maybe it will not be germane, but we are going to offer it anyway. We are going to continue with this as an issue."[27] Faced with Democratic threats to delay other important matters, Majority Leader Frist agreed to allow the vote, and the Democratic minority scored a rare victory when the Senate approved the Harkin amendment 54–45. Six Republicans joined all Democrats but one to support it.[28] The Democrats rolled the majority by attracting a handful of Republicans from the left wing of the party, such as Senators Lincoln Chaffee (R-RI) and Arlen Specter (R-PA), with an average DW-NOMINATE score of 0.18 as compared with 0.46 for Republicans voting against the provision.

It was not the only Democratic victory of the season. On the Transportation-Treasury bill, the Bush administration was rebuffed on policies governing travel to Cuba. Responding to pressure for new trading markets, both the House and the Senate approved amendments opposed by most Republicans to lift the ban on travel to Cuba. In the Senate, nineteen Republicans on the party's left wing (average DW-NOMINATE 0.39 as compared with 0.44 for the remainder of the party) joined with most Democrats to kill a tabling motion on the amendment 36–59.[29] It was then adopted by voice vote. Similarly, Bush administration proposals to privatize portions of the federal workforce were challenged. The House adopted an amendment to block the privatization proposal 220 to 198, when twenty-six Republicans joined a virtually united Democratic caucus to pass the amendment.[30] A similar amendment in the Senate failed

[27] *Congressional Record*, September 5, 2003, S11137–8.
[28] Roll Call 334, U.S. Senate, 108th Congress, First Session, September 10, 2003.
[29] Roll Call 483, House, September 9, 2003. Roll Call 405, U.S. Senate, 108th Congress, First Session, October 23, 2003.
[30] Roll Call 487, House, 108th Congress, First Session, September 9, 2003.

by one vote on near party lines, but a weaker version challenging some aspects of the administration policy passed 95–1.[31]

Senate Democrats also scored a victory on the District of Columbia appropriations bill. Republican leaders included a provision in the bill permitting the District to implement a school vouchers program. It became ensnared on the Senate floor, where voucher opponents had sufficient votes to prevent cloture on the bill. After the bill had languished for five days with little action, Republicans asked for unanimous consent to bring debate to a close and vote on the bill. Democrats objected. Senator Reid explained the Democratic position: "I think if we would take the contentious issue dealing with vouchers from this bill ... this bill would pass in a matter of not hours but minutes."[32] The Republican leadership pulled the bill from the floor rather than force the issue with a cloture vote. They brought it back seven weeks later, and it was passed quickly after the bill's managers stripped away the provision on vouchers.

The final push to pass the spending bills on an individual basis came in early November. The onslaught of Democratic amendments, slow pace of debate, and defeats on the floor frustrated Majority Leader Bill Frist. He warned on November 4th that "we're going to need to either settle them or wrap them into an omnibus."[33] Frist carried through on this threat a few days later. He announced after a meeting with Speaker Dennis Hastert and the chairs of the House and Senate Appropriations Committees that the Senate would debate individual bills through November 12 and would incorporate any remaining bills into an omnibus package after that date (*Congressional Quarterly Today*, November 6, 2003). Frist's decision worried Minority Leader Tom Daschle, who was enjoying relative success on the floor of the Senate. He explained that Democrats would be in a stronger position to influence the bills if they passed in regular order:

> The problem you always face with an omnibus bill is that it gives so much more leverage to the administration, and it plays into their hands. They will be in a much stronger position to dictate the terms and, ultimately, the language of these appropriations bills. And for that, and many other reasons, it was our feeling that we ought to pass these bills freestanding; negotiate them, as we have with a few of them, and complete our work.[34]

[31] Roll Call 407 and 408, U.S. Senate, 108th Congress, First Session, October 23, 2003.

[32] *Congressional Record*, September 30, 2003, S12173–4.

[33] Taylor, Andrew and Joseph J. Schatz. "Stevens' Promise Maintains 'Regular Order' on Spending Bills, For Now." *Congressional Quarterly Daily Monitor* (November 4, 2003).

[34] "Stakeout Media Availability with Senator Tom Daschle (D-SD), Senate Minority Leader, Prior to Senate Policy Luncheons." Federal News Service (November 11, 2003).

Daschle was also concerned because the majority's plan was to assemble the omnibus bill in a Republican-controlled conference. A majority vote of conferees was all that was necessary to approve a final bill. Democratic policy gains would be at risk, and the resulting conference report would not be amendable under the rules of both chambers.

In an effort to meet Frist's deadline, Republican appropriators brought the Commerce, Justice, and State bill to the Senate floor on November 10. The major point of controversy in the bill was over a provision that overturned a decision by the Federal Communications Commission to permit large media companies to expand their shares of the U.S. market. The provision had been added to the bill at the committee level in both the House and the Senate and had the support of Chairman Stevens (R-AK). He noted that the committee's agreement with the House meant the issue would not need to be reconsidered in conference. The Bush administration indicated it would veto the bill if the provision stood.

The bill was ultimately sidelined in the Senate by an entirely separate matter – Republican judicial nominees. Rather than debate the Commerce, Justice, and State bill, Democrats staged a nine-hour filibuster over judicial nominations. Senator Harry Reid (D-NV) explained the Democratic rationale: "In the House of Representatives, the majority party can run right over the minority party, but in the Senate it cannot be done.... This is a one-man show to indicate that the Senate cannot necessarily be run unless we work together."[35] The Democrats continued their talk-a-thon all afternoon. When they finished, Majority Leader Frist pulled the bill from the floor, and it was not considered on an individual basis again. "I can take a bill to the floor ... and if [Democrats] refuse to talk about it, debate it, discuss it, I have no choice but to pull that bill down and address it the only other way I can, and that's in a minibus or omnibus bill."[36]

By Thanksgiving 2003, all the spending bills but Commerce, Justice, and State had passed the House and Senate, but Republicans had suffered a series of embarrassing policy defeats. As promised, their next step was to create an omnibus by adding six spending bills to the Agriculture appropriations bill, which was already in conference. According to the *Almanac*, negotiators for the House and Senate initially reached

[35] *Congressional Record*, November 10, 2003, page S14288.
[36] "Press Stakeout with Senate Majority Leader Bill Frist (R-TN); Senator Rick Santorum (R-PA); and Senator Richard Shelby (R-AL)." Federal News Service (November 11, 2003).

a bipartisan agreement on the omnibus package.[37] Minority Leader
Daschle reported that he was being briefed regularly by Chairman Ted
Stevens on the progress of conference negotiations and said that Stevens
and Majority Leader Bill Frist had "both promised us that there would
not be any surprises as this legislation comes back, and there would be
very careful and close consultation."[38]

Then over the weekend of November 22–23, House Republican leaders armed with veto threats from the president stepped in and overturned
compromises that had been reached by Democratic and Republican members of the Appropriations Committee in favor of the president's position.
News reports from the time note frustration among Senate Republicans
with the tough negotiating tactics of the White House. "I think they've
had a pretty good run here," Senator Rick Santorum (R-PA) told the *New
York Times*. "[I]f you win 99 out of 100, you should declare victory."[39]
Stevens reported that White House veto threats had been used as a "club"
to win policy disputes.[40] On the Labor–Health and Human Services bill,
the ban on the administration's overtime pay rules was dropped. On the
Commerce, Justice, and State bill, the ban on media concentration that
Stevens supported was weakened in the administration's favor. On the
Transportation-Treasury bill, the prohibitions on enforcing the travel ban
to Cuba and on privatizing federal workers were removed and weakened,
respectively. On the District of Columbia bill, funding for private school
vouchers was restored in the bill. The result of the White House intervention was to give the president "victory after victory on the issues that had
stalled the seven bills."[41]

Democrats in both chambers geared up to oppose the final package.
The Democratic opposition in the House predictably went nowhere.
Under the firm rules of House debate, the conference report was passed
in short order on December 8, 2003, on a mostly party line vote of
242–176. In the Senate, where Democrats had the option of filibustering

---

[37] "Omnibus Fight Extends Into 2004." In *CQ Almanac 2003*, 59th ed., 2-33-2-34
(Washington, DC: Congressional Quarterly, 2004). http://library.cqpress.com/cqalmanac/
cqal03-835-24336-1083980.

[38] "Stakeout Media Availability with Senator Tom Daschle (D-SD), Senate Minority Leader,
Prior to Senate Policy Luncheons." Federal News Service (November 18, 2003).

[39] Stolberg, Sheryl Gay. "Congress Bows to Veto Threat on Spending Bill." *New York Times*
(November 25, 2003), 20.

[40] "Omnibus Fight Extends into 2004," in *CQ Almanac 2003*, 59th ed., 233–234
(Washington, DC: Congressional Quarterly, 2004). http://library.cqpress.com/cqalmanac/
cqal03-835-24336-1083980.

[41] Ibid.

the omnibus package, it ran into a firestorm opposition that blocked its initial passage.

Majority Leader Bill Frist first tried to call up the conference report for debate on December 9, but Democratic Leader Tom Daschle objected to the unanimous consent request and blocked the Senate from moving to the bill. Citing provisions in the omnibus ranging from overtime pay to media concentration, Daschle outlined the objections of the Democrats:

> What makes this omnibus unique is its utter disregard for the expressed will of each House of Congress. The process was an abomination, closed largely to Democrats, hidden from the light of day, written to satisfy nothing more than special interest wish lists. It didn't have to be this way. The Senate passed 12 of the 13 appropriations bills by wide bipartisan margins. The House passed 13 appropriations bills with wide margins. None of the bills posed difficulties. The only reason the process was handled this way was to ram through divisive provisions and pork spending that could never win the support of the Congress on their own.[42]

Daschle's strategy was to delay the omnibus long enough to draw public attention to provisions in the bill that Democrats felt would be unpopular with the public and abandoned by the Republicans if enough pressure was applied. It was a gamble that was unlikely to succeed, since disruptions in government services that could result from the failure to pass the bill would be politically damaging if Democrats received the blame. Still, the strategy initially went as planned. The effect of Daschle's objection was to force Frist to file a cloture motion. This delayed the vote until January 20, 2004, since the Senate was ready to adjourn for Christmas.

When January 20 arrived, Daschle rallied his party to oppose the omnibus package. Democrats decried the omnibus in speech after speech and complained that the conference had been used to insert controversial policy riders into the bill. In response, Majority Leader Frist warned that a failure to adopt the omnibus would lead to a yearlong CR and the Senate would lose all the work that had been completed on the bills in 2003.[43] The result was a clear win for the Democrats. The Republican majority needed sixty votes for cloture, and Frist secured only forty-eight.[44] Daschle carried the votes of forty Democrats (including independent Jim Jeffords of Vermont) and five Republicans.

The victory was short-lived. Behind the scenes, Democrats signaled that they had no intention of shutting down the government and would

---

[42] *Congressional Record*, December 9, 2003, S16084.
[43] *Congressional Record*, January 20, 2004, S20.
[44] Roll Call 1, U.S. Senate, 108th Congress, Second Session, January 20, 2004.

allow the bill to pass. "Our desire isn't to kill this bill, our desire is to give them a chance to fix it," Daschle said. "It is my expectation that the omnibus will pass, either fixed or not."[45] The purpose of the Democratic strategy, according to Senator Dick Durbin (D-IL), was "to register a protest."[46] Meanwhile, Republicans warned that new funding would be lost if Congress was forced to adopt a CR that extended the previous year's legislation. Majority Leader Frist claimed that any shortfalls in funding would be the responsibility of the Democrats:

> If we fail to enact this legislation, we will do very clear things. We will curtail our efforts in the fight against terrorism; it won't be as effective. We will weaken funding for our food security system if we don't pass this legislation. We will not have as secure and as strong a system inspecting our food. We will create hardships for millions of veterans, which is unnecessary. That is what this vote, in part, is about. We would put at risk millions of lives of people who suffer from AIDS and the global effort to fight one of the most moral humanitarian and public health challenges of our time. We would be shortchanging the needs of our schools, our communities, our States, and needy and disadvantaged Americans.[47]

Democrats continued their demand that Republicans remove the riders that had been added to the bill, but it was clear to both sides that Majority Leader Frist would reach sixty votes on his second attempt to impose cloture.[48] Nonetheless, Daschle took the floor in frustration to hammer home his frustration with the process:

> I worry about this precedent from the point of view of the institution. What does it mean in a democracy when 100 Senators vote, take a position, and when 435 Members of the House vote and take a position, and a cabal in the dark of night with no roll call vote can overrule that position willy-nilly, with absolutely no record, with no fingerprints, and nullify the actions taken by the bodies themselves?... But I know why we will probably get cloture today. Nobody here wants to be accused of shutting the Government down. Everybody understands the commitment that this legislation reflects in its support for veterans and for so many other things that we care deeply about. Senators are put in a very difficult position. I understand that. Do you support veterans or do you support an effort to deal with mad cow? Do you support highways and transportation or do you support an effort to confront this onerous provision eliminating overtime? Do you support housing or do you support an effort to retain the Senate

45 Pierce, Emily. "Omnibus Stalled Briefly." *Roll Call* (January 21, 2004).
46 Ibid.
47 *Congressional Record*, January 22, 2003, S155.
48 *Environment and Energy Daily* (January 22, 2004).

position with regard to media concentration? That is a tough position for anybody to be in, especially people in politics. So we may lose this cloture vote today. I suspect we will. And I understand why.[49]

When the second cloture vote was called, eleven Democrats who had voted to sustain Daschle's initial filibuster against the omnibus bill broke ranks and voted with the Republicans to end debate. Frist won the vote 61–32.[50] With the filibuster cut off, the omnibus bill was adopted by the Senate that same day and sent to President Bush for his signature. Daschle's filibuster push was the high water mark of opposition to the bill. The final vote on the bill was 65–28, with twenty-one Democrats favoring the bill and twenty-four opposed.[51]

2004

Majority Leader Frist took the lessons of 2003 to heart in 2004. In the last year of the 108th Congress, the tight limits President Bush again demanded on domestic spending were widely thought to be unrealistic in Congress. The refusal of moderate Republicans in the Senate to support the budget left it without sufficient votes to pass the chamber, and, as a consequence, Congress failed to adopt a budget resolution. These challenges were responded to in different ways in the House and Senate. In the House, all bills but one were passed in regular order. In the Senate, Republican leadership did not call votes on seven spending bills. The two chambers then created a nine-bill omnibus package that came to the floor as a nonamendable conference report (Table 5.4). Frist's strategy allowed the one-seat Republican majority to avoid more obstruction and another embarrassing series of rolls. The final bill again pushed policy in a more conservative direction than floor outcomes alone would likely have dictated, but the bill nonetheless won substantial Democratic support.

As in 2003, an important characteristic of the major policy disputes was that they pitted Democratic-leaning coalitions in both chambers against most members of the Republican majority and the Bush administration. On the Agriculture bill, the House Appropriations Committee adopted a Democratic amendment permitting the reimportation of prescription drugs from Canada, while the Senate Appropriations Committee again adopted Democratic language promoting trade with Cuba. On the Labor–Health and Human Services bill, a Democratic amendment

---

[49] *Congressional Record*, January 22, 2004, S128.
[50] Roll Call 2, U.S. Senate, 108th Congress, Second Session, January 22, 2004.
[51] Roll Call 3, U.S. Senate, 108th Congress, Second Session, January 22, 2004.

TABLE 5.4. *Legislative History of Appropriations Bills, 2004, Second Session, 108th Congress*

Bill	No Floor Vote (House)	No Floor Vote (Senate)	Bill in Omnibus
Agriculture		✓	✓
Commerce, Justice, and State		✓	✓
District of Columbia			
Defense			
Energy Water		✓	✓
Foreign Operations			✓
Interior		✓	✓
Labor–Health and Human Services		✓	✓
Legislative Branch			✓
Military Construction			
Veterans Administration–HUD	✓	✓	✓
Homeland Security			
Transportation-Treasury		✓	✓
Total	1	7	9

blocking the Bush administration's overtime pay regulations was adopted on the House floor, while in the Senate a similar amendment was adopted by the Appropriations Committee. On the Treasury-Transportation bill, the House adopted a Democratic amendment prohibiting the outsourcing of federal jobs at the subcommittee level, while amendments weakening the trade ban with Cuba were adopted on the floor. On the Senate side, amendments limiting outsourcing and weakening the Cuba trade ban were adopted at the committee level.

Frist was in a difficult position. A swarm of amendments awaited him if he brought the bills to the floor. The failure to pass a budget resolution meant all the spending bills would be open to Democratic amendments to add additional funds to them. His party risked being rolled again if left-leaning amendments were brought to a vote. And it was likely Democrats would seek votes on other politically charged matters in an effort to influence the tight presidential race between George W. Bush and Senator John Kerry (D-MA). Former Majority Leader Trent Lott sympathized with his party's predicament, noting, "51–49 is damn near impossible to manage."[52]

---

[52] "Frist's Challenges Grow in Unruly Senate." *National Journal's Congress Daily* (July 14, 2004).

By July, Republican leaders were already raising the possibility of not bringing many of the bills to the floor unless Democrats consented to time agreements that would limit amendments. Appropriations chairman Ted Stevens explained, "The trouble is non-germane amendments. We're going to get time agreements, or we're not going to take them up at all."[53] News reports from the time indicate that Republicans were considering possible endgame strategies for the year. One plan was to create an omnibus bill that would be drafted in conference and not amendable. Another was to create an omnibus that would be brought to the floor and open to amendment. Each approach had risks: "For the GOP, bringing an amendable bill to the floor means they risk having to cast votes on a range of campaign-season spending and policy proposals by the Democrats, but the alternative – namely presenting the minority party with a take-it-or-leave-it omnibus – would inflame Democrats and probably incite a filibuster."[54]

Frist's decision was to delay bringing bills to the floor individually and debate an omnibus package in a lame-duck session after the presidential election had been safely won by President Bush and Republicans had expanded their congressional majority (in part by defeating Democratic Leader Tom Daschle in a fiercely competitive race). Then Frist skipped floor debate and votes on the seven remaining bills and wrapped them directly into the conference report of the Foreign Operations bill, which had passed both chambers. Since these bills had never been debated on the Senate floor to begin with, wrapping them into a nonamendable conference report ensured that there would be no opportunity to amend them and instead required the Senate to take a single up or down vote on the resulting omnibus.[55]

Frist's strategy took a sharp toll on the ability of members to offer amendments (Table 5.5). In the freewheeling process of 2003, when the House voted on every bill and the Senate voted on all but one, House members cast 114 votes related to amendments on appropriations bills and senators cast 357. In 2004, when the House failed to vote on one bill and the Senate failed to vote on seven, House members cast 135 votes related to

[53] "Senate Appropriators Plan to Pick Up Pace This Week." *National Journal's Congress Daily* (July 6, 2004).

[54] Taylor, Andrew. "GOP Appropriations Strategy Uncertain as August Recess Looms." *Congressional Quarterly Weekly* (July 16, 2004).

[55] "Omnibus Bill Wraps Up 2004," in *CQ Almanac 2004*, 60th ed., 23–24 (Washington, DC: Congressional Quarterly, 2005). http://library.cqpress.com/cqalmanac/cqal04-836-24361-1084891.

TABLE 5.5. *Votes on Amendments in House and Senate, 108th Congress, 2003–2004*

	House		Senate	
	2003	2004	2003	2004
Agriculture**	11	18	52	0*
Commerce, Justice, and State	13	23	0*	0*
District of Columbia	4	1	1	0
Defense	2	2	61	2
Energy Water	6	7	53	0*
Foreign Operations***	10	12	11	1
Interior	16	13	7	0*
Homeland Security	5	16	35	32
Labor–Health and Human Services	6	19	66	0*
Legislative Branch	0	2	5	0
Military Construction	0	0	0	0
Transportation-Treasury	21	22	38	0*
Veterans Administration–HUD	20	0*	28	0*
	114	135	357	35

* Indicates regular appropriations bill was not brought to a vote.
** The Agriculture conference report carried the omnibus in 2003.
*** The Foreign Operations conference report carried the omnibus in 2004.

amendments and senators cast just 35. The majority's decision to abandon the regular order in the Senate created an effective closed rule for most bills in the appropriations process and shut down the Senate floor.

This strategy allowed Republicans to abide by the president's strict spending limits and to block Democratic-leaning policies for a second year in a row. These policy losses were prominently noted in the media at the time, and Democrats complained loudly about the process. Even so, the votes for final passage on the bill raise questions about the degree to which these headline-catching policy defeats reflected the broader content of the bill. In the House, the bill was adopted by a vote of 344–51, with the "no" votes coming almost evenly from Democrats and Republicans.[56] In the Senate, there was more resistance from Democrats. The Democrats' ranking member on the Appropriations Committee, Senator Robert Byrd (D-WV), took the lead in opposing the omnibus package. Calling the 3,000-page, $388 billion bill a "monstrosity" filled

[56] Roll Call 542, House, 108th Congress, Second Session, November 20, 2004.

with controversial and undebated policies, Byrd explained why he would vote against it:

> Of the nine appropriations bills in the bill, only two were ever debated in the Senate. The conference report includes a miscellaneous division that contains 32 unrelated provisions, most of which have never been considered by the Senate. There is not a single Member in this body who can say that he or she has read this bill. It contains complex and controversial matters.... Yet here we are on a Saturday, 51 days into the fiscal year, forced to vote on this monstrosity in the form of a $388 billion unamendable, unread conference report. The bill is entitled "Consolidated Appropriations Act, 2005." It should be entitled "Lame Appropriations Act, 2005."... Sadly, it has become almost an annual ritual that we shackle ourselves with these omnibus monstrosities. It is not good – not good for the Senate, not good for the American people, not good for your political system. We did in 1996, 1997, 1999, 2000, 2001, 2003, and 2004. When I was chairman from 1989 to 1994 and again in 2001, we produced 13 individual bills annually. That is the way to protect Congress's power of the purse. That is the way to protect the American people. That is the way to respect Members' rights to debate important legislation. We should not go down this road again next year. The woolly mammoth became extinct ages ago. I hope one day that the same will be said for such mammoth appropriations bills.[57]

As in 2003, a number of Democratic senators came to the floor of the chamber to decry the abandonment of provisions such as the ban on the Bush administration's overtime pay rule in the conference report, but the protests on the floor were not matched by votes against the bill. The omnibus passed later that day by a vote of 65–30 with substantial Democratic support.[58] The votes of Senate Democrats were nearly evenly split (twenty-three in favor and twenty-four opposed). Six Republicans voted against the bill as well. Democratic opponents of the bill were generally more liberal than its supporters, with an average DW-NOMINATE score of −0.46 for opponents versus −0.34 for supporters. Prominent members of the Democratic leadership, including Senators Tom Daschle and Harry Reid, voted in favor of the bill.

The overall pattern of the 108th Congress confirms the thesis that the inability of the majority party to deal effectively with delays or the threat of unfriendly amendments on individual spending bills contributes to the creation of omnibus spending bills. In 2003, Majority Leader Frist brought spending bills to the floor for debate and met a wave of

[57] *Congressional Record*, November 20, 2004, S11741.
[58] Roll Call 215, U.S. Senate, 108th Congress, Second Session, November 20, 2004.

Democratic amendments and obstruction that delayed the bills and led to embarrassing Republican rolls. In response, he worked with House leaders to form an omnibus package that limited amendments and won bipartisan support for the spending bills. In 2004, Majority Leader Frist headed off the previous year's problems by opting not to bring most of the bills to the floor for debate at all and instead wrapping them into a nonamendable omnibus package. This tactic substantially reduced amending opportunities in the Senate and again led to a package that won substantial bipartisan support.

While both packages won the support of substantial numbers of Democrats, more than 50 percent of the minority caucus opposed each bill. One reason for the opposition was that the packages overturned decisions of the floor that had been supported primarily by Democrats. But Democrats were not the only ones who suffered policy defeats. Appropriations chairman Ted Stevens also lost a policy debate when a provision he supported preventing media concentration was weakened in the 2003 omnibus. Nineteen Senate Republican who supported lifting the travel ban on Cuba that year were also rebuffed. The influence of President Bush played a major role in these policy outcomes. Virtually all policies that were in dispute in the bill appear to have been decided in favor of the president.

CONCLUSION

This case study reviews the major factors behind the creation of omnibus spending bills and the consequences of the bills at a fascinating point in time during the first term of President George W. Bush. Control of government was divided in the 107th Congress and unified in the 108th Congress. Democrats and Republicans in the Senate were each ideologically unified but retained razor-thin margins of control of the chamber during their times in the majority. The majority party was weak as a result, and the Senate floor was a treacherous environment.

The overall pattern of these four years fits well with the expectation that difficulty managing the Senate floor leads the majority to abandon the regular order and contributes to the creation of omnibus spending bills. The majority party faced frequent obstruction by the minority and the risk of being embarrassed or rolled by minority amendments. In response, it pulled bills from the floor or declined to bring them to the floor for debate altogether. Instead, party leaders created omnibus bills that attracted at least some bipartisan support and limited amendments and were adopted in Congress.

The fact that omnibus bills attracted more opposition from the minority party than in the past is noteworthy and tests the expectation that the bills are designed to win bipartisan support. On the one hand, some decisions of the floor were overturned, and policy often moved in a more conservative direction. On the other, a substantial number of Democrats consistently supported the packages. The omnibus bills were center-right, according to voting patterns, and they won bipartisan support. In addition, some of the policies that were overturned had the support of prominent Republicans such as Ted Stevens.

What factors account for the defeat of provisions that won support on the floors of the House and Senate? One likely explanation is found in the role of the president. President George W. Bush succeeded in pushing the policy contents of the bills toward his position in the early 2000s just as President Clinton had done when he was president. The success of both presidents suggests that presidential influence, rather than majority party control, best accounts for the partisan "tilt" sometimes visible in the bills despite their overall ability to win bipartisan support. As Senator Robert Byrd complained in 2004, "Omnibus bills bring the White House to the table and put them in charge."[59] Still, the president's influence did not appear to change the basic bipartisan character of the bills and the resulting packages won substantial support from Democrats.

[59] *Congressional Record*, November 20, 2004, S11742.

6

Conclusion

"To avoid an omnibus, you need to do twelve bills. Right now, the Senate ... cannot functionally do twelve bills on the Senate floor" (Staff Interview F 2012). The staff member's observation captures an essential relationship between omnibus spending bills and the power of the majority party in the Senate. The Senate majority party is likely to abandon the regular order when it is weak and faces difficulty managing the floor. Its decision to do so influences legislative outcomes in the Senate by reducing opportunities for all members to participate in lawmaking and by helping the majority to assemble a bipartisan coalition for the budget.

The majority's influence has important consequences, but there are limits to what it can accomplish. The majority party can protect its reputation by shielding members from difficult votes and passing a budget, but there is no evidence that it can systematically pursue its preferred policies. These findings show that the majority party has more influence than has been understood in the traditional view of the Senate but less than revisionist accounts would suggest. They also demonstrate that partisan models of Congress written for the House of Representatives, such as Conditional Party Government (CPG), do not accurately describe the Senate.

EVIDENCE FOR THE LIMITED INFLUENCE THEORY

The limited influence theory offers a better description of majority party influence in the Senate. This book tests four expectations arising from the theory. The first is that members prefer the regular order and desire to pass spending bills on an individual basis because it maximizes their opportunity for legislative influence. Policy makers and the records of floor debates from the 1980s through the early 2000s make clear passing bills individually is the preference of most members. "I don't ever remember starting a year where it was the majority's goal to have an omnibus bill," one staff member observed (Staff Interview D 2012). In the 1980s, Majority Leader Howard Baker (R-TN) sought to pass bills in the regular order but was unable to overcome policy disputes to bring bills to a vote on an individual basis. From the late 1980s to the mid-1990s, the powerful Democratic majority in the Senate opted to pass all bills individually and did not create omnibus bills. From the mid-1990s onward, the Republican majority frequently attempted to pass the bills individually only to face trouble doing so on the floor. Consistent with the statements of policy makers, the regular order is the preferred strategy for passing spending bills.

A second major expectation is that omnibus bills arise out of majority party weakness in the Senate. Specifically, I expect that the majority party is more likely to abandon the regular order when it is heterogeneous, has a small margin of control, and is distant from the minority party. All of these factors weaken the majority party by making it more difficult for the party to control the floor. Quantitative evidence supports these expectations. The majority party is more likely to abandon the regular order at statistically significant levels when it is small, divided, and distant from the minority. The same findings do not hold true in the House of Representatives. The House majority party is more likely to be unified on the rare occasions when it abandons the regular order, just as partisan theories of the House would predict. The results from the two chambers are strong evidence that party power functions a different way in the Senate than it does in the House.

Case studies also support the conclusion that majority party weakness spurs the creation of omnibus bills. The Republican majority was weak in the early 1980s because it had a narrow margin of control and was ideologically divided. Republicans fought among themselves on policies such as school prayer and abortion and prevented spending bills from being brought to a vote on an individual basis. Omnibus bills were first created when the majority adapted the traditional practice of passing temporary continuing resolutions (CRs) by extending them for a full year and abandoned efforts to pass bills on an individual basis after a sustained effort to do so proved to be fruitless. Majority parties were more unified from the mid-1990s and forward, but they still risked the threat of defection and more intense opposition from the minority as the distance between the two parties increased. Republican efforts to bring bills to the floor on an individual basis were met with a flood of Democratic amendments that slowed the process and forced Republicans to take difficult votes. Their response was to create omnibus spending packages in conference in order to limit amending and more easily secure bipartisan coalitions of support. The only period of time in which omnibus bills were not common in the years under study was from 1988 to 1994, when the Senate was under the control of a Democratic majority powerful enough to overcome a variety of challenges and pass bills on the floor on an individual basis.

Finally, I tested the expectations that omnibus bills reduce amending opportunities and receive bipartisan support. The quantitative evidence presented in Chapter 2 shows that abandoning the regular order sharply reduces the number of roll call votes and voice votes in the appropriations process. Not calling votes on any of the appropriations bills in the regular order reduces the amount of roll call votes to 29 percent of the normal level and voice votes to less than a tenth of their normal level. Floor debates illustrate that reducing the opportunity for offering amendments was often an explicit goal for the creation of omnibus spending bills. Chairman Ted Stevens, burned once too often by waves of Democratic amendments after bringing the bills to the floor on an individual basis, stated the problem and solution plainly: "The trouble is non-germane amendments. We're going to get time agreements, or we're not going to take [up the bills individually] at all."[1]

The finding that abandoning the regular order reduces amending may be difficult for some traditional scholars of the Senate to accept. The likely objection from this corner hinges on the idea that senators retain the technical ability to offer amendments, or to filibuster a bill to protect that right, when omnibus bills come to the floor. It is true that senators retain their traditional right to amend legislation and to filibuster a bill when the regular order is abandoned. But legalistic arguments such as these ignore the practical effect that creating an omnibus package has on the likelihood of amendments. Senate leaders understand the rules of the chamber well, and they understand how to manipulate legislative circumstances to shape the opportunity and cost to a senator of exercising his or her rights. The observation of policy makers and scholars alike is that omnibus bills reduce amending relative to what would otherwise occur

---

[1] "Senate Appropriators Plan to Pick Up Pace This Week." *National Journal's Congress Daily* (July 6, 2004).

in the regular order because of their unwieldy size and the tight time constraints under which they are brought up. In addition, omnibus bills brought to the floor as conference reports are not amendable. Conference reports could be filibustered – if senators wish to take the risk of being blamed for holding up the federal budget. Abandoning the regular order does not rewrite the Senate's rules, but the empirical evidence shows that it has a clear effect on the behavior of senators and reduces the likelihood that they will offer amendments.

The expectation that the bills receive bipartisan support also holds. Most of the time, omnibus packages receive strong support from both the majority and the minority. Within that context, there is some interesting variation that appears to be the result of presidential influence on the final policy content of the packages. President Bill Clinton partnered with Senate Democrats to force the creation of an omnibus package by slowing the consideration of individual spending bills, and the resulting package was opposed by a higher percentage of the Republican majority than Democratic minority. President George W. Bush successfully overturned policies he opposed that had been adopted on the Senate floor, and he was rewarded with higher levels of Democratic opposition. In both cases, significant numbers of senators from the party opposing the president still supported the final omnibus. The bulk of the evidence is consistent with the statements of policy makers who claim that omnibus bills are generally designed to win bipartisan support. Omnibus bills are typically massive logrolls that give something to everyone rather than vehicles for partisan policy. It is likely that there is a limit to the partisan policy gains that can reasonably be expected from them.

This account is consistent with the limited influence theory of the Senate. While omnibus bills may not be terribly useful for pushing policy in a more partisan direction, they are consequential. Abandoning the regular order and packaging bills together gives the majority party an effective way to overcome routine legislative problems and carry out its basic duty to fund the government. But there is a cost to keeping the trains running on time. Packaging bills together reduces the transparency of the appropriations process and limits the opportunity for individual members to influence legislation by reducing amending opportunities. Both the process and the resulting legislative package are widely scorned. As former majority leader Tom Daschle put it, "I think it's a symptom of the dysfunctionality of Congress these days" (interview with author, February 15, 2012). The weakness of the Senate majority party also influences the lawmaking process as a whole by shaping the way in which the House, Senate, and president work together to adopt the legislation needed to fund the federal government. It is likely that if the Senate's rules were more similar to those of the House, fewer omnibus bills would be adopted.

Finally, these findings underscore the important difference between majority party strength and influence in the Senate. The majority party's strength is a description of its strategic position in the chamber and an overall measure of its ability to meet its goals. Influence is the ability of a majority party to shift legislative outcomes away from what would otherwise occur without its intervention. The common jargon of describing a majority party as "strong" because it can influence legislative outcomes is poorly suited to the Senate. The evidence shows that the Senate majority party influences the appropriations process when it is in distress as a defensive strategy to protect itself from harm, not to go on the offense to pursue its policy goals. Equating "strength" with "influence" misstates the majority party's actual strategic position on the floor and risks leading researchers to make false assumptions about the circumstances under which influence is used and its consequences.

FUTURE RESEARCH

The once-admired appropriations process has continued its decline in recent years. Between 2008 and 2012, the Senate failed to give an individual vote to all twelve appropriations bills on three occasions. It has also been more likely to pass CRs that fund government agencies by extending the previous year's bill rather than with new legislation. On a few occasions, the powerful subcommittees of the House and Senate Appropriations Committees have failed to report their assigned bills. All of these factors point to the fact that the regular order – long under strain – may finally have broken down for good. As Senator Daschle noted, "There's almost an expectation now that omnibus bills are regular order" (interview with author, February 15, 2012). If this is the case, Congress is entering uncharted new territory. One important question for future research is whether party characteristics will have the same relationship with abandoning the regular order in the future that they have had in the past. The relationship may start to disappear if members no longer think of the regular order as the default way in which appropriations bills should be passed.

Future research should also address the roles that the House of Representatives and the president play in managing the appropriations process. Quantitative findings suggest that traditional partisan theories of Congress may explain why the House abandons the regular order. I also outline a new theory of presidential involvement in the appropriations process called "opportunistic bargaining." Future research should aim to explain the strategic choices facing members of the House and the president in the appropriations process and what the costs and benefits are of abandoning the regular order or creating omnibus packages for them.

Finally, the most important task for scholars of the Senate is to develop a partisan theory of the chamber. This book provides ample evidence that the partisan theories such as CPG do not find empirical support in the Senate. An effective partisan theory of the Senate should identify the conditions under which majority party influence is used and its consequences. The creation of such a theory will benefit the research of Congress overall by demonstrating how the House and Senate are different and contributing to the understanding of parties in legislative politics generally.

CONCLUSION

Lawmaking in the United States is the result of the combined effort of three distinctly different institutions: the House, the Senate, and the executive branch. Elected officials in each institution have their own incentives and work within unique institutional environments. Accordingly, each leaves a distinct imprint on lawmaking. For the last thirty-eight years, the persistent inability of the Senate majority party to adopt appropriations bills on an individual basis on the Senate floor has made the creation of omnibus packages more likely. While many factors influence the creation of omnibus spending bills, the weakness of the Senate majority party is a persistent theme.

The growing frequency of omnibus bills has pushed the traditional appropriations process to the brink of collapse. Absent changes to the Senate's rules or a substantial change in the characteristics of the two parties, it is unlikely that the process will recover anytime soon. In November of 2013, Majority Leader Harry Reid signaled the beginning of a move to reform the Senate's procedures when he exercised the so-called nuclear option and eliminated the requirement to seek sixty votes in the Senate to approve presidential nominations. It remains to be seen whether senators will adopt further changes to the filibuster to ease the passage of legislation. The key issues facing reformers are how far they wish to walk down the road of reform and whether it is possible to preserve the individualism of the Senate without also creating the kinds of opportunities for delay and minority activism that have contributed to the creation of omnibus spending bills. One hundred years ago, members of a gridlocked House of Representatives faced a similar choice when deciding whether to create new rules to prevent dilatory tactics. They opted to create a strong system of majority party control that has powerfully shaped the institution and reduced minority influence. Making the Senate more efficient will require a similar effort – and potentially fulfill senators' fears of making the chamber more similar to the House of Representatives. In coming years, we will see whether senators will judge that increasing the Senate's productivity is worth that outcome.

Works Cited

Aldrich, John. 2011. *Why Parties? A Second Look*. Chicago: University of Chicago Press.

Aldrich, John, and David W. Rohde. 2000. "The Republican Revolution and the House Appropriations Committee." *Journal of Politics* 61 (1): 1–33.

——. 2001. "The Logic of Conditional Party Government: Revisiting the Electoral Connection." In *Congress Reconsidered*, ed. Lawrence Dodd and Bruce Oppenheimer, 269–292. Washington, DC: CQ Press.

Berry, William, and Stanley Feldman. 1985. *Multiple Regression in Practice*. Edited by Michael Lewis-Beck. Newbury Park, CA: Sage Publications.

Binder, Sarah. 1996. "The Partisan Basis of Procedural Choice: Allocating Parliamentary Rights in the House, 1789–1990." *American Political Science Review* 90 (1): 8–20.

——. 1997. *Minority Rights, Majority Rule*. New York: Cambridge University Press.

——. 2003. *Stalemate: Causes and Consequences of Legislative Gridlock*. Washington, DC: Brookings Institution Press.

Black, Duncan. 1958. *The Theory of Committees and Elections*. New York: Cambridge University Press.

Brady, David, and Craig Volden. 2006. *Revolving Gridlock: Politics and Policy from Jimmy Carter to George W. Bush*. Boulder, CO: Westview Press.

Cameron, Charles and Nolan McCarty. 2004. "Models of Vetoes and Veto Bargaining." *Annual Review of Political Science* 7:409–435.

Cox, Gary, and Mathew McCubbins. 2005. *Setting the Agenda: Responsible Party Government in the U.S. House of Representatives*. New York: Cambridge University Press.

Davidson, Roger, Walter Oleszek, and Frances Lee. 2012. *Congress and Its Members*. 13th ed. Washington, DC: CQ Press.

Den Hartog, Chris, and Nathan W. Monroe. 2011. *Agenda Setting in the U.S. Senate: Costly Consideration and Majority Party Advantage*. New York: Cambridge University Press.

Evans, Diana. 2004. *Greasing the Wheels: Using Pork Barrel Projects to Build Majority Coalitions in Congress.* Cambridge: Cambridge University Press.

Fenno, Richard. 1966. *The Power of the Purse: Appropriations Politics in Congress.* Boston: Little, Brown and Company.

        1973. *Congressmen in Committees.* Boston: Little, Brown and Company.

        1989. "The Senate through the Looking Glass: The Debate over Television." *Legislative Studies Quarterly* 14 (3): 313–348.

Fiorina, Morris. 1989. *Congress: Keystone of the Washington Establishment.* New Haven, CT: Yale University Press.

Gailmard, Sean, and Jeffrey Jenkins. 2007. "Negative Agenda Control in the Senate and House: Fingerprints of Majority Party Power." *Journal of Politics* 69 (3): 689–700.

Green, Matthew and Daniel Burns. 2010. "What Might Bring Regular Order Back to the House?" *PS: Political Science and Politics* 43 (2): 223–226.

Hall, Richard. 1996. *Participation in Congress.* New Haven: Yale University Press.

Hanson, Peter C. 2014. "Abandoning the Regular Order: Majority Party Influence on Appropriations in the United States Senate." *Political Research Quarterly* 67 (3).

Hanushek, Eric, and John Jackson. 1977. *Statistical Methods for Social Scientists.* Edited by Peter Rossi. Orlando, FL: Academic Press.

Hayward, Steven. 2009. *The Age of Reagan: The Conservative Counterrevolution, 1980–1989.* New York: Crown Forum.

Holtz-Eakin, Douglas. 2004. *Reforming the Federal Budget Process.* CBO Testimony. Washington, DC: Congressional Budget Office.

Jacobson, Gary. 2009. *The Politics of Congressional Elections.* 7th ed. New York: Pearson Longman.

Jones, Charles. 2005. *The Presidency in a Separated System.* 2nd ed. Washington, DC: Brookings Institution Press.

Keith, Robert, and Allen Schick. 2003. *Introduction to the Federal Budget Process.* Washington, DC: Library of Congress.

Kiewiet, D. Roderick, and Matthew McCubbins. 1991. *The Logic of Delegation: Congressional Parties and the Appropriations Process.* Chicago: University of Chicago Press.

Koger, Gregory. 2010. *Filibustering: A Political History of Obstruction in the House and Senate.* Chicago: University of Chicago Press.

Krehbiel, Keith. 1992. *Information and Legislative Organization.* Ann Arbor: University of Michigan Press.

        1998. *Pivotal Politics: A Theory of U.S. Lawmaking.* Chicago: University of Chicago Press.

Krutz, Glen. 2000. "Getting around Gridlock: The Effect of Omnibus Utilization on Legislative Productivity." *Legislative Studies Quarterly* 25 (4): 533–549.

        2001a. *Hitching a Ride: Omnibus Legislating in the U.S. Congress.* Edited by Samuel Patterson. Columbus: Ohio State University Press.

        2001b. "Tactical Maneuvering on Omnibus Bills in Congress." *American Journal of Political Science* 45 (1): 210–223.

Lee, Frances. 2009. *Beyond Ideology: Politics, Principles, and Partisanship in the U.S. Senate*. Chicago: University of Chicago Press.

LeLoup, Lance. 2005. *Parties, Rules and the Evolution of Congressional Budgeting*. Columbus: Ohio State University Press.

Madonna, Anthony. 2011. "Winning Coalition Formation in the U.S. Senate: The Effects of Legislative Decision Rules and Agenda Change." *American Journal of Political Science* 55 (2): 276–288.

Mayhew, David. 1974. *Congress: The Electoral Connection*. New Haven, CT: Yale University Press.

Monroe, Nathan W., and Jason Roberts, eds. 2008. *Why Not Parties? Party Effects in the United States Senate*. Chicago: University of Chicago Press.

Nelson, Dalmas H. 1953. "The Omnibus Appropriations Act of 1950." *Journal of Politics* 15 (2): 274–288.

Neustadt, Richard. 1990. *Presidential Power and the Modern Presidents: The Politics of Leadership from Roosevelt to Reagan*. New York: MacMillan.

Oleszek, Walter. 2007. *Congressional Procedures and the Policy Process*. 7th ed. Washington, DC: CQ Press.

Polsby, Nelson. 2004. *How Congress Evolves: Social Bases of Institutional Change*. New York: Oxford University Press.

Poole, Keith T., and Howard Rosenthal. 2007. *Ideology & Congress*. New Brunswick, NJ: Transaction Publishers.

Rae, Nicol, and Colton Campbell. 2001. "Party Politics and Ideology in the Contemporary Senate." In *The Contentious Senate: Partisanship, Ideology and the Myth of Cool Judgment*, ed. Nicol Rae and Colton Campbell, 1–18. Lanham: Rowman and Littlefield.

Riker, William H. 1982. *Liberalism against Populism: A Confrontation between the Theory of Democracy and the Theory of Social Choice*. San Francisco: W. H. Freeman and Company.

Schick, Allen. 2007. *The Federal Budget: Politics, Policy and Process*. 3rd ed. Washington, DC: Brookings Institution Press.

Schickler, Eric. 2000. "Institutional Change in the House of Representatives, 1867–1998: A Test of Partisan and Ideological Power Balance Models." *American Political Science Review* 94 (2): 269–288.

Schickler, Eric, and John Sides. 2000. "Intergenerational Warfare: The Senate Decentralizes Appropriations." *Legislative Studies Quarterly* 25 (4): 551–575.

Shepsle, Kenneth A., and Mark Bonchek. 1997. *Analyzing Politics: Rationality, Behavior, and Institutions*. New York: W. W. Norton and Company.

Shepsle, Kenneth A., Robert P. Van Houweling, Samuel J. Abrams, and Peter C. Hanson. 2009. "The Senate Electoral Cycle and Bicameral Appropriations Politics." *American Journal of Political Science* 53 (2): 343–359.

Shepsle, Kenneth, and Barry Weingast. 1981. "Political Preference for the Pork Barrel: A Generalization." *American Journal of Political Science* 26: 86–111.

Silverstein, Gordon. 2009. *Law's Allure: How Law Shapes, Constraints, Saves, and Kills Politics*. New York: Cambridge University Press.

Sinclair, Barbara. 1986. "Senate Styles and Senate Decision Making, 1955–1980." *Journal of Politics* 48 (4): 877–908.

2002. "The '60-Vote Senate': Strategies, Process and Outcomes." In *U.S. Senate Exceptionalism*, ed. Bruce Oppenheimer, 241–261. Columbus: Ohio State University.

2005. "The New World of U.S. Senators." In *Congress Reconsidered*, ed. Lawrence Dodd and Bruce Oppenheimer, 1–22. Washington, DC: CQ Press.

2012. *Unorthodox Lawmaking: New Legislative Processes in the U.S. Congress.* Washington, DC: CQ Press.

Smith, Steve. 1989. *Call to Order: Floor Politics in the House and Senate.* Washington, DC: Brookings Institution Press.

2005. "Parties and Leadership in the Senate." In *The Legislative Branch*, ed. Paul J. Quirk and Sarah A. Binder, 255–278. New York: Oxford University Press.

2007. *Party Influence in Congress.* New York: Cambridge University Press.

2010. *The Senate Syndrome.* Washington, DC: Brookings Institution Press.

2014. *The Senate Syndrome: The Evolution of Procedural Warfare in the Modern U.S. Senate.* Norman: University of Oklahoma Press.

Stein, Robert, and Kenneth Bickers. 1994a. "Congressional Elections and the Pork Barrel." *Journal of Politics* 56 (2): 377–399.

1994b. "Universalism and the Electoral Connection: A Test and Some Doubts". *Political Research Quarterly* 47 (2): 295–317.

Stewart, Charles. 1989. *Budget Reform Politics: The Design of the Appropriations Process in the House of Representatives, 1865–1921.* New York: Cambridge University Press.

Wawro, Gregory, and Eric Schickler. 2006. *Filibuster: Obstruction and Lawmaking in the U.S. Senate.* Princeton, NJ: Princeton University Press.

Weingast, Barry. 1979. "A Rational Choice Perspective on Congressional Norms." *American Journal of Political Science* 23 (2): 254–262.

Wildavsky, Aaron, and Naomi Caiden. 2004. *The New Politics of the Budgetary Process.* 5th ed. New York: Pearson Longman.

Wlezien, Christopher. 1996. "The President, Congress, and Appropriations, 1951–1985." *American Politics Research* 24 (1): 43–67.

Index